Self-Service Data Analytics and Governance for Managers

Self-Service Data Analytics and Governance for Managers

NATHAN E. MYERS

GREGORY KOGAN

WILEY

For general information on our other products and services or for technical support, please contact our Customer Care Department within the United States at (800) 762-2974, outside the United States at (317) 572-3993, or fax (317) 572-4002.

Wiley publishes in a variety of print and electronic formats and by print-on-demand. Some material included with standard print versions of this book may not be included in e-books or in print-on-demand. If this book refers to media such as a CD or DVD that is not included in the version you purchased, you may download this material at http://booksupport.wiley.com. For more information about Wiley products, visit www.wiley.com.

Library of Congress Cataloging-in-Publication Data is Available:

ISBN 9781119773290 (hardback)
ISBN 9781119773313 (ePDF)
ISBN 9781119773306 (epub)

Cover image: © imetamorworks/iStock/Getty Images
Cover design: Wiley

SKY10026398_042121

Contents

Preface

The breadth and scale of data are growing exponentially, and the growth of data is impacting the shape of organizations. According to the "On Risk 2020" report by the IIA, "Organizations face significant disruption driven by the accelerating pace of technology and the growing ease of mass data collection." Executives are placing increased reliance on the abundance of data in their decision-making process. A number of factors are driving the steep growth of data: data and metadata created and captured from the Internet of Things (IoT), increasingly interconnected supply chains, proprietary company information generated in unified ERPs, and the increasing number of third-party cloud data sources available for subscription and consumption. Organizations have available far more data than ever before.

The rise of data analytics is transforming business functions in an accelerated pace. This transformation is driven by managements' strategic goal of evolving their organizations to being data-driven, interconnected, and innovative in their approach to unlocking insights from the rapidly increasing volume of data. While data analytics is an extremely broad category of technologies and disciplines, self-service analytics has recently emerged as a significant driver of accelerated digital transformation. At the heart of digital transformation in accounting, finance, and operations functions is the move from manual spreadsheet-based data processing to structured, robust, and efficient automated processing using self-service analytics tools. Business professionals who spend their days assembling and enriching information from disparate sources in spreadsheets, performing routine formulaic processing steps, comparisons, and aggregations, now have data analytics tools at their disposal to rapidly automate the least value-added portions of their roles.

Even though automation techniques through core IT systems have existed for decades, the defining features of the new wave of self-service analytics automation is that it is "small." Small automation is relatively inexpensive from a capital investment perspective compared to multi-million-dollar enterprise IT investments. Self-service data analytics offers flexible, no-code, low-cost processing capabilities that are directly accessible to process owners outside of IT. Without the need to involve IT or to await the technology investment cycle, self-service data analytics solutions can be developed and implemented in only hours or days – directly by those overseeing the process. Such capabilities allow for dramatic acceleration of routine processes and reduce the likelihood that manual processing errors are introduced. Perhaps most importantly, they transform the role of business professionals who can reclaim time to focus on higher-order data analysis, the implementation of improved controls, or on other emerging business priorities. These benefits taken together amount to a quantum leap forward for organizations intent on truly harnessing data capabilities and optimally deploying human capital.

While self-service data analytics deployments can improve process control and efficiency in the finance function, they also markedly impact the internal control environment. In the past, the control environment which safeguarded the enterprise from IT general and application risks was centralized around the core technology stack. As processing capabilities are now placed directly into the hands of end-users to import and analyze data, structure processing steps, and export outputs, the risk environment has been dramatically shifted. Robust internal control governance built around systems over several decades has been side-stepped by increased data analytics processing outside of systems, necessitating a commensurate shift in governance. We will systematically inventory the body of existing regulatory guidance, legacy IT governance precepts, and data governance and model governance frameworks to identify foundational principles which must be extended to forge a data analytics governance framework. Building upon existing governance literature, we will outline the first comprehensive, fit-for-purpose, and actionable data analytics governance framework for managing the governance triad: project governance, risk governance, and investment governance.

Three governance disciplines are required to sustainably scale self-service data analytics: project governance, risk governance, and investment governance. Project governance provides a framework to ensure that efforts have the right stakeholder support and that solutions satisfy requirements and are tested to a high standard. Importantly, project governance also mandates the maintenance of an adequate audit trail to enable process assurance capabilities. Risk governance is a framework for the assessment and management of risks introduced by individual builds – and the portfolio, as a whole. Automation builds can be assessed according to unique risk scoring dimensions, allowing the risks introduced to be recognized and well understood. Armed with full transparency, the organization can actively prioritize risk response strategies for higher risk analytics builds in the portfolio. Investment governance is a framework providing for detailed cost and benefit analysis, weighing the expected efficiencies of analytics deployments against the cost and effort required – such that firm resources and investment dollars flow logically to the best opportunities. Investment governance ensures that projects selected for implementation provide adequate return on investment (ROI).

It is not enough to theoretically discuss the application of data analytics in accounting, finance, and operations. We will discuss common use cases and take readers through our approach to process discovery to uncover opportunities to employ analytics for control and efficiency. We will demonstrate the application of one prominent data analytics tool, Alteryx, to common use cases through our practical case studies. To build familiarity with the features and functionality on offer, we will demonstrate the application of data analytics to real problems that managers are likely to face, and we will introduce them in an extremely approachable way for the consumption of a broad audience with varied levels of data analytics exposure. We will suggest ways to industrialize the data analytics function to achieve the scale required to optimize expected program benefits. The use of self-service data analytics in accounting, finance, and operations functions is relatively new and rising to prominence. A comprehensive governance framework entirely suited for self-service data analytics programs has not yet been established. Accordingly, in this book, we will draw from more mature and established frameworks (data governance, system governance, and model governance) to build a foundational governance model that can grow with your footprint, as your organization embarks on its inevitable digital journey.

Acknowledgments

Throughout the development of this book, we were privileged to have sincere and valuable advice from contributors, reviewers, and peers in the data analytics for finance and accounting research and teaching area, as well as industry change practitioners at leading organizations. These individuals provided us with invaluable perspective, recommendations, feedback, and constructive review.

Sean Adams

Douglas Boyle
University of Scranton

Kevin Dow
University of Auckland

Daniel Gaydon
University of Scranton

David Greene
Indiana University

Dana Niblack

Dan Palmon
Rutgers University

Ray Pullaro
Long Island University

Vernon Richardson
University of Arkansas

Edward Rogoff
Long Island University

Marcia Watson
Trinity University

About the Authors

Nathan E. Myers, MBA, CPA, Six Sigma Black Belt, has over 20 years of public accounting and investment banking experience at flagship organizations including Ernst & Young, Morgan Stanley, UBS Investment Bank, Credit Suisse, and JP Morgan. He received both his bachelor's degree in Accounting and an MBA in Accounting from the Indiana University, Kelley School of Business. Much of his career has been spent in finance functions as a controller and as a change manager for products such as FX spot, forwards, and options, securities lending, margin, and equity finance at global investment banks, building scalable controls and delivering strategic technology change. In the recent past, his career has evolved from owning a portfolio of large-scale technology change, to putting data analytics tooling into the hands of users to drive aggressive digital transformation. Nathan has worked to build rigid data quality standards to drive rich and accurate datasets as inputs to processing, has managed robotic process automation (RPA) portfolios, and has scaled end-user data analytics across organizations to capture control and efficiency benefits. He has seen firsthand the requirement to build and maintain close governance over these toolsets, as they rapidly proliferate across banks and large organizations. He resides on Long Island, New York, with his wife, son, and daughter.

Gregory Kogan, CPA, is a professor of practice in accounting at Long Island University, focusing on teaching undergraduate and graduate courses in accounting and finance. He has experience as an auditor at Ernst & Young and as a controller at Tiger Management. He received his MBA from Rutgers Business School in Accounting and a Bachelors of Science in Computer Science from Rutgers University. He is currently pursuing his doctorate in Business Administration at the University of Scranton with the research focus of data analytics in accounting.

While in public accounting, Gregory worked on major clients in the asset management industry, gaining exposure to auditing hedge funds and private equity funds. At Tiger Management, he led the day-to-day accounting and finance operations of a long/short equity start-up hedge fund as the controller of the fund. While at Long Island University, he spearheaded the launching of an MBA program that delivers graduate business education to a leading US banking institution. At Long Island University, he has been leading the effort of integrating data analytics into the accounting curriculum. Gregory resides in Manalapan, New Jersey, with his wife, daughter, and son.

Introduction

The breadth and scale of data are growing exponentially, and this growth of data is impacting the shape of organizations. Across industries, many companies have entire departments and functions devoted to processing vast numbers of data points into information, for delivery to internal and external stakeholders. Along with the growth of data, data analytics technology and tooling are advancing at a breakneck rate to process it, to identify and understand relationships and trends, and even to make predictions on future outcomes, before displaying them neatly in low-latency dashboard views for ultimate consumption by managers, executives, clients, counterparties, and regulators.

Data analytics is coming to the fore as an exciting strategic and tactical enabler of higher-order analysis and value creation through insight generation and automation of manual processes. Data analytics includes a number of analytics tools, technologies, and buzzwords readers will have heard thrown about more and more over the last 5 to 10 years: robotic process automation (RPA), machine learning (ML), artificial intelligence (AI), text mining technologies like natural language processing (NLP), optical character recognition (OCR), and intelligent character recognition (ICR), along with neural networks, logistic and linear regression analysis, and many more. At the most basic level, these are disciplines enabling descriptive techniques to understand past events and their drivers and to gain insight through the extraction of data trends. These technologies can allow us to forge more structured and intelligent processing steps, and at their sexiest, they can enable predictions, trigger recommendations or prescribed actions, and prompt informed decision-making.

More data analytics and automation tools are available to perform routinized tasks in the data-to-information processing chain than ever before. Digital transformation features in the concerns of most Fortune

500 CEOs, and while companies report that the chief goals of digital transformation are to understand their customers better or to improve products or services, quite often there are more practical motivations for digital transformation, particularly in finance, accounting, and operations functions. The goals are to build capacity and create efficiencies through automating routinized processes, improve process stability and control by structuring the work performed outside core systems, and to optimize human capital resources by reducing the proportion of low value-added processing tasks in their workday.

Many large firms employ dozens, hundreds, or even thousands of employees, who spend their days enriching, processing, transforming, and perhaps to a limited degree, even analyzing data in Microsoft Excel. They may work in a variety of functional silos in the organization, whether as product controllers, entity controllers, or accountants within the CFO organization, whether they work in an operations function, or whether they work in a business management or business intelligence function rolling up to a COO – or in any other part of the organization. Spreadsheet processing continues to dominate in accounting, finance, and operations functions, but the thick and lengthy manual processing tail performed outside of systems highlights the shortfall of core technology platforms in meeting users' needs. Advancements in data analytics and automation tooling delivers viable alternatives, with the potential to supplant and dethrone Microsoft Excel as the default business processing tool, and perhaps finally relegate it to where it belongs – one of several quick and dirty tactical tools available for selection if and as required, but not the default go-to, where the majority of processing teams live, day by day.

When we think of AI, data science, and related disciplines, for many of us, the most leading-edge advanced analytics capabilities come to mind – the ability to detect anomalies in financial data, the ability to detect and flag high-risk patient test results for further review by medical practitioners, and any of a host of proven use cases for descriptive and predictive analytics. While these represent striking and momentous opportunities to employ data analytics to great effect, we submit that these higher-order applications are the exception rather than the rule. The bread and butter use cases that will offer predictable and quantifiable benefits for rapid adoption of data analytics are the opportunities that exist in spreadsheet-driven environments to structure processes in self-service data analytics tooling. Data analytics is not always a theoretical predictive rocket science employing code-based technology and advanced algorithms to solve complex problems. It is the body of solutions that organizational leaders must cultivate and have at hand to forge ahead in their digital journey, at whatever pace is consistent with digital transformation goals and objectives. The development of practical data analytics tools has led to billions of dollars of investment across many service industries, aimed at building core competencies, increasing competitive advantage and organizational efficiency, doing more with fewer employees, or reducing employee costs and footprint.

It is this last goal that the authors predict will prompt a surge in adoption of data analytics tooling in the next five years, across medium to large-scale enterprises. In many organizations, the cost of employees is the most significant expense on the income statement. Managers are motivated to structure their spreadsheet-based processes in a more mature and robust way. By reducing the manual processing performed in Excel, managers can stabilize and lock down spreadsheet-driven processes into more repeatable, structured, and time-efficient processing steps. By minimizing both process variance and time spent performing routinized processing steps, spreadsheet-based jobs of the past will evolve to remove the most manual and least value-added steps in the processing chain. While this book cannot but introduce and acknowledge many more advanced data analytics capabilities and technologies to provide the backdrop, the focus of this book is largely around one subset of the emerging tool suite, self-service data analytics.

Self-service data analytics is an important growing subset of the suite of data analytics tools that is emerging as a focal point of digital transformations across large companies. It is distinct from the other sets of tools in the analytics toolkit in important ways. First, self-service tools are typically built in off-the-shelf vendor products with which individual operators, not technologists, can interact and configure directly, due to their ease of use. Process owners, with no prior technology background and that may have never seen a piece of code, are well equipped to lay out a customized, automated process, armed only with their knowledge of the raw data inputs and the processing steps they routinely perform in spreadsheets. Intelligent source data parsing and drag-and-drop operations replace SQL and Visual Basic commands, enabling the most inexperienced, inexpert, if not maladroit and bungling of us to quickly roll up our sleeves, forge and test processing steps, and implement a processing workflow, all in an afternoon ("small" automation). Benefits cases based on control and efficiency are self-evident to those performing processing, and the decisions to invest time in structuring spreadsheet processes into automated workflows are directly in the hands of operators and their managers.

The benefits of self-service data analytics tools include increased process stability, reduced dependency on the often over-subscribed technology function, improved time-to-market – and the instant relief as capacity is recaptured through process automation. Removing the technology function from the critical path is an important end that has led to a raft of self-service and user-configurable tools spanning processing and reporting. Data democratization, or the widespread availability and accessibility of critical datasets throughout organizations, is a significant driver behind the growth of self-service data analytics, as operators sitting directly on top of business processes are well-placed to unlock data value if provided with the tools and capabilities to harness it. Perhaps chiefly, work that was previously unstructured, risky, and manual-intensive can now be structured in a tool, emulating system-driven processing. Laborious and time-consuming spreadsheet processing can now be easily replaced with tactical application-driven processing, leading to time savings and efficiency.

We all know that systems ("big" automation) are integral to nearly every job across nearly every industry, much as mechanization was a game-changer for manufacturing during the Industrial Revolution. In our digital and information age, where vast data is captured, stored, transformed, and processed for use to inform business decisions, core technology systems offer both coded processing and considerable mature technology governance, tied up with a bow and a ribbon. Systems are a central hub for structured development – offering data storage and processing operations, long lists of features and functionality, they offer user experience (UX) styles, and perhaps a rich reporting suite – but importantly, they quietly serve unnoticed as a centralized funnel around which to build internal controls and governance to ensure the accuracy and stability of processing.

The fact that systems are widely subscribed to in an organization ties many operators to enveloping control frameworks built around them. Thanks to mature system governance, many systems are designed with embedded internal controls such as those that ensure appropriate user entitlements, automatic system reconciliations and check totals to ensure data integrity, and perhaps even workflows providing for required supervisory approvals. Critically, many companies already enforce robust change governance around technology deliveries, including the mandated production of key project development artifacts such as documented requirements, evidence of test scripts and testing results, evidence of sign-off, and post-implementation reviews following a release. However, with the development decentralization that results from putting low-code, no-code tooling in the hands of users throughout the organization, governance frameworks built around systems will ignore an increasing segment of solution development and processing. This is one factor leading to a rift we are referring to in this book as the self-service data analytics governance gap.

This book is unique, because it is written not for data scientists or those with PhDs in statistics, mathematics, or neural sciences. It is not written for machine learning experts or AI specialists. This book is written for managers at large organizations, where there are pockets of operators – or likely entire functions – performing manual processes in spreadsheets. This edition will be valuable for managers that are increasingly under pressure to cut costs, produce more, and overall to do more with fewer hands. We will introduce process discovery methods to identify manual pain points and opportunities to capture efficiencies across functions, we will demonstrate how to size and cost these efforts, how to quantify the benefits cases, and how best to compare projects to assess priority. We will showcase prominent tools in action, as we take our readers through case studies featuring common use cases that they are likely to encounter in their own processing plants. The process consistency and stability benefits, which result as manual work done outside of systems is structured in tools, will be crystallized for the reader. Further, the reader will walk away convinced of the need for an overarching governance framework to protect the value created by the analytics portfolio. Our readers will surely have heard about AI and some of the disciplines within it, they may have heard about data analytics and understand that it is transformative, but they will benefit from a clear introduction to the language of data analytics, and they will benefit from simple demonstrations of emergent data analytics technologies. Finally, they will be armed with ideas on how to influence the approach, the course, and the speed of their organization's digital progression.

A subset of readers may be further along the digital transformation journey at their respective organizations. They have been exposed to common use cases for analytics tooling, they may have assembled a project portfolio, or perhaps even adopted self-service tooling across their organizations. These readers will benefit as the basics are clarified and reinforced, and they will appreciate the pains we have taken to present complex subject matter colloquially, as though we are explaining it to a trusted friend. Perhaps readers have already witnessed risks introduced by the unchecked proliferation of self-service analytics, in an environment where fragmented legacy governance frameworks better suited to *system* development have failed to close the coverage gap. In months of research prior to writing this book, your authors failed to identify an existing comprehensive governance framework suited entirely for data analytics or self-service data analytics portfolios. We resolved, therefore, to examine the existing body of frameworks and guidance and extend key principals to create and present an actionable governance runbook to optimize control over data analytics portfolios in this book – the first of its kind. In an era of increased accountability to internal auditors, external auditors, and regulators, we want to provide readers with the means to protect portfolio value through risk identification and mitigation and prepare you to meet the inevitable scrutiny head-on.

In the following chapters, we will take a practical approach to familiarizing readers with data analytics technologies and practices: we will discuss the rise of big data, whether from the internet of things (IoT) or the increasing body of digitized text from optical character recognition (OCR) or intelligent character recognition (ICR), the large data arrays that can be interacted with through natural language processing (NLP), subscribed to with ready-made application programming interfaces (APIs), and visualized with customizable interactive dashboarding solutions. From there, we will move on to explain the ways processing has evolved to digest the increasing body of available data. We will highlight decentralized, crowd-sourced distributed ledger technology (DLT) and blockchain, as well as cloud computing as a shift in the consumption model for storage, data subscription, and software. We will define AI as the nebulous pursuit of technologies that may ultimately emerge to emulate human thinking, capabilities, and interactions, encompassing all of the disciplines above – and more.

Having provided a backdrop to ease readers into our key topics, we will discuss data analytics disciplines that are rapidly evolving to supplant routinized manual spreadsheet operations. We will walk through robotic process automation (RPA) use cases and describe how RPA is being widely adopted to capture efficiency for (repetitive and stable) data capture and manipulation. We will briefly touch on machine learning and predictive analytics as advanced areas of analytics. Likely, the most immediate opportunity to transform processing will come about from the widespread adoption of self-service data analytics, which will emerge as a theme throughout this book. Putting low-code/no-code capabilities directly into the hands of process owners to automate extract, transform, and load (ETL) steps and to perform formulaic calculations, extensions, and comparisons will lead to a growth pattern and a pace of change never before encountered in the legacy system development environment. We will further devote a chapter to demonstrating the use of Alteryx, an increasingly prevalent tool that is rapidly transforming data analysis, processing, and reporting, to bring you firmly aboard the journey.

You may wonder just where to find promising opportunities to deploy data analytics tooling in your own organizations. We will propose methods for surveying processing operations to uncover use cases with significant benefits warranting prioritization and investment, matching tools to opportunities, and deriving an achievable digital roadmap. We will discuss the levers that can be pulled to increase control and drive efficiency, and decisions that can be made to adapt the organization to expectations that routine processes can be accelerated and streamlined to build capacity, unlock value, and to enhance decision-making. Finally, we will get you thinking about how to prepare your organization for the impending seismic shift, by establishing key governance procedures now, to maintain control as your organization adopts self-service data analytics and business intelligence tooling.

One key contribution of this book to the body of data analytics literature and discourse is our broad-based digest of existing governance frameworks and the systematic revelation of a significant governance gap that must be addressed, as data analytics saturates our respective organizations. There are any number of relevant and overlapping frameworks that cover portions of IT governance and even portions of data analytics governance in the finance and accounting environment. However, no single framework exists that is fit for the universe of self-service data analytics builds. We will draw from mature system governance, model governance, data governance, process governance, SOX 404, COSO IC (internal control framework for the financial reporting process), COSO ERM, and COBIT 2019 (ISACA) frameworks, and even the AICPA's Statements on Auditing Standards – and distill fundamental governance principles that can be extended more suitably to govern data analytics portfolios. Building on such principles, we will call out recommended action steps that will help managers to satisfy them. Such action steps will be presented in the form of two checklists that readers can take back to their own organizations and implement straightaway. This must be done early and determinedly, so it is in place and can play a formative role in safeguarding your organization, as it embarks on what we believe to be an inevitable digital journey.

No matter which segment of readers you fall into, our goal in writing this work was to present you with a plain-language digest of the mosaic of developing analytics disciplines that warrant your attention. All pretense aside, we offer you our viewpoints and perspectives, with all deference to the insight and views of others that are concurrently embracing these same forces of change. We acknowledge that we cannot get our arms around the growing body of data analytics technology in this work of several hundred pages, alone. It can be fairly said that in the pages to follow, we barely scratch the surface. However, our goal is not to provide a comprehensive treatment of an extremely broad subject area that advances in leaps and bounds day by day. Rather, we set out to distill for you the significant developments in the space, to provide detailed discussions of key topics relevant to universal management goals of control and efficiency, and to empower you to succeed as the imminent data analytics–led digital transformation overtakes us. Best wishes for the journey!

CHAPTER 1

Setting the Stage

Impact

The breadth and scale of data are growing exponentially, and the growth of data is impacting the shape of organizations. In a number of industries, there are multiple departments spanning many functions who process vast numbers of data points into information for delivery to a number of internal and external stakeholders. Along with the growth of data, data analytics technology and tooling are advancing at a break-neck rate to process it, to understand trends, and even to make predictions on future outcomes, before displaying results neatly in low-latency dashboard views for ultimate consumption by managers, executives, clients, counterparties, and regulators. Increasingly, data analytics and automation tools are available to perform more of the routinized tasks in the data-to-information processing chain than ever before. Digital transformation features in the concerns of most Fortune 500 CEOs, and while companies report that their top goal regarding their digital transformation is to understand their customers better or to improve products or services, in practice, there are more practical motivations for digital transformation in finance, accounting, and operations functions. The goals are to build capacity and create efficiencies through automating routinized processes, improve process stability and control by structuring the work done outside core systems, and to optimize human capital resources by reducing low-value-added processing tasks.

It is useful to introduce typical environments where self-service data analytics tools can be adopted to great effect. There is a vast number of companies who employ dozens, hundreds, or even thousands of employees, who spend their days in Microsoft Excel. They may work in a variety of functional silos in the organization, whether they are product controllers, entity controllers, or accountants within the CFO's organization, whether they work in an operations function, or whether they work in a business management or business intelligence function rolling up to a COO or another part of the organization. Microsoft Excel continues to dominate the data processing world in the accounting, finance, and operations functions, but a thick and lengthy manual processing tail performed outside of systems highlights the shortfall of core technology platforms in meeting users' needs. Advancements in data analytics and automation tooling may finally represent viable alternatives, with the potential to supplant and dethrone Microsoft Excel as the default business processing tool, and perhaps finally relegate it to where it belongs – one of several quick and dirty tactical tools available for selection if and as required, but not the default go-to, where the majority of processing teams live, day over day.

In many organizations, the cost of employees is the most significant expense on the income statement. Intellectual capital is carefully cultivated and is very often the strongest asset from which we derive our competitive advantage and stand out from our peers. Why then is our precious bandwidth being wasted on administrative tasks or those tasks that do not push us to use our full potential? It is in the best interests of organizations to free up their people assets from the rigors of routine, mundane tasks which are not befitting of our intellectual capacity and/or skillset. How can managers safeguard the focus of their employees from the burdens of low value-added task overload? The answer may be that these tasks are ripe for automation.

We all know that systems ("big" automation) are integral to nearly every job across nearly every industry, much as mechanization was a game-changer for manufacturing during the industrial revolution. In our digital and information age, where vast data is captured, stored, transformed, and processed for use to inform business decisions, core technology systems offer coded processing and considerable mature technology governance, tied up with a bow and a ribbon. Systems are a central hub for structured development – offering data storage and processing operations, long lists of features and functionality, they offer user experience (UX) styles, and perhaps a rich reporting suite – but importantly, they quietly serve unnoticed as a centralized funnel around which to build internal controls and governance to ensure the accuracy of processing output, financial accounting, and management reporting. The fact that systems are widely subscribed to in an organization ties many operators to enveloping control frameworks built around them. Thanks to mature system governance, many systems are designed with embedded internal controls such as those that ensure appropriate user entitlements, automatic system reconciliations and check totals to ensure data integrity, and workflows may even provide for required supervisory approvals as required. Critically, many companies already enforce robust change governance around technology deliveries, including the production and retention of key project development artifacts such as business and functional requirements, evidence of test scripts and testing results, evidence of sign-off, and the completion of post-implementation reviews following a release.

Emergence of Data Analytics

However, a game-changing add-on is now available. Data analytics is coming to the fore and emerging as an exciting strategic and tactical enabler of higher-order analysis and value creation through insight generation. Data analytics includes a number of analytics tools, technologies, and buzzwords you have heard thrown about over the last decade (perhaps not at parties or on date night, but you have heard them nonetheless): robotic process automation (RPA), machine learning (ML), artificial intelligence (AI), text mining technologies like natural language processing (NLP), optical character recognition (OCR), and intelligent character recognition (ICR), along with neural networks, logistic and linear regression analysis, and many more. At the most basic level, these are tools meant to enable descriptive techniques to understand past events and drivers, to gain knowledge through the extraction of trends, to forge more intelligent processing steps, and to inform decisions. Analytics at its sexiest enables predictions to be made and even for actions to be recommended, in response to scenarios encountered.

The ability to detect anomalies in financial data, the ability to detect and flag high-risk patient test results for further review by medical practitioners, and any of a host of proven use cases for descriptive and predictive analytics – these represent huge opportunities to employ data analytics. In many cases, these are enabling models run outside of core technology systems. Data science and data analytics encompass these and many other solutions. It is not always a theoretical predictive rocket science employing complex code-based technology and advanced algorithms to solve complex problems. It is the body of solutions that organizational leaders need to cultivate and have at hand to forge forward in their digital journey, at whatever pace is appropriate to meet digital transformation goals and objectives. This pursuit has led to billions of dollars of investment in technology across many service industries, aimed at building core competencies, increasing competitive advantage and organizational efficiency, doing more with fewer employees, or reducing employee costs and footprint.

It is this last goal that the authors predict will prompt a surge in adoption of data analytics tooling in the next five years, across medium-to-large scale enterprises. Managers are looking to structure their spreadsheet-based processes in a more mature and robust way. By reducing the amount of unstructured processing performed manually in Excel, managers can stabilize and lock down spreadsheet-driven processes into more automated, repeatable, structured, and time-efficient processing steps. By minimizing time spent in performing routinized processing steps, and by minimizing process variance through emulating system processing, the spreadsheet-based jobs of the past will evolve to remove the least value-added steps in the processing chain. While this book cannot but acknowledge many of these data analytics capabilities and technologies, its focus will be around one subset of the wide body of data analytics disciplines – self-service data analytics.

See Exhibit 1-1, which illustrates how productivity can be built through the reduction of time spent for the performance of routinized processes. This can be achieved by enlisting self-service analytics capabilities to address many of the routine steps performed daily, which are highlighted in the list at the left of the diagram.

EXHIBIT 1-1 Building Daily Productivity

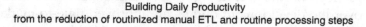

Building Daily Productivity
from the reduction of routinized manual ETL and routine processing steps

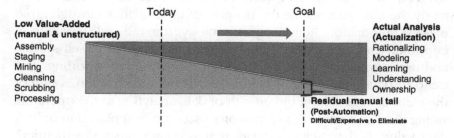

Remember that it is realistic to assume that there will always be some measure of a manual processing tail that is expensive or even impossible to eliminate, but the idea is to move as far to the right along the continuum as possible. The end result is to recapture processing time spent on low value-added steps, to allow for a greater proportion of the day to be spent on value creation.

Self-Service Data Analytics

The self-service data analytics toolset is an important growing subset of the suite of data analytics tools that is emerging as a focal point of digital transformations across large companies. It is distinct from the other sets of tools in the analytics toolkit in important ways. Self-service tools are typically off-the-shelf vendor products with which individual operators, not technologists, can interact and configure directly, due to their ease of use. Process owners that have no prior technology background and that may have never seen a piece of code are well equipped to lay out a customized, automated process, armed only with their knowledge of the raw data and the processing steps they previously performed in spreadsheets. Intelligent source data parsing and drag-and-drop operations replace SQL and Visual Basic commands, enabling the most inexperienced, inexpert, if not maladroit and bungling of us to quickly roll up our sleeves, forge and test processing steps, and implement a processing workflow, all in an afternoon ("small" automation).

The benefits of self-service data analytics tools include a reduced dependency on core technology when individuals have little influence over the development queue, an improved time-to-market and reduced "wait" in the core technology stack backlog – and importantly the ability to realize the benefits of time-savings through rapid process automation. Removing technology from the critical path is an important end, in itself, and this goal has led to a raft of self-service and user-configurable tools spanning processing and reporting. The trend of data-democratization throughout the organization is one of the main drivers behind the growth of data analytics, as the operators sitting directly on top of business processes are best placed to unlock data value. Perhaps chiefly, work that was previously unstructured, risky, and manual-intensive is now in a tool, emulating a system-driven process. Laborious and time-consuming spreadsheet processing has been replaced with nearly instantaneous computer-driven processing, leading to time savings and efficiency. Of course, there are drawbacks to these tools as well. A significant portion of the pages ahead will be focused on assessing, managing, and mitigating the risks introduced by widespread proliferation of this tooling, through the prescription of a foundational governance framework.

More immediately in this chapter, we will discuss a day in the life of operators, highlight that much of the work performed by operators and analysts is not in fact analysis, but low-value-added data staging, enrichment, and processing activities. We will also look at the processing landscape from the perspective of managers, who are increasingly under pressure to cut costs, produce more, and overall to do more with fewer hands. Then we will take a top-down strategic view from the perspective of executives who are motivated to uncover opportunities to drive efficiency across functions and silos, who share an interest in minimizing unstructured spreadsheet work across the plant, and who may be more directly accountable to internal auditors, external auditors, and regulators. They may also influence the approach, the course, and the speed of the organization's digital transformation. We will discuss the levers they can pull to increase control and to drive efficiency, and the decisions they can make to adapt the organization to expectations that routine processes must be structured and accelerated, that the focus of people resources must extend beyond low value-added mundane processing steps, and that higher-order pursuits such as unlocking data value and the enhancement of decision-making are of prime importance in the new age. Last, we will introduce one of the key topics of this book, which is the need to fill a noted governance gap, as data analytics builds saturate our respective organizations.

There are any number of relevant and overlapping frameworks that cover portions of IT governance and even portions of data analytics governance in the finance and accounting environment. However, no single framework exists that is fit for the universe of self-service data analytics builds. We will draw from mature system governance, model governance, data governance, process governance, SOX 404, COSO IC (internal control framework for the financial reporting process), COSO ERM, and COBIT 2019 (ISACA) frameworks, and even the AICPA's Statements on Auditing Standards – to sketch a foundational governance model that your organization can implement and build upon as necessary. This must be done early and determinedly, so it is in place and can play a formative role in safeguarding your organization, as it embarks on its inevitable digital journey.

Let's look at the environment from the perspective of the employee.

Employee/Analyst/Operator Perspective

Generically, these operators are analysts, though very often, actual analysis is only a sliver of their day, compared to the time spent on the raw processing steps they are expected to perform, prior to generating output for evaluative analysis. Such processing steps likely include capturing information from a number of sources, enriching the data to assemble suitably rich datasets, before completing further processing steps and transformation steps to yield final outputs in the form of information and reports. It is really only at this point that the operator can embark on true analysis in earnest.

Such outputs are often validated against prior periods to attempt to identify any abnormalities or errors. There may be key ratios that are calculated, observed, and compared to get comfort that the output is correct. There may be other sanity checks and detective controls performed to ensure process effectiveness and the integrity of deliverables. We will refer to these broadly as analytical review procedures, and we will assume that these procedures are partially about quality control and error detection, but also partially about understanding the business better, so that value can be added as a true business partner. It is these latter analytical processes that lead to actualization – ensuring high-quality outputs, owning your numbers and outputs, and gaining insights into the business through analysis.

If an organization is large enough to be layered, a pecking order emerges. More junior, if not entry-level, staff will be buried in the assembly of information and information processing. Over time, if they are good, they will strive to get faster, better, and more efficient at assembling and processing data. Those who are able to get their head above water enough to truly understand what the processing outputs are telling them, and those who can glean critical insights surrounding the business, may gain visibility and be recognized as true process owners. With luck, they may graduate to being a reviewer, supervisor, or manager – sampling the butter with a critical and experienced eye, instead of churning all day. This is the aspirational path to advancement for many in the analyst ranks, whether across finance or accounting functions, operations functions, or any of the business analytics or reporting roles that pepper the ranks of large organizations.

In times of great flux from business growth or volatility, departmental reorganizations, regulatory demands, or other external pressures, operators may find themselves quickening the pace to get their heads above water, only to be rewarded with more of the same work to drown them anew. *Take a deep breath, because you are about to be pushed right back under the surf, until you bed things down yet again at a higher plateau of utilization, with even less time to perform actual analysis, to learn, and to add value to your business.* Just when the operator begins to get to a point where they have learned enough about what their own deliverables and end-products are telling them about the business to begin to add value, they may be asked to cover another 20 accounts, or take on 20 more processes, or to produce five more weekly deliverables.

Very often, processing pain points to the need for additional system features and functionality. Organizationally astute analysts will articulate the need and route the demand item to the core technology demand queue, with the hope that it will introduce time savings, when it is eventually delivered. Such hopes can be dashed with the slash of a red marker, as requests are buried at the bottom of an interminable wish list, when higher priority initiatives take precedence, or when requestors lack the influence to argue for the relative priority of their requests. This is the reality of the environment in which many operators find themselves each day. Later, we will propose that self-service data analytics is one of the few tactical levers that can be pulled to lock down the data preparation, transformation, and processing steps in a stable, controlled manner, and to capture efficiency in the form of time savings. For now, let's look at the same environment from the perspective of managers.

Managers' Perspectives

Some managers have come up the ranks in the career progression outlined above; they may have started as an analyst and sharpened their technical skills at a faster rate than others, such that they were able to successfully execute their workload, but even more, they learned from their outputs, demonstrated value to internal clients, and ultimately moved up. Others may have been hired externally and brought into the organization, and may be less aware of the processing steps and rigors that their teams undergo each day. Similarly, *existing* managers within the organization may have been asked to assume ownership of a function, and may again be less familiar with the processes required to generate departmental deliverables. Irrespective of which of these profiles is most applicable, managers will be expected to deliver an increasing number of accurate and conforming deliverables, these days without the free hand to hire additional resources to meet increasingly stringent demands.

Most managers are focused on minimizing process variance to ensure consistent quality of outputs. In the mature systems-based environment, they insist that as much processing as possible is performed within systems, and that system outputs require little manipulation, in order to generate deliverables. Deliverables requiring complex, multi-step, and unstructured Excel-based operations introduce significant risks. Accordingly, astute managers track the progress of the technology backlog, ensure that they weigh in on the prioritization queue, and shepherd their must-haves through project stages to a scheduled release. In this way, they can ensure that the systems environment supports their processing needs. They would prefer to use well-documented, prescribed and controlled system features and functionality to perform the lion's share of processing, rather than relying on unstructured manual processing steps. The goal is to extract output from systems that is as close as possible to final form for departmental deliverables.

However, often the core technology systems have a lengthy backlog of competing priorities that may have been built up over years, that can be difficult to navigate, and which can result in significant delays in the delivery of needed features and functionality. Many readers will have felt the disappointment when they learned that a promised sprint or release has been postponed, or when they learned that the all-important and long-awaited Phase 2 of a large-scale strategic technology delivery is below-the-line for the year, left unfunded on the shelf. Does that mean that teams must continue to work in an inefficient and unstructured way, until such time as the technology investment is revisited in the next investment cycle? Perhaps not. In the section Arguments for Self-Service Data Analytics Tooling, presented later in this chapter, we will provide a preview of self-service data analytics options and introduce an approach that managers can take to structuring work with analytics-assisted tooling while they await the needed system enhancements.

Control is not the only concern of today's managers. In an environment where increasing work demands are being placed on the talent pool, with downward pressures on the organizational cost-base and footprint, managers are preoccupied with the capture of efficiency. Across large departments, each daily hour saved can contribute to headcount avoidance, in the event that the increased productivity allows existing staff to accommodate additional demands without making a hire. Even in a stable demand environment, efficiency is a prime motivator. In the event that the hours saved sum up to a full headcount equivalent, one full-time employee can then be redeployed to another function altogether.

Now, let's look at the organization from the perspective of executives.

Executives' Strategic Perspectives

To get a full perspective, it is useful to understand the concerns of divisional executives or even C-suite executives who are charged with leading efforts to unlock the value of data, managing divisional footprints, and driving organizational efficiency. They have a keen interest in setting the pace of digital technology adoption and deployment. They can directly influence the approach, course, and speed of the organization's digital journey progress. Of course, they have more control over resource pools and technology budgets across functions than do managers. While often removed from the day-to-day processing operations of their constituent teams, they share an interest in structuring unstructured work across the plant, and in minimizing the likelihood and business impact of process failure, given their accountability to internal auditors, external auditors, regulators, clients, and investors.

Divisional executives will be interested in all key measurements that communicate the health of their business. From sales and market share on the revenue side, to the cost and expense side of profitability metrics, they will be motivated by data points and trends that point to organizational fitness and longer-term value creation. In service organizations, efficiency is measured not by inventory turns and asset turnover but by productivity measures like cycle times, process completion times, failure rates, and straight through processing (STP) ratios, just to name a few. Of course, executives spend much of their time managing and remediating failures and exceptions, which impact the business considerably, when they are bubbled up to visibility. We are speaking in broad terms here, and in no way are we minimizing other important metrics that executives may actively manage like social responsibility, employee diversity, employee satisfaction, and the many other critical measures they consider. The point is that, to the extent that executives can be brought to see the potential for introducing processing efficiency across an organization, to the extent that they understand the very real impact of process failure on client relationships, audit results, and even on their stream of information for decision-making, they can be brought into the tent as active champions and sponsors of a digital course that drives the organization forward in leaps and bounds.

Due to the organizational resources they have at their disposal, there are many levers they can pull to increase control and to drive efficiency, and to unlock data value to enhance decision-making. If the total cost of the many processing departments measures in the millions of dollars, a fractional savings is a worthy objective to be excited about. If an innovation is developed in one part of their organization that has wide applicability and opportunities for replication across the shop, it is their responsibility to put in place an overarching clearinghouse apparatus to capture and scale these opportunities. Perhaps most critical of all is that executives feel convinced that risks are well documented and understood across the enterprise, and that strong policies and procedures are in place to guide the organization in active risk management.

In Chapter 5, we will discuss further the need to address risk through active risk governance, as operators themselves develop processing solutions with the employ of self-service data analytics tools.

Arguments for Self-Service Data Analytics Tooling

The data analytics toolkit is growing at a rapid pace, with many off-the-shelf tools that can be customized to perform routinized processing tasks. By shoehorning an unstructured process into a self-service data analytics tool, analysts and operators can structure work into a repeatable process that is stable, documented, and robust – even tactically mimicking a system-based process. Self-service analytics is a form of business intelligence (BI) in which line-of-business professionals are enabled to perform queries; extract, transform, and load (ETL) and data enrichment activities; and to structure their work in tools, with only nominal IT support. Self-service analytics is often characterized by simple-to-use BI tools with basic analysis capabilities and an underlying data model that has been simplified or scaled down for ease of understanding and straightforward data access.

Earlier in this chapter, in the section Employee/Analyst/Operator Perspective, we described the plight of end-users who spend a disproportionate amount of their time performing data staging, data preparation, and routinized processing activities, instead of spending their time gleaning meaning and trends from their outputs through value-added analysis. We discussed that they may have little influence over the prioritization queue for technology demand items, let alone an ability to influence the budgeted dollar amounts approved during the annual technology investment cycle, often leaving their efficiency needs unmet by core technology. We discussed the overlapping, but slightly different perspective of managers, surrounding the need to increase control and reduce processing variance and failures, by structuring work in tools. We also discussed their motivation to capture efficiency, in order to meet additional demands being placed on resource-constrained departments. Here again, managers are often at the mercy of the technology investment cycle budgets and priorities, which may be likely to leave their needs unmet in the short term. Finally, we discussed the landscape from the perspective of C-suite and divisional executives, who wish to minimize the number and impact of highly publicized catastrophic processing failures and the number of audit points levied by internal and external auditors, and who could be enticed to embrace any edge offered in strategic decision-making that paves the way for organizational success. The authors submit that a program of "small" automation through self-service data analytics could serve the needs of all of these stakeholders.

End-user analytics tools and business intelligence tooling can be readily deployed to automate small bits and pieces of processes in and around systems. Importantly, the involvement of core technology teams is not required to build them, as they would be for a far larger application rollout. When vendor software licensing costs are weighed up against time savings, the average cost of employees, and the additional productivity that can be enjoyed as a result of tool deployment, a significant return on investment (ROI) is evident. End-user tooling can be engaged by virtually everyone in an organization that is able to identify appropriate use cases and to navigate the increasingly accessible and user-friendly functionality.

Operators and analysts can target the low value-added steps in their processing chain for analytics-assisted automation, allowing them to realize efficiency benefits in short order, even while strategic change requests work their way through the backlog and "wait" queues. Managers gain from the structured, stabilized, and regimented processing that results from centralizing processing steps in a tool. They can improve process controls, while improving cycle time and building capacity. Finally, executive-level strategic leadership can directly benefit from widespread adoption of self-service data analytics. From reduced client and regulatory impact of failed processing incidents to improved audit results, from capturing efficiency to sourcing descriptive and predictive information to improve decision-making – all of these arguments will be persuasive to division-level executives and functional heads. As self-service analytics champions, these leaders can do much to instill a proactive and empowered mindset across the organization. They can influence the reallocation of core technology investment budget dollars to the funding of a centrally sponsored data analytics program. Perhaps most importantly, they can promote and encourage innovative thinking throughout the enterprise.

Need for Self-Service Data Analytics Governance

Having set the stage, it is now appropriate to introduce one of the key topics of this book, which is the need for strong self-service data analytics governance. Many readers may already have begun to replace their spreadsheet-based end-user computing (EUC) tooling with tactical data analytics tools. We have already discussed the significant benefits available in putting flexible, user-configurable tools into the hands of users. Once the seal has been broken, expect widespread deployment at scale.

Skip ahead two years and suddenly you feel exposed. Which builds are being relied upon by regulators? Which builds are relied upon by customers? Did the individual who put them in place have adequate knowledge of the underlying processes to build reliably and effectively? Were they well versed with the data analytics tools and technologies deployed? Were such builds adequately tested? Precisely how many builds exist across the organization? If key software vendors raise the price of basic licenses, is any of the work salvageable for migration to a new platform? You are being challenged by key internal clients on the quality of the financial deliverables that your team prepares, but you learn your team has simply been taking analytics build outputs at face value. They no longer understand the longhand processing steps that have been automated, as the team has experienced significant turnover over the last two years. This has resulted in the tools effectively becoming "black boxes," where the transformation steps embedded in them are obscured and difficult to decipher. You fear that your organization has fallen into a common trap; by moving away from regimented technology release cycles toward a decentralized change model, you have lost control.

Governance, or lack thereof, is perhaps the strongest harbinger of control and stability, in an environment where self-service data analytics is prevalent. Effective governance is particularly critical due to the expected growth pattern of data analytics adoption, once the floodgates are opened. Without the benefit of governance to keep pace with the decentralization of development capabilities, organizations can find themselves struggling to demonstrate process effectiveness; they may not have clear visibility into the degree to which they are dependent on off-the-shelf software applications; they may lack adequate information upon which to base risk assessments; or they may get it abjectly wrong. Governance must provide guidelines aimed at ensuring the quality and integrity of processing inputs; that processing solutions implemented are appropriate, adequately tested, and operate effectively; that minimum standards of project documentation are met; and that risk assessment and mitigation activities can be demonstrated in the thoughtful deployment of analytics tooling.

The shift from centralizing processing within systems to the decentralized development model, where end-users are equipped to independently source data and to flexibly structure processing without the involvement of IT, necessitates a commensurate shift in controls. In the past, the controls safeguarding the enterprise from various IT general and application risks were centralized around the core technology stack. With the advent of self-service data analytics tools, increased development capabilities are placed directly into the hands of end-users. Controls embedded in systems are rendered irrelevant, to the extent that processing is done outside of them. This evolution has dramatically shifted the risk environment.

Effectively, the robust governance that was built around systems has been side-stepped, now that systems are no longer the critical path for an increasing number of data analytics–assisted processes.

A risk mitigation framework is needed that would address the real-location of control risk to the end-user in the decentralized processing environment. Since process owners, themselves, oversee many facets of their processing, it is not appropriate for IT alone to administer and maintain governance for data analytics programs. As a complement to systems governance, a framework must be developed to pull together the mature elements of system controls to marry them with the unique profiles, risks, and capabilities of emerging self-service data analytics tools. This framework must be threaded and interconnected throughout the firm, championed and sponsored by firm leadership, and must provide for robust *project* governance, *investment* governance, and *risk* governance.

In the following chapters, we will take a very practical approach to getting readers comfortable with data analytics technologies and practices: surveying operations to uncover use cases with significant benefits warranting prioritization and investment, matching tools to opportunities, and deriving an achievable digital roadmap. We will introduce you to emerging technology that is markedly transforming the processing environment. Later, we will demonstrate the use of one prominent data analytics tool, Alteryx, to bring you aboard the journey. Perhaps most importantly, we will get you thinking about how to prepare your organization by establishing key governance steps now, so that you maintain control as your organization adopts self-service data analytics and business intelligence tooling at scale. In months of research prior to writing this book, your authors failed to identify an existing comprehensive governance framework that is suited entirely for self-service data analytics. Accordingly, in this book, we will draw from more mature and established frameworks (data governance, system governance, and model governance) to build a foundational governance model that can grow with your footprint, as your organization embarks on its inevitable digital journey.

CHAPTER 2

Emerging AI and Data Analytics Tooling and Disciplines

Companies pursue digital transformation as part of an overall overhaul of business models, as legacy models no longer apply in the current technology-driven environment. As notable technology companies have disrupted entire industries over the past two decades, service companies have pursued digital transformation to remain relevant, develop a competitive edge, and to integrate successful technology innovations into their overall strategy. Many companies regard data as one of their most valuable assets, and digital transformation initiatives are often centered around creating systems and processes to unlock this value. Some of the top reasons that organizations undertake the effort is to unlock data value, to better understand their customers, and to improve products and services. Within finance, accounting, and operations functions, digital transformation initiatives have been more focused on value creation through process control, efficiency savings, and improved reporting.

The low-hanging fruit in finance, accounting, and operations functions is to automate unstructured manual spreadsheet processes using self-service analytics tooling and robotic. process automation (RPA) to increase control and to capture process efficiencies. Enhanced processing and reporting can be achieved by ingesting high-quality data into self-service analytics tools for enrichment and automated processing, before outputs are communicated visually with low-latency, interactive dashboards. Cost savings can be realized by freeing up human capital from the manual and repetitive performance of routinized processes. Further, manual processes performed in spreadsheets are error-prone, and resulting errors can cascade into other dependent processes and continue to proliferate undetected. The reduced dependence on spreadsheets for manual processing can reduce the possibility of introducing errors and can thereby improve the expected quality of processing outputs. These two goals – control and efficiency – are the key motivations for organizations to adopt automation tooling and will be the predominant focus of this book. However, there are additional motivational factors as well.

Increased job satisfaction and full resource actualization can occur when employees focus on tasks that enhance value for the organization, rather than on mundane, redundant, and low value-added processing steps and activities. By reducing the proportion of time that individuals spend on the manual tail performed outside of systems (data staging, cleansing, enriching, reformatting, and processing), relative to the time spent performing value-added analysis to generate actionable business insights, employees can more readily create value. Organizations benefit through increased process stability and productivity, while employees benefit from increased focus, increased engagement, and true process ownership. In some cases, advanced analytics can be applied to use machine learning and artificial intelligence models for decision-making. New applications of advanced analytics emerge daily and are limited only by the collective imagination, but in large spreadsheet processing plants, "small" automation efforts aimed at improving control and realizing efficiencies and cost savings one process at a time will come to the fore. Self-service data analytics tooling can enable these efforts and will largely be the focus of this book.

Introduction to Data Analytics Tooling

A decade or more into the data analytics era, many readers will have heard reference to a number of data analytics disciplines and technologies. Some of them have highly technical and sexy sounding names, while others may sound vaguely familiar, if lackluster. In the following pages, we will provide a very high level introduction to a handful of key data analytics technologies, with which managers should be familiar. They all form the living backdrop against which specific analytics applications have emerged. Only a small subset of these are considered to be self-service data analytics tools, but all of these have been successfully demonstrated to add value, when applied appropriately to use cases with adequately rich benefits at scale. In the following sections, we will introduce some of the data analytics disciplines and technologies that have matured and risen to prominence. Note that these abbreviated introductions only scratch the surface of the suite of emerging technologies marching under the broad banner of data analytics.

Internet of Things

One of your authors was a houseguest in a luxury Manhattan apartment roughly 15 years ago, in 2005. He recalls being shown around and impressed that previously stand-alone items were now connected and controlled by the internet. One specific appliance that caught his eye was the refrigerator, which featured a small TV monitor on its door. The homeowner explained that with his "connected" fridge, he was able to maintain an inventory of what necessities were on hand and could easily make a list of the items he needed to purchase. He could even place an online order to have those items delivered. This was an amazing step forward at that time.

Now, any number of items in our homes are connected to the internet – smart TVs, thermostats, security cameras and home alarms, door locks and garage door openers, lightbulbs, a variety of Amazon Alexa and Google Home hubs, stereos and speaker systems, and far more. Looking forward another 15 years, we predict that readers of future editions of this book may not even recall the age when these connected "things" were not in our homes and relied on to provide the weather forecast, to recommend items for our shopping lists, and to consume streaming podcasts, music stations, and video content. Clearly, we are interacting with and consuming data at an unseen level, but on the flip side, we are generating consumer data at an explosive clip.

The "internet of things" (IoT) is one of the factors that is driving the data explosion. All of these connected items are generating colorful data on consumer choices, our buying patterns, and our individual routines. When do we check the weather? When do we leave for work and typically return at home after our workday? When do we turn up the heat or cool our homes down? How many times did the garage door go up and down throughout the day? What movement was captured and logged near the back door on our connected security camera? What do we order when we have our meals delivered? If you consider the vast array of high-velocity data types and the number of observations being collected, it is easy to see how the term "Big Data" was coined. How your organization mobilizes to connect to this data for logistical and client relationship benefits will set the tone for success in the next decade. How you, as an individual, can adopt emerging technologies to get on board in the new digital landscape will position you for personal success along this time frame.

Cloud Storage and Cloud Computing

We have already described that data is being captured at a rate never before seen. Some say that today, companies like Amazon, Google, and others know what we need before we do. They capture data surrounding how we shop, what we buy, our online browsing patterns, our spending patterns, and the likely order of our transactions. One consequence of harnessing the enterprise utility of customer data is that data volumes have multiplied and exploded over the last 10 to 15 years. In many cases, enterprises require data storage that far exceeds what can be accommodated with their own hardware in their own facilities. Further, the number of operations performed on the data has increased commensurately. However, with advances in connectivity, the availability of capacious networks, increased speed of information transmission, and advances in data security, companies may elect to upload their data to data centers outside of their organization in the cloud, to be administered by cloud service providers (CSPs).

Some of the largest CSPs, such as Amazon Web Services, Microsoft Azure, IBM, Google Cloud Platform, Salesforce, Alibaba, and Oracle, offer not only storage but computing, security, and enterprise software services. It is easy to see that there is a virtual ecosystem to be managed, including not only Big Data but also the hardware, specialty software, and analytical methods required to unlock its value. This ecosystem includes other ancillary components, including security and encryption, computer processing, and a host of tools and solutions to transform supply chains and to enhance customer experience. Companies must face the decision as to whether to continue to build and grow their own technological capabilities in-house or to subscribe to one or several focus-built and ready-made cloud services available in the marketplace, or perhaps to consume services from several CSPs, which is an increasingly likely choice.

Since the advent of cloud computing, many companies no longer deem it necessary to purchase licenses and install software for dozens of required programs on every individual connected machine across an enterprise. Instead, every computer on a connected network can subscribe to and run software that is *housed* in the cloud to process data that is *stored* in the cloud, assisted by the expertise of CSPs. A user may only pull down fully processed information and outputs, as required for local consumption. It is important to introduce the cloud, given some of the largest service providers are packaging up tools and expertise surrounding some of the subject technologies of this book – artificial intelligence, machine learning, and analytics, to name a few. Let's begin by providing an introductory overview of artificial intelligence.

Artificial Intelligence

Artificial intelligence (AI) is one of the broadest and most all-encompassing of the data analytics references the reader will hear. It is the over-arching theory and science of development of computer systems and processes that can consider facts and variables to perform processes that typically require human intelligence and the uniquely human capability of learning new things and applying them. Any number of sciences and disciplines are brought to AI such as mathematics, computer science, psychology, and linguistics, among many others. One need only picture the ways that humans think, interact, and understand one another to perform daily tasks to see the breadth of fields, disciplines, and specialty branches of learning that must be brought to bear.

At one time, this term included virtually all the individual technologies that will be introduced in this chapter, in one form or another. However, once the loosely organized science gives birth to a proven discipline, the emergent capability is purged from the definition of AI and can stand alone. Therefore, AI is by definition the nebulous and nondescript potential technologies that may ultimately emerge to emulate human thinking, capabilities, and interactions. Prior to building critical mass and emerging successfully as individual disciplines, optical character recognition (OCR), intelligent character recognition (ICR), speech recognition, observing any combination or sequence of variables for compound decision making, language translation, robotic process automation (RPA), neural networks and machine learning – all of these lived in the vague, blurred, and ambiguous land of potential to emulate human-like capabilities – artificial intelligence.

Blockchain and Distributed Ledger Technology

The next technology we will introduce in this chapter is distributed ledger technology (DLT) upon which blockchain is based. In order to transact digitally and with confidence, the ownership chain of assets of value must be trackable and auditable. If we think about all the transactions our companies engage in, one activity that often represents manual work and a break in straight through processing (STP) is verifying transactions when questions arise after-the-fact. Think of the number of reconciliations performed across accounting, finance, and operations functions in business today. Often, reconciliations are aimed at comparing and agreeing things like transactions, assets, securities, and account balances to confirm the true state of a ledger. A reconciliation is essentially the comparison of two datasets to either confirm their agreement or to identify any exceptions or *breaks*. Once exceptions are identified, countless hours of investigation can follow, tracing the exceptions back to transactional source data to confirm which of the two data sets under comparison are correct, and to take the necessary resolution steps to correct the faulty dataset. What if this could be solved in a different way?

Distributed ledgers contain different types of shared data, such as transaction records, attributes of transactions, credentials, or other pieces of information worthy of retention and validation. Blockchain technology allows a network of computers to agree at regular intervals on the "true" state of a distributed ledger. On a blockchain, transactions are recorded chronologically, forming an immutable chain, and can be made private or public, depending on how the technology is implemented. The ledger is distributed across many participants in the network; it does not exist in only one place. Instead, copies exist and are simultaneously updated with every fully participating node in the ecosystem. Therefore, a blockchain emerges as a single validated source of truth. Suddenly, a decentralized network can achieve broad consensus about the state and authenticity of a block's contents. Each participant in the network can verify the true state of the ledger, contribute to maintaining the accuracy and authenticity of the ledger, and subscribe to the resulting dataset as a golden source of truth. This technology can be used to transact at low cost, or to reduce reconciliation efforts and minimize the costs of resolution steps.

What if counterparties to transactions were both (or all) participants on the same distributed ledger? If they each (or all, respectively) agreed on the validity of ownership or asset movements, and each subscribed to the resulting golden source of truth, would there be a need for the vast numbers of after-the-fact reconciliations or the audits that are undertaken to resolve exceptions? Would there be an opportunity for exceptions to emerge at all? So goes the theoretical benefits case for distributed ledger technology to the accounting, finance, and operations functions in large organizations.

Use cases abound for distributed ledgers and blockchain. In accounting and finance functions, there are a number of opportunities to harness this to settle and reconcile transactions more efficiently than is done currently. Think of the processes undertaken by your own organizations to research the completeness of transactions, the accuracy of balances, or the true state of ownership. Have a think about the number of reconciliations and comparisons performed in your own office to get a sense as to whether there are opportunities to gain efficiencies by consuming a single source of truth that has been validated through consensus of participants. In logistics, benefits can accrue from leveraging an immutable audit trail of goods as they move through the economy – as supplies move to manufacturers, through the goods production process, as finished goods move out the door to distributors, and how they pass logistically through shipment and delivery to consumers. Other use cases arise in identity and authentication. It is clear that distributed ledger technology will change the way we do business in the future. This technology is in no way the focus of this book, but we want readers to be familiar with key disruptors that are shifting the landscape in the new digital age.

Robotic Process Automation

One of the tools that has gained prominence is robotic process automation (RPA). Robotics, or Bots, for short, can be used to automate routine processing steps that were previously done by humans. RPA is most appropriate for highly routinized or transactional processes or for the routinized portion of more complex processes. Obvious benefits of RPA can be measured in three ways:

1. In many cases, the cost of software licenses required to maintain the Bot can be less than the costs to maintain the number of employees they can replace. This is often, but not always true.
2. Given that Bots, by definition, structure processes that were previously unstructured and manually performed by operators, they can lead to increased control and process stability.
3. Bots can perform processes at speeds unrivaled by humans, when appropriately configured. This means that work which previously required a full day to perform (or many equivalent workdays to perform, in cases where an entire team performed the task in the legacy environment) can be accomplished in minutes – or even seconds.

Data entry is often a prime candidate for this technology, when the target source data for input can be found in a consistent array. Imagine for a moment that a receivables clerk routinely captures an extract of received cash from a bank statement, traces the amount back to a receivables balance, and then formulates a cross-asset journal entry in the general ledger to debit cash and credit accounts receivable. If we assume that there is connectivity between the Bot software and all component systems related to the process, and if we assume that there is a high-quality mapping of customer static allowing the operator to relate the enterprise name on the bank statement to the accounts in the receivables master, and if we assume that adequate controls surrounding this process can be built to ensure it is rigorous and stable, this process may be a great candidate for a Bot.

Today, readers may be interacting with Bots without even being aware. Individuals may engage Chatter Bots (Chat Bots) in any number of platforms. Chat Bots are NLP-intensive applications which are programmed to perform human-like on-line chat conversations. Customers interact with them in much the same way as they would, were there a live operator on the other end of the line. The software would respond to social and conversational queues like "Hello" and respond in kind ("Hello, Reader!"). They would also perform a classification to understand what information is being requested and what operations are required to respond most appropriately. These are heavily used by support teams and can multiply the bandwidth of existing staff. Of course, there are limitations. The Bots must be explicitly programmed to respond to written queues, meaning that each response must have been explicitly provided for, as the program is developed. The Turing Test was developed to test the ability of a machine to interact in a way that is indistinguishable from a human. On this scale, many Chat Bots today fail to convincingly resemble humans, but they can be used to great advantage when requests are highly predictable and standardized.

Complex software installations can be performed by a Bot, given that the number and order of steps are discrete, finite, and well understood. Reconciliations, which occupy many in accounting, finance, and operations, can readily be performed by Bots. Any number of activities that require the merging of data from any number of systems, departments, or processing outputs can benefit from a Bot, though in many cases there are ready-made tools available for ETL use cases that are better suited to this task.

There are general rules of thumb that allow reviewers to confirm that a process is viable for RPA. In order for it to be viable, as a starting point the target data attribute needs to be mastered consistently such that it appears in the same format, placement, or field on a page, file, or screen. If it is being captured for entry elsewhere, the Bot must be able to readily interface with the destination application and to navigate to the target field for entry. More complex processes can represent a challenge for Bots, where instability of input formats and locations is introduced. Any processes which require qualitative discernment would likely be out of reach for independent Bot processing. However, Bots in a first pass could wade through processing queues, process only qualifying transactions in scenarios where prerequisite values and criteria are met, and surface all other nonconforming transactions to an exception queue for the human operator, when they warrant scrutiny and discernment. *Sure, it is cherry picking, but does it add up to appreciable savings? In many cases, the answer is yes.*

Another way to deal with complex processes is to break them down to a series of the most basic discrete steps. For the simpler steps in the processing chain that are viable, Bots can be deployed for rapid execution, leaving the more complicated processing steps in the value chain to an operator (who now enjoys a bit more time to perform them). A much-repeated folly is to promise your stakeholders that an entire process from A-to-Z can be automated. Very often it is simply a matter of time until a time-sucking challenge is encountered that endangers the delivery as a whole, or at least the perceptions of the delivery. In reality, for virtually all automation projects, there is very often residual manual tail of work left unautomated by the effort.

One alternate approach is to embrace this fact from the start and to employ a modular approach to automation, by narrowly defining the scope of Bots within a process chain. The scope of the Bot could be defined to be only a very narrow sliver of the overall process. An example may be that when product controller performs a reconciliation of trade blotter positions to general ledger positions on T+1, they perform 27 steps across several systems, many of which involve discernment, judgment, and the benefit of their considerable experience and expertise. Within the process overall, there are only several individual steps which are well suited for RPA. For example, two steps that are critical and must be performed without exception, are: (1) download an extract of yesterday's trade activity from the risk management system, and (2) launch the general ledger application and set the value date to the prior day. These narrower scope processes can be successfully automated with a Bot, even though the remainder of the processing steps may be overly complex or unsuitable for automation. By modularly defining the scope of the Bot and deploying them for limited use, the time-to-market can be hastened, versus spinning your wheels attempting to automate the process from head to toe (*chasing a unicorn*). The individual savings on any given day may be small, but the benefits can be considerable, if the same functionality can be reused with only minor customization. (You have now built an application launch Bot for the general ledger. Need a Bot to launch any other applications? Simply rinse, adapt, and repeat). The benefits can add up when there is wide applicability and abundant replication opportunities for modular functionality to be redeployed to the benefit of hundreds or even thousands of employees across an enterprise.

At the time of this writing, the robotics platforms of four companies dominate, although this is a moving target. The industry-leading platforms are as follows: Automation Anywhere, Blue Prism, UIPath, and NICE. These names are less important than gaining an appreciation for the underlying technology and the appropriate use cases to which they are best applied. For now, remember that Bots are best deployed for stable and repetitive processes that exhibit very little variance.

Machine Learning

Machine learning (ML) is the subset of artificial intelligence (AI) that is focused on the study of computer algorithms that improve automatically through experience. Machine learning algorithms build a mathematical model based on samples of data observations or *training data*, to make decisions or predictions, without being explicitly programmed to do so. Above, we introduced RPA, which relies on very regimented coding of specific operations, depending on explicit variables. With machine learning, a number of samples are analyzed to understand the relationships of inputs and to determine how outcomes are derived. The more training data that is pumped through the model, the better the algorithm should get at predicting the "right" answer. Machine learning algorithms are used in a wide variety of applications, such as email filtering and computer vision, where it is difficult or infeasible to develop conventional algorithms or code to predict and specify needed tasks.

This morning, one of your authors arose an hour earlier than normal to get in a jog on this pleasant June day. As he pulled the phone off the charger, a message on the screen read that the phone was scheduled to be fully charged at 5:45am. The change in schedule had clearly thrown off the charging fairy, as the battery power read only 94% charged. One hour and a good jog later, the author then launched his thermostat app to turn down the AC, before getting in the car to begin the commute. Once in the car, the same phone displayed a message indicating that there was light traffic to the train station, a journey which was predicted to take 8 minutes. A prompt came up to allow for quick directions to the train station, which was hastily declined. Afterall, the authors are brilliant not only with data analytics and governance books, but with getting themselves to the train station, even without the benefit of GPS-assisted instructions.

It is easy to see machine learning in action, in just the first 90 minutes of the day. It is not exactly clear which of the author's observed activities or *features* were used to trigger his phone to make suggestions, but it is clear that routine daily actions observed and logged over time had served as training data and had ultimately resulted in a number of predictions about subsequent activities or *labels*. Clearly, the phone knew the time the alarm was set for, at what time the commute begins, and where your author's car is left for the day.

There is a scale of maturity for machine learning capabilities, beginning with descriptive analytics to look at what has happened in the past with data aggregation and mining, moving forward to diagnostic analytics, to understand the drivers of the target outcomes. Moving further along the continuum, we get to predictive analytics to help us to project from past observations what will happen in the future, based on statistical forecasting models, and on to prescriptive analytics, which uses optimization and simulation algorithms to advise on possible outcomes and to determine what actions should be taken. In the phone example above, the machine learning model is far out to the right, even approaching prescriptive analytics. The model was able to predict the next actions and to prescribe what to do about them – launch the driving directions app, as you are in the car and headed to the train station!

It is likely that analysts will encounter less mature models, where they would be pleased just to draw correlations that are difficult to uncover with simplistic traditional analysis tools. The analyst may be looking for descriptions of the *X*s observed in the case of *Y* outcomes, or perhaps explanations of the *Y*s from observed *X*s. However, it is thought that the true value can come in an algorithm *understanding* a large number of observations such that it can make predictions about the future. Taking it a step further, by tying the predicted outcomes to prescribed action steps, we approach true artificial intelligence, enabling us to best deal with encountered scenarios in a data-driven and methodical way.

Optical Character Recognition/Intelligent Character Recognition

Optical character recognition (OCR) is a means of using software to convert images of typed, handwritten, or printed text into machine-encoded text, from a number of formats – scanned documents, photos of documents, or even from subtitles, captions, or text superimposed on an image. As a practical matter, OCR is often used to digitally capture books or other documents with consistent and universally recognizable fonts. OCR is often a component of document management software (DMS) that can be used to go paperless. Many readers may use DMS programs to allow them to take a snapshot of transaction receipts with their phones, and the software will capture and categories transactional details like the items purchased and the vendor, directly from the image. Other images that we work with can be tailored to our needs better with OCR. Common examples include Adobe Acrobat document images, which are common for locking down documents into a stable, read-only format, prior to distribution. Using OCR capabilities can allow for more flexible digital archiving, can make them searchable, and can even allow users to copy and paste from the created body of machine-encoded text, once it has been extracted from the image.

Intelligent character recognition (ICR) is a very similar technology, on the surface. It also enables the extraction of text from images. However, it has an added dimension of complexity: the ability to learn more complicated and non-standard fonts, and importantly – even human handwriting. Whereas OCR tends to be appropriate for easily understood typewritten text, being able to learn, recognize, and understand the free-est of free-text forms is another skill altogether. The ability to continuously learn from training data makes it significantly more sophisticated and often more costly to deploy. Organizations that wish to be able to capture and archive large volumes of information from images should evaluate the level of customization and flexibility required to process the target body of data, being conscious of the complexity and costs involved in moving along the capability spectrum from OCR to ICR.

Natural Language Processing

Natural language processing (NLP) is a dimension of artificial intelligence that enlists linguistics and computer science to improve how computers can capture, analyze, and process large volumes of human language data. Efforts in this area have centered around speech recognition, language translation, natural language understanding, and natural language generation. This is perhaps the area of artificial intelligence which has been in existence the longest, spanning decades of work in the field.

In our discussion of robotic process automation (RPA) in a previous section of this chapter, we described in some detail how Chat Bots can multiply the efforts of existing customer service staff by engaging users to extract common demands and then locating appropriate information to provide in response. Chat Bots leverage NLP to "understand" those demands. Other popular assistants in use today are reliant on NLP to enable commands to be invoked.

For many of us, informal conversational English can be quite different from explicit computer language demands. "Hey Siri, can you place a call to order pizza from that place on Main Street we ordered from last week?" is a natural language request that needs to be *classified*, or broken down, to answer such questions as Q1: "What does the user want?" – A1: The user would like me to place a call, or at least to locate a phone number. Q2: "Place a call to (or get a phone number for) whom?" – A2: A pizza restaurant that is in the user's call history, with an address on Main Street, Q3: "If my classification fails, or any of my actions do not appear suitable, relevant, or of value, is there any other related information I can provide to better assist the user?" – A3: Provide pizza options from nearby restaurants.

NLP is all about being able to structure, classify, and understand meaning from volumes and volumes of unstructured data. If we think about how much information is available on the internet, could not the internet be a valuable and rich dataset containing a nearly infinite number of observations for virtually any study? If you were the CEO of one of the largest social media sites, do you think you could benefit from digesting at any point in time, the millions of posts that are published in your ecosystem? Remember, these posts are both the lifeblood of your livelihood, but they may also represent the biggest liabilities to your reputation and ultimately threats to your profitability. Perhaps even worse, could a reckless failure to draft guidelines on appropriate online behavior, to actively monitor the body of content published on your site, and to implement policies and procedures to appropriately respond to any behaviors that are counter to your guidelines introduce regulatory risk? Could they prompt regulatory action, potentially impact your business model, and compromise your long-cultivated self-determination and independence? *GULP!*

In the above example, getting assistance from a finely tuned NLP model, to process informal vernacular in posts, to glean meaning from content, to perform classification to determine whether posts are appropriate, and finally to flag as exceptions any posts deemed inconsistent with usage guidelines, could be a very valuable tool to have at your disposal. Equipping an NLP model to extract, structure, and classify messages, all while continually improving the outcomes, is integral to allowing humans to interface with computers on our own terms.

Self-Service Data Analytics

We have introduced self-service data analytics as an important growing subset in the suite of data analytics tools that are rapidly saturating the finance, accounting, and operations functions across organizations. In most cases, these tools are off-the-shelf vendor products with which individual operators, not technologists, can interact and configure directly, due to their drag-and-drop ease of use. Process owners, rather than coders and technologists, can build workflows in a tool that can replace many of the unstructured spreadsheet processes they perform each day, or at least replace *many* of the processing steps embedded within such processes (*always remember the residual tail*). In this section, we wish to highlight self-service data analytics as an indispensable evolving discipline that is rising to prevalence across medium-to-large organizations. This specific subset of data analytics will be one of the key focal areas of this book.

The flexible, customizable, and low-code, no-code capabilities offered by self-service data analytics tools allow process owners to very quickly structure a workflow to extract source data for processing, whether selected and consumed from systems or arriving in free text, as a clean data array in a flat file or a spreadsheet or as an image for OCR/ICR data extraction. Once data is extracted and ingested, it can be transformed (joined or enriched with data from additional datasets, filters can be applied, mathematical operations completed, and field order or file format can be changed) before the data outputs are loaded to another system for further processing, or perhaps to a visualization application or dashboard for display.

These functions are commonly referred to as extract, transform, and load (ETL) capabilities. ETL represents some of the most common use cases for self-service data analytics tools. If you think about what operators in your respective organizations are doing in spreadsheets all day, it is very often starting with one or several system extracts, then enriching them further by joining together a number of other flat files or spreadsheet files, performing any number of operations on the dataset, before transforming data to a specific output format such as a report, or the required format for load to another tool. As a last step, the enriched and transformed dataset can be either input directly to another system or tool or transmitted via any number of delivery methods.

Many readers that carry out their processing work in spreadsheets day in, day out could likely save time and reduce errors, if processes are migrated to a regimented workflow in self-service data analytics tools. If you think about the accounting, finance, and operations departments in your respective firms, how many office workers are spending a good portion of their days doing exactly these things? Are there hundreds? Are there thousands? What if one to two hours per day could be saved for each of them by adopting self-service data analytics tools? Would that free up thousands of hours? Could your organization save millions of dollars? *Now we have your attention!*

Of course, many of these steps could be eliminated by adding additional features and functionality to core systems. If there was interoperability between systems upstream, such that datasets were adequately rich within core systems, users may not be required to enrich them downstream outside of systems. No longer would they need to open six spreadsheets and use key fields and VLOOKUPs to pull back all the data required for a given processing operation. If system reporting suites were adequately rich and flexible, operators could forego the "transformation" steps they perform outside of systems to reorder fields or to reformat system outputs.

The authors submit that in no way should tactical self-service tooling replace the core tech backlog delivery. Managers should continue to push the change apparatus in their respective organizations for the delivery of processing functionality in strategic applications. We have already discussed that lengthy wait times often accompany a full core tech backlog; however, there is no need to suffer while you wait. In many cases, process owners, themselves, can quickly structure their own processes in self-service analytics tools, like Alteryx, for example, dramatically reducing the time spent performing processing in spreadsheet-based end-user computing tools (EUCs), and can even reduce their number altogether. In Chapter 4, we will prescribe a control point to ensure that all tactical self-service data analytics builds can be cross-referenced back to an enhancement request in a strategic core technology system backlog. This ensures that tactical builds are a stopgap measure with a limited shelf-life, until the strategic solution can be delivered behind it.

In the meantime, tactical builds can pave the way for strategic change by forcing end-users to systematically think through and articulate requirements. The tactical builds can also serve as working proofs of concept for the requested system enhancements and can be used to demonstrate the required functionality, as part of the requirements package handed off to technology. Further, once built, the tactical tool can be run in parallel, to assist with user acceptance testing (UAT), as the strategic enhancements are developed in core systems behind it. This can significantly speed testing cycles and allow for additional and more comprehensive testing and testing coverage by reducing the required testing lift with the assistance of the tactical tooling.

There is one final point to make about self-service data analytics. They are not meant to be a bandage for a broken, overly convoluted, or an inefficient process. Process owners should map out their processes from start to finish, preferably with swim lanes to readily identify inter-functional touchpoints with other parties and stakeholders (see the section Process Map (Swim Lanes) in Chapter 7 for an example of this artifact). They should take the opportunity to highlight and eliminate any low value-added steps, where possible. They should ask the Whys to understand the root causes and rationales for any accommodation steps in workflows. Only when process owners have distilled and rationalized their processes down to eloquent simplicity should they embark on a tactical automation project with data analytics tools. The idea is not to take the pain out of a broken process with tactical automation, so that it is smoothed over and forgotten, and left to age with all of its pimples and warts, out of sight, out of mind. After all, pain points have a way of festering when left unaddressed.

Dashboarding and Visualization

As a freshman at Indiana University in the mid-1990s, one of your authors took an Introduction to Business class taught by Professor Tom Heslin. He didn't have to tell you he was from Brooklyn, as his accent stood quite apart in southern Indiana, but he loved to work his Brooklyn origins into his lectures two or three times each Thursday evening anyway, and his students loved him for it. Oddly, by contrast, he never mentioned that he was a Navy veteran and a World War II war hero. We did know that he had come to the Indiana University Kelley School of Business to teach and to give back, after a lengthy career at Bell Labs. He was no-nonsense and full of energy, and had a way of giving students punchy one-liners that would stick. Several come to mind, but one was "You gotta have a plan!" which he employed liberally to drill into his students that they must exercise forethought, be purposeful in their actions, and leave little to chance. But importantly for this section, when introducing the concept of business controls to bright-eyed freshman, he said "You can't manage it if you can't measure it."

It is this last aphorism that has really stuck. This is mentioned because in all of our businesses, there are key metrics that are actively managed (and frequently reported) to allow individuals, managers, or executives to closely monitor process performance. These measures are referred to as key performance indicators (KPIs) and are used to measure and report on the health and performance of an organization, a division, a function, or even a process within them. They tend to be some of the most widely reported numbers for internal audiences, and a portion of them may find their way to external stakeholders and regulators. A whole book could be written on how to make a thoughtful selection of KPIs for a given process, in order to convey health across a number of dimensions. However, for purposes of this book, we will assume that these have been arrived at separately and are effectively conveying business performance to allow for active and rigorous management. What we do want to cover in this section is the ways that KPIs can be compiled and displayed efficiently through the use of dashboards and visualization tools.

Most, if not all of our readers will be familiar with common temporal data visualization formats – bar charts (to show value comparisons), line charts (to show time-series movements), scatterplots (to show large numbers of observations), and sparklines (for trending). Some may be familiar with hierarchical visualizations like tree diagrams, sunbursts, and ring charts. A more select few will be familiar with multidimensional data visualizations that can communicate more than one variable for each observation. Examples of multidimensional data visualizations include pie charts and stacked bar charts that show observation values relative to the whole, and Venn diagrams that can show observations that meet either one or both of two population definitions or constraints. Visualizations are widely in use to make both interpretation and comparison of KPI observations as easy as possible to understand at a glance, or at least in a handshake, rather than after a prolonged study.

Dashboards build on data visualization by pulling together all critical KPIs that are necessary to manage an enterprise, a business, a department, or even a process, in a single view. Measuring and displaying multiple business indicators together can offer context that communicating a single fact or value alone can fail to do. They are built to deliver the key and necessary performance metrics in a visually rich frame that can provide stakeholders with an instant comprehension and more complete understanding of the relative health of business processes.

Anyone who has ever owned the production and distribution of a metrics dashboard or scorecard would likely tell you that they are surprisingly thought- and labor-intensive to produce and maintain. From gathering and agreeing the KPIs that best convey the full picture, to the design and layout of each individual component metric in a visualization, to structuring the page layout to feature the most key of the key metrics prominently – all of these design steps represent a lot of work. When there are multiple recipients, it is always a challenge to navigate the conflicting preferences of each, and we all know that recipients are never bashful about suggesting additions or format changes. We have all been to meetings that have been sidetracked completely by the one audience member who spends the bulk of the session asking questions surrounding the format of the visualizations or the array of components and their order on the page, rather than engaging in a productive discussion on how to improve any of the key metrics. Beyond the design, perhaps even more time-consuming are the maintenance steps that are required each time the metrics dashboard is to be communicated. The slides must be dusted off and refreshed with the updates that have occurred across any of the dimensions from any of the various data sources. From there, date headings must be refreshed, any changes that have been requested must be made, and of course commentary must be updated, before it is sent off.

Over the last decade, a number of dashboarding and visualization vendor tools have emerged to simplify dashboard design, to enable the efficient capture and assembly of KPIs, and importantly to allow for low-latency refresh of visualizations on demand. Key among them are Tableau, QlikView and Qlik Sense, SAP Business Objects, IBM Cognos, Microsoft Power BI, and Oracle BI. This is an ever-moving list, but these are names readers should recognize, as they represent prevalent and widely subscribed visualization platforms – and they are increasingly tied to business intelligence and data analytics.

The evolution from flat reports on continuous form paper that had the perforated strips with holes on each side, if anyone remembers folding them over, licking the edges, and tearing them off (sorry team, yes one of your authors licked the edges to get a cleaner tear, while your second author claims not to have and cringes in disgust— you'll never know which was whom), to brighter reports featuring better fonts and some color graphs and visuals that we got accustomed to in the 1990s and 2000s, to the highly flexible, visual, dynamic, and interactive digital dashboards we have today that convey business intelligence insights is startling – and game-changing. We cannot introduce significant emerging and enabling data analytics technology without making mention of the advancements in data visualization and dashboarding that puts key information in the hands of end-users and decision-makers in an intelligent, versatile, and insightful way.

Discussion with Paul Paris – CEO, Lash Affair

"How did you first learn of the AI components and technologies that are Social Listening?"
I first learned about Social Listening AI technology during a lecture given by a PA-based firm called Monetate back in the Spring of 2015. At the time of the lecture we were still essentially a startup and we were more focused on foundational steps to build our company. However, AI captivated me from that moment onward, and I began to watch developments in the space much closer. The potential to get inside of our customers' heads to improve our products and services sounded like a game-changer. As our company grew to a stage where we were ready, we immediately plugged in. Frankly, we knew that to be a trend-setting and best-in-class company, we needed to be on the forefront with cutting edge technology like AI Social Listening. How could we not?

"How have you employed artificial intelligence and applied data science for Social Listening?"
At Lash Affair, anything we can do to isolate and uncover consumer trends and brand sentiment will give us an edge. Our

company is growing quickly, and more than ever before, we need our hands directly on the pulse of our customers. We want to be the very best in our industry and want to set the bar very high when it comes to exceeding customer expectations. How do we understand those expectations? Well, of course, we don't have time to devote to personally trolling social media sites for posts related to our industry, products and services, and our brand in particular (although we admit to trying every day). However, we have armed ourselves with a serious data analytics dashboard, which gives us the reach to be able to scour the enormous social media landscape for relevant data points that can help us to understand how we are doing with our customers – and with influencers.

"What specific AI components are employed for Social Listening?"

Web-data capture is instrumental to helping us to cast a wide net based on search criteria we use to define relevance. This technology is important to allowing us to capture an enormous number of target observations. From there, we work with machine learning analysts and consumer intelligence experts to extract and understand the tone of posts. With enough timely observations, we can interpret and even get ahead of sentiment about both our brand and trends in the industry. Once we have relevant data, NLP technology is enlisted to translate the informal vernacular of social media participants in posts. After all, few bloggers use straightforward and easy-to-interpret affirmative statements like, "My brand sentiment for Lash Affair products and services is extremely positive – on the very far right of the brand sentiment continuum." Instead, we need to be able to analyze a vast number of sentiment observations and classify each as "positive" (+1) or "negative" (–1), or somewhere in between along the spectrum. Imagine an algorithm that assigns numerical values to the series of observed adjectives being used to describe excitement about our brand, recent customer experiences, and customer loyalty to help us gauge prevailing consumer sentiment. By charting sentiment observation values in time-series, we can spot trends. To get at it involves feeding tons of training data through the machine learning classification algorithm, so that it begins to interpret observations as predictably and reliably as if I personally was in the chair, reading each post, and graphing each sentiment observation as it comes in.

"What do you do with the summarized customer sentiment information?"

The obvious benefit is that we can put our own bias aside to listen to what our customers and target market are saying. Where an opportunity to improve is highlighted, we proactively make changes to better meet the needs of our customers. Where we are doing things that are extremely positively received, we do more of it! One way we can directly react is through engagement. Our service provider gives us an added drill-down capability that allows us to hone in on specific observations that appear as outliers, whether positive or negative. We then have the opportunity to respond through an active feedback loop. We can reinforce positive sentiment and respond to or even turn around negative sentiment through this channel. The other key component here is having a highly trained internal team to take swift action when the time comes. Our Google review stats are proof that we understand the importance of keeping consistent excitement around the Lash Affair brand. Data analytics capabilities have given us a giant advantage in getting this done.

Paul Paris, CEO at Lash Affair.

www.lashaffair.com

Conclusion

In this chapter, we have mentioned a number of important emerging analytics tools. We discussed the vast explosion of data that we have witnessed, partially due to the "internet of things" and all of the various connected objects we interact with each day. Cloud storage and cloud computing have emerged to efficiently store, access, and interact with this flooding sea of Big Data. We introduced artificial intelligence as a broad subject, encompassing many fields of study, that is an incubator for data analytics technologies and disciplines. From it have emerged OCR and ICR, as well as natural language processing and language translation disciplines. We highlighted blockchain and distributed ledger technology as an important means of crowd-sourcing consensus to agree to the true state of ownership for assets, or to agree to the golden source of truth that many can subscribe to and consume, to eliminate the need for reconciliation and to reduce investigative efforts that are undertaken to resolve differences between disparate sources of data. We discussed the role of robotics in performing structured, repetitive processes quickly and more efficiently, in the reduction of manual-intensive tasks that distract humans from focus, higher-order analysis, and actualization.

Your mind was already blown, your teacup was nearly empty except for a bit of floating sediment, and then . . . self-service data analytics was introduced to lend structure to spreadsheet-based processing steps, to build efficiency, and to bridge the gap until strategic systems can deliver needed interoperability or enhancements! Critically, we submitted that the move toward self-service analytics represents a de facto decentralization of change, from being *in* systems, to being *around* or *outside of* systems and far more focused on automating individual spreadsheet-based processes. We pointed to the rise of self-service data analytics as putting digital instruments of change directly into the hands of process owners, rather than only in the hands of technologists. Finally, we have stressed the inroads made on dashboarding and visualization to communicate processing results and key business performance metrics in a way that gives color and context to the numbers being presented.

Having introduced these key enabling analytics technologies, we will ask the readers to consider how they have an obvious impact on their daily lives. Clearly, you will have interacted with many of these with some frequency. We have provided only a high-level introduction to these topics here, when volumes can and have been written on each of these, individually. The idea was to take some of the fear out of these buzzwords and to show how they are beginning to change the way we live, what we know about consumers and customers, how we transact business, and how we perform our daily jobs.

In this chapter, we treated self-service data analytics as if it is just one of many in a new breed of intelligent analytical tools – and that is true. But they are a worthy focal point for the majority of this book, as they represent a seismic shift in how change is delivered across large organizations. The impact of the shift can be seen both in how we work individually and the pace of process change and digital advancement across organizations. These tools are steering technology budget allocations toward the licensing of off-the-shelf tools, and they are influencing the size and shape of the technology arm of organizations. Clearly, they are impacting how we staff our processing functions and the new skillsets that are valued. This set of tools is driving an observable shift in large organizations across a number of dimensions.

This evolution comes with significant benefits, but also with significant risks. As the pace of change accelerates, the need for strong overarching governance is most pronounced. In Chapters 3, 4, and 5, we will describe how the introduction of self-service data analytics tools will open the floodgate for rapid adoption. We will demonstrate how the shift to decentralized change renders much of the governance apparatus that may be mature in legacy system-centered organizations as incomplete, if not superfluous and irrelevant. We will systematically highlight the gap in available governance frameworks, when it comes to structuring controls around self-service analytics builds and tooling. Most critically, we will draw essential elements from a host of fragmented and overlapping governance models and extend them to forge a new, dynamic, and comprehensive governance framework to fit the new landscape of self-service change.

CHAPTER 3

Why Governance Is Essential and the Self-Service Data Analytics Governance Gap

As described in Chapters 1 and 2, organizations are leveraging analytics and automation tools today more than ever. The adoption of technological innovation is driven by the promises of more stable and efficient processing, an attractive projected return on investment (ROI), and for the capture of competitive edge by early adopters. Even while analytics solutions confer obvious benefits to finance, operations, and accounting functions that have historically relied on manual spreadsheet processing to supplement system features, functionality, interoperability, and reporting gaps, they also introduce a new set of risks to the organization.

Readers must not doubt that data analytics tooling is quickly becoming indispensable to publicly traded companies and high-performing organizations, more generally. Not only do they perform core processing activities, but they are relied upon to inform management decision-making. Further, for accounting and finance functions in particular, their output is likely to be highly regulated. While the benefits of "small" automation are clear and ever-growing as more use cases are discovered, supporting governance foundations have not closely followed; most organizations that have embraced digital transformation may be operating under fragmented legacy governance structures that have failed to keep pace with the growth in data analytics tooling and the changing face of technology. Worse yet, governance may be an afterthought, even as build after build creates dependency after dependency, incrementally adding risk to the data analytics portfolio and to the organization – all in a governance vacuum.

This chapter will begin by introducing governance and explaining why it is critical. We will highlight the risks to which a lack of governance discipline can give rise, in an environment where data analytics is rising to prominence. For public companies specifically, adequate controls over financial reporting must be forged and thoroughly documented. Section 404 of the Sarbanes–Oxley Act requires public companies' annual reports to include an Internal Control Report asserting that adequate internal controls structures exist, and auditors must attest to the accuracy of this assertion. In cases where flawed tooling has been deployed outside of a robust governance framework, the door could be opened to an adverse finding of material weakness in internal controls, amongst other unfavorable outcomes.

In the case of finance and accounting processing, a governance breakdown can lead to process instability in the short term and increase the likelihood of adverse regulatory examination results, accounting restatements, and even financial penalties in the form of fines from the Securities and Exchange Commission (SEC) or other regulatory bodies in the long run. While material weaknesses may ultimately be corrected – hopefully in time to prevent a negative effect on company profitability – a finding of material weaknesses in the publicly filed SOX 404 internal control attestation report could cause reputational damage to public companies. Such risks must be mitigated through the establishment of a robust overarching governance framework to ensure investments in tools and technology flow to the best available opportunities; to ensure the effectiveness of implemented solutions; and to monitor, assess, and mitigate the risks introduced to the environment by the implementation of new technology and capabilities.

Importantly, the ever-growing body of analytics and automation builds represent process change, they represent investments in tooling, and very often they represent new risks – they are at the very epicenter of the goals and concerns addressed by governance. How is it possible that new data analytics builds in many cases manage to live outside of the fragmented legacy frameworks that predate their emergence? In the following sections, we will introduce and analyze the body of existing regulatory guidance, IT governance frameworks, internal control frameworks, and risk management frameworks, to demonstrate that they leave an appreciable governance gap that must be addressed. In Chapters 4 and 5, we will draw from and extend the existing guidance and frameworks to forge a comprehensive project governance, investment governance, and risk governance framework that is wholly applicable to emerging data analytics tools and disciplines.

Governance Is Essential

The governance of new analytics and automation build deployments is critical. Governance should generally provide for accurate source data inputs, comprehensive details of where tooling exists in the organization, evidence of risk assessment to consider such factors as the number of downstream dependencies and the likelihood and impact of process failure, and finally should provide consistent policies and practices aimed at evidencing quality workflow development throughout project phases, through the production and retention of prescribed project documentation artifacts. Importantly, a valid and empowered body must be in place to oversee these practices.

Before we begin to introduce the existing guidance and mature governance frameworks that can be referenced and extended to weave a comprehensive data analytics governance framework in Chapters 4 and 5, we will spend the next several sections demonstrating why governance must cover the full data analytics value chain spanning from inputs through to and beyond processing, covering inputs, processing quality, required change artifacts, risk assessments, and risk mitigation plans. The absence of governance along any of these dimensions can result in severe exposure. Let's look at each in turn to get a picture of why governance is of paramount importance for a growing data analytics portfolio.

Inputs

The GIGO adage (Garbage In, Garbage Out) reminds us that the quality of processing outputs can only be as good as (or worse than) the quality of inputs to the process. Input quality is largely governed by data governance. Data governance can be defined as the loose set of internal firm policies and practices that enterprises undertake to oversee the operation and evolution of critical capabilities to manage their data assets. Data governance policies can shift the organizational mindset to value data assets in a manner more consistent with how the organization manages its financial assets. Such policies are aimed at the cultivation of practices that ensure that data are properly captured, maintained, and protected.

In finance and accounting functions, the existence of poor data quality and the need to manage it is exemplified by the fact that in financial institutions, entire reconciliation teams are dedicated to the problem. Were it the case that the process inputs were correct to start with, we could expect to see a dramatic repurposing of entire teams! Incidentally, a number of data analytics tools (e.g., Alteryx) have reconciliation functionality that can assist in structuring comparisons and in exception identification. Other vendors like Informatica have developed platforms that enable the testing of input quality to specifically identify data quality exceptions, based on business rules that can be easily configured. Possibly the best way to illustrate the importance of getting control over data is to provide an example of what the reader may face, in the absence of governance.

Imagine that tomorrow you walk in to find that any preventative input quality controls and detective controls such as reconciliations have all been summarily done away with. The starting data array, upon which many processes are based, is plagued with holes and inconsistencies, and nonconforming and duplicate records abound. Irrespective of the quality and precision of the processes built upon this data, it is difficult to imagine that the resulting output can be relied upon – or add any value whatsoever. It is easy to foresee severe adverse consequences to overall process quality. Where many critical deliverables are dependent on this array as an input to processing, problems can cascade throughout the organization. In the best-case scenario, any number of outputs will be flawed or incorrect. In the worst case, depending on the specific data in question, how it is being used, and the intended audience, more severe adverse outcomes may result, up to and including economic loss, reputational damage, and financial reporting misstatements.

We will touch on the importance of data quality governance later in this chapter in the section entitled Data Governance, but it is important to demonstrate the need for input governance at the start of the chapter, to convince you that strong controls are critical path for process inputs to ensure that processing starting points are valid, and that well-considered data governance procedures must be adhered to in furtherance of this goal.

Process Quality

If valid high-quality inputs are fed into a process, we are off to a good start. However, the processing steps must likewise be stable, performant, and consistent with requirements to arrive at quality outputs. A mature governance program will ensure not only that builds are based upon consistent high-quality inputs, but also that all processing steps based upon them perform as intended. This is the heart of data analytics governance. To get comfort that "small" automation is effective, we will need a number of foundational artifacts, controls, and procedures to ensure that builds are operating soundly prior to deployment.

Particularly as build complexity increases as data analytics capabilities grow and mature, having a backbone of controls in place to ensure build quality becomes essential. Defining roles and responsibilities to ascribe adequate project team accountability, establishing required minimum testing procedures, and ensuring that adequate project artifacts are in place – all of these are integral to processing effectiveness. Let's imagine for a second that no such governance guidelines are in place. A complex build leveraging several input files and containing dozens of processing steps is implemented. At some later point, build effectiveness is called into question. Without clearly documented requirements that can be reviewed against delivered functionality and absent a detailed record of the testing procedures carried out, or evidence of business sign-off at the right level, confidently standing in support of the build would be just as difficult as identifying the source of failure.

One could essentially be flying blind, not knowing whether the failure is due to faulty input data, whether processing steps were performed incorrectly, or where exactly in the workflow that a failure point may have occurred. Without the ability to identify failures or to understand root causes – whether due to poor process design, the matching of an inappropriate solution to the use case, or whether it is down to flawed execution – there is not a leg to stand on. We cannot affirmatively state that the build meets requirements, we cannot attest to user acceptance, and we cannot demonstrate that the configuration works effectively in the production environment. In such a case, we have little hope of salvaging any value from the effort; it would only be appropriate to discontinue use of the tool with urgency, perform rework to retrofit governance procedures and artifacts – or worse yet, discard it altogether and start again.

Firm-Wide Build Inventory

What happens if naked (ungoverned) data analytics deployments continue unchecked, with the hyper-organic grow pattern we expect to see as tooling is rolled out across organizations? What if an adequate record is not kept of where such tools exist? This could lead to a lack of understanding of key dependencies. As key processing outputs are themselves used as inputs to other downstream dependent processes, many deliverables – if not entire value chains – could be fowled, in the event that a single upstream build is flawed. Similarly, what if management is unaware of the extent to which single-software solutions have been deployed across the plant. Clearly, the extent to which a key vendor dependency has emerged should inform the vendor management process. It may also weigh in to a build/buy decision, in the event that the company is considering investment in a proprietary alternative suite of tools.

Finally, imagine the uncomfortable attention that could be drawn, as internal or external auditors become aware that, unbeknown to senior managers, new data analytics builds are being quietly relied upon for critical operations or in processes related to the generation of financial reporting outputs? The auditors will rather quickly determine that a review is in order, and they may ask to review the firm-wide build inventory to understand the risk assessment methodology and to ensure that adequate controls exist over the portfolio. However, here again, without an adequate record of where tooling has been deployed, management is flying blind. For all of these reasons and many others, a governance mandate that requires that a firm-wide build inventory is maintained with adequate detail is absolutely critical.

Risk Assessments

As alluded to above, organizations must vigorously manage the risks introduced by any appreciable process change, whether the change is realized through the introduction of data analytics builds into workflows or from any corner, for that matter. The first step to risk management is identifying risk drivers. What are the factors driving risk? How prevalent are they? What is the likelihood that the risks will result in process failure? If process failure occurs, how quickly can we detect the failure? What is the likely impact of failure in financial terms? In reputational terms? Only when the answers to these questions are developed can an organization formulate risk mitigation strategies to manage and mitigate risks that come with a scaling automation program. It is worthwhile to note that the firm-wide build inventory is a required starting point to build upon, for the creation of the risk assessment. What are we assessing, after all?

There are any number of risk drivers that could be identified by an organization as important. Input availability or quality, the intended consumers of build output (senior management, regulators, investors), the number of downstream processing dependencies, the ability to detect process failure or output anomalies – these risk drivers are just several of any number that should be considered as individual build risk or aggregate portfolio risk is assessed. Let's compare two tactical workflows that you learn have been recently developed and deployed in your processing plant, to understand how these factors may figure in to driving disparate risk assessments between the two.

First, imagine that an individual spends two hours each day on a control that has been implemented to ensure that the general ledger is accurate and complete. At the end of the day on T+0, an email is received from the trading desk that contains the trade blotter, or the record of trading activity conducted throughout the day. The next morning, the operator must ensure that the overnight batch process successfully captured all trade activity sourced from the risk management system downstream in the general ledger, to ensure completeness and data integrity. At start of day on T+1, the operator downloads the activity that has posted overnight in the general ledger, formats it for an easy comparison, and then pulls in the trade blotter activity received the evening before via email, and performs a comparison. Any exceptions identified are raised with technology, trading, and operations, and they are ultimately resolved.

The operator has heard about "small" automation tooling and works with a project team to build an Alteryx workflow that allows for the swift normalization of the data to the required format for comparison, performs a join of the two datasets using the trade identifier as a primary key for comparison, and instantly identifies any exceptions for later resolution. The tooling can perform the two-hour process in minutes, irrespective of the trade volume on a given day. After several testing cycles, she is convinced that the tooling is performant and is excited to realize the time-saving benefit from the project. Of course, this reconciliation is an important detective control, but she is convinced that there are compensating controls that could detect a process failure. In the worst-case scenario, if a trade was not captured in the general ledger even on T+1, she would detect it the following day when she compared the mark-to-market profit and loss (pnl) from the risk management system to the unrealized mark-to-market pnl in the ledger.

Now, let us imagine that a separate finance workflow is produced in Alteryx and distributed quite broadly across the organization with the use of a distribution list. Ultimately, this output is consumed as an input to many further processes, only one of which is known. The COO team use this report, along with two others it is enriched with, before the enriched dataset is transformed into a new format and loaded to a management dashboard. The management dashboard is used by executives to understand current financial performance and to formulate short-term strategy. The dashboard is also used by the financial reporting team as the primary source from which to draft footnotes to the financial statements (which happen to be audited by a Big Four accounting firm). Of course, audited financial statements form a key component of the SEC Form 10-K, which is published for consumption by regulators and by analysts and investors on the street.

Might the second build warrant increased focus and a more aggressive risk mitigation and management approach than the build in the first example? In the reconciliation example, a single user was dependent on the build output. There were secondary detective controls that provide alternative assurance that process failures would be captured and corrected the following day. The second build by contrast was consumed not only by a broad indeterminant audience that may be included on the email distribution list, but also by senior management who even use the output for strategic decision-making. Additionally, the target audience includes external auditors, investors, shareholders, and the SEC.

You can readily see that without the capture of risk drivers, and the careful consideration of each build in a risk assessment matrix, it may be difficult to identify the second build as the riskier of the two – one which warrants increased testing, possibly supplemental controls as part of a risk response strategy, and rigorous process documentation that can withstand later scrutiny. Now, imagine that six months down the line, there are not two Alteryx workflows in production, but 200. A strong governance practice would ensure that risk drivers are captured and that each build is assessed against them, that necessary compensatory controls are implemented, and that due focus and consideration are given to high-risk builds.

Rationalizing Fragmented Governance

As firms begin to adapt legacy IT governance, regulatory guidance, and other existing governance standards to the new data analytics tools, it becomes increasing important that a comprehensive governance framework is woven as a superstructure to which all analytics builds are subject – cross-functionally and across divisions, rather than applicable only to one silo. Even within the same firm, it may be that there are several concurrent, competing, and conflicting governance structures in place. A single definitive standardized framework can ameliorate this, by providing a well-suited governance solution for analytics and automation practitioners. This will remove any confusion or duplication of effort on the part of project teams, so that they can focus on meeting a single standard to a high level – and get on with their delivery.

Perhaps one of the most powerful capabilities of self-service analytics tools such as Alteryx, Xceptor, and many others is the degree to which they are customizable in creating process automation solutions. As we will demonstrate in a case study in Chapter 6, Alteryx provides extremely flexible functions to allow users to structure any number of unique processing steps in various sequences. Given that each "small" automation deployment results in a unique customized solution, when we project the growth rate as these tools begin to scale up, an organization could end up with dozens, hundreds, or even thousands of customized analytics builds, each having a unique design and risk profile.

While there is no doubt that flexibility is what makes analytics tooling so broadly applicable in structuring processes and driving efficiency, the many uses and broad applicability also pose a tremendous control risk. Core systems may feature embedded controls that were either specified in advance of deployment or have been built up incrementally in response to risk events over time (think limit checks, range checks, validity checks, check digits, check totals, duplication checks, and others). Further, as we have already described, systems have long been subject to mature IT governance structures and controls. Given that tactical automation may have emerged outside of governance, solutions do not benefit from the scrutiny that larger system investments undergo. Absent a governance structure, self-service tooling may forego the rigorous approvals that core technology changes often call for. Solutions may not be vetted by internal audit and other risk stakeholders. Builds will not be subject to established and mature governance controls, as they sit apart from core IT, and by definition live in the cracks that are left by system controls and system-based processing governance.

Without the cadre of functional specialists to raise any concerns for discussion and to offer any workarounds that can increase the likelihood of success, something is lost. The establishment of an adequately senior governance committee with broad functional representation can function as the needed sounding board. The committee can serve to simulate the same level of input and scrutiny for tactical solutions that would come as a matter of course, when hundreds of thousands of investment dollars and significant resources are at stake for a traditional technology investment. By harnessing the guidance and input of the governance committee, more junior project teams and process owners can benefit from more thoughtful solution design that is dotted with process assurance control points.

The risks of operating under a fragmented analytics and automation governance model can be extensive. The very real chaos that lacking governance foretells is also unique in a decentralized end-user driven environment, where a single chink in governance armor can lead to broad-based risk, should users fail to adhere. Remember, there is even more at risk than process failure and all of the consequences that can come with it financially or operationally. Incubation-stage data analytics automation programs often have one chance to build a stream of successes; one misstep leaves them with an ill-fated and uncertain future, if the organization loses confidence in the ability of the program to implement stable and quality outputs in place of longhand processes. Should the program be painted in a negative light through a highly publicized failure, digital transformation could be set back months, if not years. At least in the initial stages, as data analytics gains a foothold, the governance committee is a custodian and caretaker of a fragile charge to covet and nurture, until it has legs of its own.

In short, while analytics tools and technologies unlock tremendous value by allowing for routine processes to be automated, this value must be protected through a ready framework that allows for regimentation of the process of change, the identification and mitigating of risks identified, and quality delivery after vigorous testing and acceptance procedures. The program must be carefully cultivated and stewarded by governance committee members and sponsors, as only at scale does investment in these capabilities begin to reap promised ROI. A robust governance framework is essential to cautiously scale the analytics and automation program.

Mature Governance Frameworks

Our research has pointed to a number of existing frameworks, regulatory pronouncements, and industry guidance that warrant discussion in this chapter. In the following sections we will discuss various mature internal control governance, IT governance, data governance and model governance, and risk governance frameworks, and examine how they are applicable to tactical automation and analytics builds, over which no unified framework exists today. Where existing governance frameworks fall short, we will outline the existing gaps, distill principles from the rules, and set the stage to stand up a bespoke data analytics governance strategy that will be discussed in the following two chapters, respectively.

Data Governance

Data governance is an amalgam of internal firm policies and procedures deployed to oversee the operation and evolution of critical capabilities to manage data assets. Data governance policies seek to treat organizational data like an asset and to cultivate practices that ensure that data are properly captured, maintained, and protected. Given that *all* processing outputs are reliant upon accurate, clean, and consistent datasets as we made clear Inputs section earlier in this chapter, there are some foundational data governance goals we must introduce. We will highlight 10 notable goals of data governance, amongst others which must be carefully considered:

1. **Accuracy:** Data attributes (and records taken as a whole) are correct. Any calculated values or fields must have integrity. For obvious reasons, if data are inaccurate and cannot be relied upon, they are of little value. Accordingly, data accuracy is one of the primary goals of data governance.

2. **Completeness:** A golden record is a collection of attributes that together describe an entity or a transaction. Some fields are required, whereas others may be optional or nice-to-haves. A customer database has little use if Customer Name (or a unique Customer Identifier as stand-in) is missing from a record, whereas "Address Line 2:" may not be required. One goal of data governance is ensuring that records are complete with respect to required attributes, so that the full factual and descriptive value of data records can be realized.

3. **Consistency:** Organizations run into trouble when there are multiple data masters for the same attribute. An example is if customer data is mastered in two systems, and value differences emerge in overlapping attributes included in both datasets. In some cases, the differences can be small with minimal impact

(49 Bell Street versus 49 Bell St.). In this example, both observed values may result in the successful delivery of correspondence or merchandise. In other cases, the disparities can be opposing or contradictory, and the effects can be detrimental and expensive to resolve. In effect, by not specifying a single golden source of data, we are inviting future discrepancies that will ultimately require reconciliation and exception management. Data redundancy should be eliminated, golden sources should be specified, and controls and rigors should be built around a single location.

4. **Conformity:** Certain fields must adhere to prescribed formats. In the United States, zip codes follow a five-digit convention (XXXXX), with more specificity offered by an optional four-digit suffix (XXXXX-YYYY). Therefore, all values for US zip codes that stray from these formats would indicate a lack of conformity and integrity. Similarly, in the United States, phone numbers are comprised of a three-digit area code, a three-digit prefix, and a four-digit line number, for a total of 10 digits. A record containing a truncated 6-digit phone number would be indicative of non-conforming data in the array. Ensuring that data attributes conform to validation guidelines is a goal of data governance.

5. **Uniqueness:** Certain fields are primary and foreign keys in a relational data model. Primary keys must be unique in a given table. Foreign keys in the parent table are primary keys in another (child) table, and reference a specific and unique record in the child table. These features allow for the accurate relation of tables. Imagine you are reviewing a table that captures and describes transactions. For three transactions during the month, the client (foreign key) is "ABC." While the client is not unique in the Transactions table, it should be unique in the Client table. In the event that in the client table there are several clients with "ABC" as the client identifier, we cannot describe the transaction correctly and specifically. Accordingly, for certain key field attributes, ensuring primary key uniqueness to preserve relationship integrity is a goal of data governance.

6. **Timeliness:** Input data must be available in time for process start. Imagine that transactions in a sales ledger post with an overnight batch on T+1. The earliest that a monthly sales report

can be generated would be not at the end of the last business day of the month, but the following morning, after the batch has processed. Now imagine that the sales data misses the cutoff for the batch. In that case, even on T+1, there would be a gap for the last day of the month. A clear trend is a preference for low-latency data refresh over nightly batch-driven processes, but for accounting applications with their many monthly, quarterly, and annual cycles, it is important that data is timely, and accordingly timeliness is one aim of data governance.

7. **Digital Security:** For many organizations, information is one of the enterprise's most valuable assets. In an environment where cyber threats continually probe for control weaknesses, and where there are an increasing number of emergent threats to data security, strong governance frameworks are increasingly relied upon to protect the value of enterprise data and sensitive information. From material non-public information (MNPI) to medical records, from employee pay rates and HR records to personally identifiable information (PII) such as credit card and Social Security numbers – there is no shortage of examples of sensitive information that must be safeguarded by rigorous controls. The protection of proprietary, client, or private data is a prime goal of data governance.

8. **Availability:** End-users need access to the right data to fuel their processing needs. Information is only valuable when it can readily be accessed and applied. Governance can highlight opportunities to ensure the right data are available to users.

9. **Authorized and Appropriate Use:** A further goal of governance aimed at ensuring that data is used appropriately for authorized purposes. Data distribution standards, procedures, and entitlements must be established in consideration of this goal.

10. **Regulation Compliance:** Many of the concerns for compliance with regulations come from the Authorized and Appropriate Use goal above, but it is worth calling out that strong governance is required to ensure that organizations are in compliance with all applicable regulations. Organizations may be subject to fines and sanctions, in the event that data are used inappropriately.

While many data governance focuses are of paramount importance to the overall governance of data, including ensuring that there is one primary golden source of each type of data in the firm, and that data attributes are properly standardized across business functions, two of the most critical data governance initiatives applicable to the finance function pertain to cloud data storage and data privacy. While COSO IC (2013), COSO ERM (2017), and COBIT 2019 all address various aspects of data management in terms of prescribing data integrity goals and objectives, the guidance regarding cloud data management and data privacy emerged from two COSO thought papers:

1. Managing Cyber Risk in the Digital Age by COSO (2017)
2. Enterprise Risk Management for Cloud Computing by COSO (2012)

The guidance in the two thought papers provides recommendations on how to secure data operations in the cloud and how to protect data from cybersecurity threats. While data governance is of keen importance in ensuring data quality throughout the firm, and it can be argued that all processes built on data assets benefit from data governance, these COSO thought papers do not offer a wealth of principles we can leverage and repurpose in forging a comprehensive data analytics governance framework. With the insights of COSO thought leaders, we acknowledge it as self-evident that organizations must have *adequate data* that is *properly accessible in the cloud*, and that is *properly protected*.

However, these papers do not go far enough in prescribing comprehensive governance procedures for data analytics portfolios. While the format and quality of data is of course essential to data analytics and automation (remember the GIGO adage – Garbage In, Garbage Out), we need to distill these frameworks to derive actual rules – where the rubber meets the road. The data likely to be sourced for data analytics processing is more specific than *firm data* and may have unique governance requirements. Often, data analytics leverages large finance and accounting datasets that may conform to the general standards of data governance provided by the COSO thought papers, but they may still require further data scrubbing, enrichment, and reformatting for bespoke processing – beyond what is prescribed by data governance policies at the organization level. Data governance includes essential and widely applicable umbrella policies that do much to standardize datasets, clarify control practices and procedures, codify roles and ownership, and to safeguard data security. However, at most, they lay crucial groundwork on which to build more detailed and actionable data analytics governance policies that apply not only to data as process inputs, but extend to the automated processing steps built upon clean and well-organized data assets.

COBIT Framework for IT Enterprise Governance

While the COSO frameworks provide guidance on the establishment of controls and risk governance across the organization, COBIT (Control Objectives for Information Related Technologies) is a framework created by ISACA for information technology (IT) management and IT governance. The COBIT 2019 framework seeks to create alignment between enterprise goals and IT utilization and to provide an avenue for IT governance, where IT-related processes' performance can be measured, risk-assessed, and monitored. The COBIT framework provides a much-needed bridge between management's business goals and the governance of IT processes and assets. In fact, each of the 40 governance and management processes in the COBIT framework must be aligned to enterprise goals. Conversely, enterprise goals themselves must relate to IT alignment with business goals. By prescribing alignment goals (goals set by organizations to align IT to the business), the COBIT framework seeks to ensure that IT is integrated with and directly supports the business, while minimizing risk and maximizing value through delivery.

While the COBIT framework is essential to creating IT governance throughout the enterprise, many precepts have limited applicability to data analytics governance. In part, this is due to the fact that strictly speaking, IT are not critical-path for many data analytics builds, given the rapid proliferation of self-service data analytics tools. In such cases, the business and technology apparatus become one and the same, given process owners themselves build the automation workflow, independent of the core technology function (using a self-service Alteryx ETL build deployment as an example). As such, the explicit alignment between the business and IT is not necessary. The process owner must individually align technology goals (or goals of the analytics build) to business goals – in a single step.

Not to be irreverently cast aside, with only a minor shift in thinking, the COBIT goal-alignment process can be extended to data analytics and automation governance. In the digital process-driven environment, a different type of alignment must be achieved. Digital transformation projects must universally be linked to overall functional goals. Stated functional goals such as process stability based on quality inputs, high-quality deliverables, and importantly, resource optimization or efficiency – these must be demonstrably supported by each digital transformation project, irrespective of the analytics tooling that is invoked. Some organizations may go a step deeper in specifying guidelines on what must be delivered and even the methods of delivery. They may set standards for model transparency, mandate process assurance capability or automated controls testing, or set minimum standards of process documentation. Whatever the goals may be, each data analytics tooling deployment, whether from RPA, self-service automation, AI/machine learning, or dashboarding/ visualization – all deliveries must demonstrate a clear link to one or many of the stated functional goals, in order to be allowed to progress.

Your organization may have a multitude of additional or varied goals, but a control point must be put in place to allow only projects that support them to move forward. We will further extend the COBIT framework to create an alignment matrix between functional goals and digital transformation opportunities in Chapter 5. The discipline of preparing the matrix can force the evaluation of the projects against functional goals to ensure they are aligned for each project under consideration. This should also allow for the ready identification of any projects which do not align to organizational goals, so that they may be rejected from the backlog and die an ignoble death.

Other parts of the COBIT governance framework are relevant to data analytics deliveries: the maintenance of governance frameworks, itself, is one of the precepts of COBIT Chapter 4 – Governance and Management Objectives – Detailed Guidance. Section 4.1 Evaluate, Direct, and Monitor gives us investment control principles to draw from, such as controlling to ensure promised benefits are delivered and suggested resource optimization controls. At the end of the day, companies operate from a position of investment dollar and resource scarcity. It is imperative that a framework is in place to ensure that *both* flow logically to those initiatives that promise optimal benefits.

Finally, given that expected project costs and benefits are often based on anecdotal estimates, investment control procedures call for a review of the accuracy of such estimates to gain confidence that expected costs and benefits cases being put forward are valid, and that the prioritization process has integrity. This can be done retro-spectively at project completion by comparing benefits realized to benefits promised, and by comparing actual cost of the development effort to that provided during the prioritization phase, to ensure that both are in line. Where large disparities emerge, they should be investigated and understood. If benefits realized consistently fall short of benefits promised, many organizations learn to apply a dis-count factor to promised benefits, prior to prioritization. Similarly, if costs consistently exceed estimates, a buffer factor can be applied before prioritization. In this way, over time, the organization should be able to increase accuracy of cost and benefits estimates for the projects undertaken.

Sarbanes–Oxley Act

In the introduction to this chapter, we cited SOX 404 as one of the regulatory guidelines that can be relevant to internal control over accounting and financial processes in public companies. Section 404 of the Sarbanes–Oxley Act mandates that public companies engage an external auditor to provide an audited report attesting to the effec-tiveness of the internal controls over financial reporting. Further, SOX also mandates per section 302 that company management provide a detailed documentation of controls over financial reporting and cer-tify the effectiveness of the internal controls. Certain companies that do not meet the accelerated filer requirement (market capitalization less than $75 million) may avoid the independent auditor attestation requirement contained in section 404 (b), but they are still subject to the management documentation requirement. While SOX 404 com-pliance can be burdensome for companies from a financial cost per-spective, particularly for smaller companies, clear benefits to market efficiency arise from the regulations. Per the SEC and the AICPA, SOX

404 has had its intended impact. It has improved the accuracy and reliability of public company financial statements by reducing accounting misstatements and even fraud.

While SOX mandates that management document internal controls and auditors attest to their effectiveness in preventing errors and fraud, the legislation does not specify a framework for use to assess and document internal controls. In theory, companies may select from various internal control frameworks to assess their internal controls, as long as the framework produces adequate control documentation. In practice, the COSO Internal Control Framework is the most widely adopted internal control framework by far. The COSO Internal Control Framework was first issued in 1992 to guide companies on the documentation of internal controls. In 2013, an updated framework was issued to reflect the evolution of accounting information systems in *the information age*, which began in the late 1990s. Thereafter, most public companies have adopted the COSO 2013 Internal control framework to assess and document their internal controls for SOX 404 compliance purposes. We will discuss the COSO Internal Control Framework in more detail in the following section of this chapter, COSO Internal Control Framework.

Section 302 of the SOX Act is another main feature of the legislation that has dramatically impacted companies' compliance requirements related to internal control effectiveness over financial reporting. Section 302 requires companies' principal executives (CEO and CFO) to certify each annual report. The certifications required by the CEO and CFO include the following:

- Based on their knowledge, there are no material errors or fraud in the financial statements and related disclosures
- The internal controls over financial reporting are operating effectively in preventing material errors in the financial statements or fraud.

The additional accountability forced upon executives for ensuring that accounting outputs are correct and free of material misstatement has led to additional emphasis on the risk assessment and governance of financial processes and related internal controls. The annual internal controls certifications required of top management are designed to ensure that internal controls oversight is robust. The SOX legislation has gone far in pushing companies to document key financial processes and to build more structure around them. As systems and process complexity is growing and evolving, management is likely to motivate their accounting functions to ensure that internal controls feature in *every* process.

While SOX legislation can clearly be relevant to the governance of analytics, it only covers the subset of processes and outputs that relate to financial reporting. In other words, if analytics processes relate only to operations such as marketing, or other uses that do not contribute to financial reporting outputs, SOX would not be applicable. For analytics processes outside the scope of SOX, companies are not required to document related internal controls and assert their effectiveness. As we described above, another limitation of the legislation is that it leaves the "how" to govern completely open. The legislation does not provide specific governance precepts that can be applied to data analytics portfolios. Even when the processing and outputs *are* related to financial statements, it is up to companies to determine an approach to document and test internal controls. SOX legislation provides only general guidelines that could be extended to govern analytics programs. In the future, regulators such as the SEC, or even the Public Company Accounting Oversight Board (PCAOB), itself established by the Sarbanes–Oxley Act, may issue further and more detailed guidance prescribing governance frameworks for analytics programs. In the meantime, organizations are left to themselves to independently formulate adequate governance frameworks and controls to ensure the success of their analytics programs.

COSO Internal Control Framework

In the above section, we introduce the COSO Internal Control Framework as a widely used framework by public companies, partially in response to the SOX 404 legislation. The COSO Internal Control Framework was created by the Committee of Sponsoring Organizations of the Treadway Commission (COSO). COSO has the support of five professional accounting associations: American Institute of Certified Public Accountants (AICPA), American Accounting

Association (AAA), Financial Executives International (FEI), Institute of Internal Auditors (IIA), and Institute of Management Accountants (IMA). The COSO Framework is widely viewed as a benchmark for the design, execution, and evaluation of internal controls and risk management procedures and is referenced extensively in the United States.

Key portions of the COSO Internal Control Framework standards that are relevant to data analytics governance can be found in the COSO Information and Communication section (Principles 1 and 2), and COSO Monitoring section (Principles 1 and 2):

Applicable COSO Information and Communication principles:

- **COSO Information and Communication principle 1:** The enterprise obtains or generates and uses relevant quality information to support the functioning of internal controls.
- **COSO Information and Communication principle 2:** The enterprise internally communicates information, including objectives and responsibilities for internal controls, necessary to support the functioning of internal controls.

Applicable COSO Monitoring principles:

- **COSO Monitoring principle 1:** The organization selects, develops, and performs ongoing and/or separate evaluations to ascertain whether the components of internal controls are present and functioning
- **COSO Monitoring principle 2:** The enterprise evaluates and communicates internal control deficiencies in a timely manner to those parties responsible for taking corrective action, including senior management and the board of directors, as appropriate.

The COSO Internal Control framework (2013) prescribes crucial guidance that applies to data analytics and automation governance, touching on both data quality in the Information and Communication principles 1 and 2, and extending to processing output. First, it prescribes that the enterprise ensures that financial data be of quality, and it specifies that data must be: sufficient, timely, current, correct, accessible, protected, verifiable, and retained. The framework also requires the use of relevant and appropriate data sources, which is of critical importance to data analytics and automation, where data sources can introduce significant risk. The framework mandates that the enterprise adequately evaluates and assesses data sources, and based on management's assessment, selects those that are most reliable, relevant, and useful.

Second, the framework dictates that enterprises document their internal control objectives and communicate those objectives broadly throughout the firm, and it provides for the establishment of clear roles and responsibilities over internal control objectives. This guidance is clearly relevant to the data analytics automation environment, where process automation is implemented by process owners, often operations, finance, and accounting specialists, along with some involvement by technology teams. The establishment of control objectives over automated processes, and the creation of well-carved-out, coordinated, and comprehensive ownership roles for those responsible for carrying them out is critical. Due to the interdisciplinary nature of automation and analytics projects (RPA, machine learning, dashboards, self-service process automation), guidance in this area requires collaboration between technical and finance teams, in order that *both* finance and technology control objectives are incorporated into the overarching control oversight process.

While there is clear potential to automate data analytics controls through the introduction of automated testing procedures or the establishment of command center dashboards to monitor performance of analytics processes, it may be more challenging to perform controls and achieve control objectives in areas where processing is based on complex and obscured algorithms (RPA and advanced decision making – AI/ML, as examples), where coded algorithms and processing steps may be less transparent. In such cases, an alternate "black box" testing approach can be elected. With this approach, models can be confirmed as effective, when test inputs fed to the model successfully yield expected outputs once processed, for the algorithms under review. Even without observing individual processing steps and mathematical operations contained within the "black box" line-by-line, the determination can be made that the model is operating as intended, from input to output, as a whole.

COSO ERM (2017) – Integrating Strategy with Performance

COSO ERM (2017) has certain components that are similar to COSO Internal Controls (IC) (2013); however, while COSO IC's primary purpose is to provide internal controls that contribute to quality financial reporting, COSO ERM is predominantly focused on managing and optimizing organizational risks in pursuit of operational excellence. It promotes transparency and the surfacing of risk, and it drives organizations to create risk response strategies. While both frameworks are concerned with identifying risks, monitoring them, and deriving effective mitigation responses, COSO ERM adds additional guidance on how to perform the following:

- Link risk to performance, and critically, to measure and quantify organizational risk appetite (COSO ERM Principle 10)
- Agree risk measures and metrics, formulate risk responses and mitigation strategies, and employ them to optimize performance (COSO ERM Principle 11)
- Examine root causes of identified risks that are causing performance variability (COSO ERM Principle 11)
- Establish risk transparency throughout the organization, so that higher-order risks can be prioritized (COSO ERM Principle 12)
- Create a portfolio view of the risks and manage risk-level awareness at various levels of the organization (department-level, business unit-level, and organization-level) (COSO ERM Principle 14)

On the control side, key benefits of digital transformation in the finance, accounting, and operations functions include promoting risk transparency and optimizing risk through increased process stability and reliability (it is acknowledged that often a primary motivation is the pursuit of efficiency benefits, over and above the control benefits). The COSO ERM is a highly relevant governance framework to data analytics, given it provides for risk identification and assessment, ongoing risk monitoring, and risk responses and mitigation strategies. However, while COSO ERM provides general guidelines, the framework does not detail specific steps to achieving these goals in the data analytics environment.

As the processing environment involves various data flows, data abstractions, models, and automation of routine accounting processes such as reconciliation and data aggregations, a comprehensive fit-for-purpose governance framework must be developed, to include a detailed and annotated runbook providing for the assessment of input risk, process risk, and output reliability, based on the unique characteristics of data analytics tooling. While COSO ERM falls short of providing detailed steps to do so, we will develop actionable guidelines in Chapter 4. In Chapter 5, we will leverage and extend the fundamental principles of COSO ERM (2017) to risk governance for self-service data analytics tooling.

SAS No. 1, Section 210

In preparing to write this book, your authors encountered guidance that we believe is important to governance, from the Statement on Auditing Standards No. 1, as issued by the American Institute of Certified Public Accountants' (AICPA) Committee on Auditing Procedure. Why is SAS No. 1, section 210 important? This section explains that independent auditors must be adequately trained and demonstrate proficiency to perform an audit. The minimum standards for audits include the principle that individuals performing the audit must in fact be qualified to do so. We stress that this is a principle, not a rule, in that it is extensible more generally, outside the specific context of auditing. In Chapter 4, we will build upon this logic to assert that individuals who develop or even use data analytics tools must similarly be adequately trained and demonstrate skills and proficiency with the tooling in practice.

There are some limited writings dealing directly with analytic models that are worth mentioning and that can be drawn upon. Clearly, we are at an inflection point, where both academia and professional practice have begun to acknowledge the reliance placed on data analytics tooling across enterprises. In his article in *Internal Auditor*[1] magazine, Allan Sammy provides four points of guidance around the analytic skills competency required of those who structure longhand processes in analytics tools. His first four points relate to controls to ensure that analytics developers have appropriate education and sufficient experience in data science and data analytics to perform their roles. Sammy suggests that organizations provide adequate funding for related training to ensure that employees' skills are kept up-to-date, and that only those individuals with appropriate knowledge and skills are assigned to projects suited to their competencies. Finally, Sammy rightfully explains that developers must understand the full context into which they are introducing tooling. They must understand business requirements and be working from documented success criteria.

The principal at play is that for any endeavor that is to be relied upon in earnest, skilled and competent operators must be equipped with solid training. Further, adequate supervision is required to ensure that training or experience shortfalls can be overcome. Sammy's article along with the AICPA's Committee on Auditing Procedure have provided us with some personnel threads that we will weave into our project governance framework in the following chapter.

SAS 70, SSAE 16, SysTrust Engagements

In the system environment with which most readers are likely familiar, build effectiveness and system integrity can be evaluated in well-defined, tried-and-true ways. The reader can find significant literature on this topic, and there is a well-cultivated body of approaches used in practice by external auditors to provide system assurance (see SysTrust engagements, SAS 70, SSAE 16). SAS no. 70 was the definitive guidance from the AICPA for nearly two decades, which described auditing standards for service organizations who represent that they have performed an in-depth review of their controls over information technology and related processes. SAS no. 70 was relevant where a company places reliance upon outputs from a third party. The idea is that the *user* organization has more confidence in the accuracy of the third-party data, if the controls have been adequately examined within the *provider* organization.

SysTrust services were jointly developed by the AICPA and the Canadian Institute of Chartered Accountants (CICA) to give comfort over systems supporting a business activity. They provided three measures for system reliability, as follows: availability, security, and integrity. The authors duly note that uptime and availability is a key measure of system performance, and system security is increasingly critical, given the trending toward cloud computing and internet connectivity for enterprise platforms. However, we are particularly interested in the "integrity" principles, as they are most relevant to establishing foundational data analytics governance. Processing integrity refers to getting comfort that processing is complete, accurate, timely, and authorized. An overarching data analytics governance program must vigorously address this goal.

We can intuit much from the SAS no. 70 examination as regards adequate core internal controls. In 2011, Statement on Standards for Attestation Engagements (SSAE) No. 16 took effect to supersede SAS no. 70 with a new attestation standard (AT 801). Both are important to consider and can be drawn from to build controls over data analytics. In much the same way, if you view your organization as a prime *user* of data analytics build outputs, you will want to gain assurance that adequate controls are in place over the analytics function as a *provider* of processing outputs. The SysTrust Processing Integrity principle similarly provides guidance we can draw from, in the purpose-built analytics governance framework presented in Chapter 4.

Model Risk Governance

Models are increasingly essential inputs to critical business decisions, but what are they? Models use quantitative theories and algorithms to arrive at estimations, inputs, and conclusions for business decisions and enterprise management. Estimations can derive from statistical or mathematical theories of various complexity as in models, but they can also derive from subjective assumptions as in qualitative models (QMs). Model risk governance is a set of policies and procedures that outline oversight and control over models and the risks they are likely to introduce.

While there are an increasing number of applications for models, there is a commensurately increasing number of risks that are posed by models and estimations. Models may have fundamental flaws due to implementation errors, any unreasonable assumptions used, or limitations in their methodology. Models may also introduce risks if they are inappropriately used, outside the scope for which they were conceived, designed, and tested. There could be flaws in the execution of otherwise sound and robust model logic. Errors in any of these dimensions could introduce significant financial, reputational, or even regulatory risk. These risks must be identified, evaluated, and mitigated through strong overarching governance. Some model risk governance procedures of note have been prescribed by regulatory bodies, to ensure models perform effectively. We will introduce the guidance in this chapter and then extend relevant points for our comprehensive *project* and *investment* governance topics in Chapter 4, and our *risk* governance topics in Chapter 5.

The Federal Reserve and the Federal Deposit Insurance Corporation routinely examine banking institutions' compliance with model governance guidelines, as prescribed by the Federal Reserve in SR Letter 11 – 7 (Supervisory Guidance on Model Risk Management). The model risk governance guidelines specified include the following directives:

- Keep an inventory of all models that are in use
- Document model development, testing, validation, implementation, and any subsequent modification
- Identify roles and responsibilities regarding model oversight
- Ensure input integrity

Furthermore, the Federal Reserve recommends that when certain key risk management functions such as accounting, operations, or compliance are outsourced to third-party vendors, that the following due diligence be performed to manage outsourced risk to third-parties (Federal Reserve – Guidance on outsourced risk – SR 13 - 19):

- Perform risk assessments
- Exercise due diligence in the selection of service providers
- Review contract provisions and considerations
- Perform incentive compensation review
- Conduct active oversight and monitoring of service providers
- Formulate business continuity and contingency plans

Additionally, the Federal Reserve recommends that organizations consider the following risks while managing outsourcing arrangements: Compliance risk, Concentration risk, Reputational risk, Country risk, Operational risk, and Legal risk.

Model governance is highly applicable to data analytics and automation efforts. Many of the principles and practices that have been codified and integrated to model governance are applicable even to analytics builds not meeting the strict definition of models. Whether or not an analytics workflow meets the definition, ensuring a configuration inventory is maintained, ensuring the performance of input verification, maintaining project documentation surrounding the development, testing and modifications of builds – all of these requirements prescribed for model governance are best practices for analytics builds beyond models.

While many similarities exist between models and data analytics and automation workflows, the distinguishing characteristics of models is that they contain mathematical computations, algorithms, and/ or quantitative theories. They may also reference estimates or probabilities, which is another determining factor, in contrast to the remaining universe of data analytics workflows. Many data analytics builds deployed across finance, accounting, and operations functions may perform simple extract, transform, and load (ETL) or automate routine processes such as reconciliations, aggregations, and selections. These builds, as examples, often lack mathematical computations, algorithms, or estimates; they by definition fall outside the scope of model governance and can fall through the cracks. It may be that self-service ETL builds outnumber those builds that meet the definition of models, across many large organizations, leaving a significant population of tactical builds to live out in the cold – in the considerable gap in governance.

Given the pace of growth for data analytics use cases in finance, accounting, and operations process automation and as the web of dependencies grows when data analytics configuration outputs are referenced as inputs to many other downstream processes, the need to redress this gap with an inclusive overarching framework is front and center. Whether or not builds qualify as models, they are sure to feature their own risks and complexities. Well-considered governance is essential to the controlled introduction of data analytics to an organization. Drawing the line to exclude a growing proportion of data analytics builds can allow for the resurgence of risks that had largely been eradicated through the maintenance of mature governance frameworks, including model governance. Of course, a comprehensive data analytics governance framework will include additional tenets beyond those prescribed by model governance; however, they will not be discarded. We consider and build upon model governance and the other guidance and frameworks we have introduced in Chapter 3, as we prescribe a data analytics governance framework in the next two chapters.

Self-Service Data Analytics Governance Gap

In the preceding sections, we presented and discussed a number of frameworks and pronouncements that relate to data, models, internal controls, and IT governance. We have shown that existing regulations and mature governance frameworks provide guidance that is at least partially applicable to the new self-service analytics environment, and that principles drawn from them can be extended to data analytics governance to some degree. Our research failed to uncover a single gilded framework that fits the bill to comprehensively cover all facets of data analytics governance, but the frameworks listed in Exhibit 3-1 provide the best references we could identify that collectively hint at an outline for governance in the new decentralized self-service analytics environment. The principles gleaned from the existing guidance on internal controls, IT governance, and data governance are essential, but we have demonstrated that there are gaps in the frameworks, due to narrow scope of coverage or a lack of actionable and detailed steps. Exhibit 3-1 summarizes these gaps and limitations, as underscored in the preceding sections.

Structures Needed to Fill the Governance Gap

Thus far in the chapter, we have introduced the body of existing frameworks and guidance that lay out some internal-control guardrails, but they have been widely focused on IT governance, with some exceptions. Importantly, we have demonstrated (and reinforced in Exhibit 3-1) that there are gaps and rifts in legacy structures, into which data analytics tooling can fall. In a decentralized environment where users, themselves, are provided with low-code, no-code analytics development capabilities, we cannot rely upon the governance

EXHIBIT 3-1 Relevant Guidance and Frameworks and the Data
Analytics Governance Gap

Frameworks & Guidance	Data Analytics Governance Gap
Data Governance	Data governance precepts apply to data quality and integrity standards, but these guidelines do not go beyond ensuring quality inputs. Data governance does not extend further to control processing based on them.
COBIT	COBIT provides a framework for ensuring alignment between IT and the Enterprise but is centered around the Enterprise IT infrastructure. Self-service analytics is "light IT" that falls outside of the IT governance apparatus.
COSO IC	While COSO Internal Control provides a framework used to assess internal control risks, the scope is limited to financial reporting-related outputs. Further, no detail is provided for the construction and maintenance of controls in the new processing environment.
COSO ERM	COSO ERM provides a framework on how to assess, document, and monitor risk in the organization and can be extended to the analytics environment; however, COSO ERM fails to specify the specific risks to manage for data analytics portfolios.
SAS No. 1, section 210	SAS No. 1, Section 210 mandates that auditors are equipped with adequate skills, training, and supervision to execute their mandate. This principle can be extended to developers of data analytics tools who must likewise be adequately trained. However, skills and training of operators, alone, does not constitute comprehensive data analytics governance.

(continued)

EXHIBIT 3-1 **Relevant Guidance and Frameworks and the Data Analytics Governance Gap** *(continued)*

Frameworks & Guidance	Data Analytics Governance Gap
SAS No. 70, SSAE 16, SysTrust Engagements	SAS 70 and SSAE 16 provide guidance on required controls where user organizations place reliance on third-party providers. A loose parallel may be drawn between external providers and the analytics function as providers of information for the user organization (though they are one and the same). SysTrust provides key measures for system reliability: availability, security, and integrity. These are relevant to analytics governance, but do not go far enough.
SOX 404	SOX 404 is the primary legislation that governs the area of effective internal controls, but applies only to controls surrounding financial reporting outputs for public companies, leaving out of scope a significant portion of non-financial processes where data analytics is being deployed.
Model Risk Governance	Model Risk Governance, used in the financial services industry, applies where models perform mathematical operations or are based on probabilities or estimations. While a portion of self-service analytics builds meet the narrow definition of models, a significant portion, if not a majority, of data analytics applications are out of scope.

spanning IT alone. The existing IT governance can be side-stepped, as there may be little to no involvement of the core technology function in the application of data analytics, depending on the tooling applied. A new broad-scope governance apparatus must be forged, to cater to the new environment and to seal the void left by legacy governance structures across the organization. In the remaining pages of the chapter, we will discuss at a high level the new purpose-built structures, policies, planning steps, and oversight that must be introduced, to carefully govern the analytics portfolio and to fill the governance gap.

Governance and Oversight

As an analytics program scales up, an organizational structure needs to be established that governs program activities, procedures, and deliverables. Oversight structures with sponsorship from senior management must be installed, such as a governance committee to oversee the activities of the analytics program. From an organizational strategy perspective, projects must be aligned to the goals of the overall organization as must be the level of program funding. Benchmarks must be established for project prioritization and for defining and measuring success. Centralizing these efforts within the purview of a governance body with senior management support and oversight gives analytics programs the best prospects to develop, grow, and scale. With proper leadership and structural support in place, a body comprised of process owners, development teams, as well as governance and control specialists can best establish procedures for project governance, investment governance, and risk assessment and mitigation efforts.

The goals of the analytics program must be aligned not only to the organization's overall strategy but also to management's expectations for the pace of digital transformation. More immediate goals may include the generation of efficiency or may be oriented to increased controls and process stability, or some combination of both. The targets set and the expected pace of transformation must inform the level of investment. Sponsors must ensure the program is resourced rationally, in light of program expectations.

Direct costs may include software licenses, providing for the upskilling and deployment of operators and developers, and the support and resourcing of process discovery efforts to uncover and capture opportunities. Of course staffing the governance function with appropriate sponsorship, process owners, developers, core technology representatives, and control specialists comes as at a cost, whether explicit or manifesting as an opportunity cost.

A detailed discussion of how to manage and sponsor the organization's governance committee will be provided in Chapter 4, in the first section, Securing Sponsorship and Establishing the Governance Committee.

Planning and Alignment

Guidelines must be established for both project selection and the thoughtful prioritization of automation opportunities. This point was touched on more generally in the Governance and Oversight section, but setting project selection and prioritization criteria in light of organization goals and constraints, risk tolerance, promised benefit, and ROI is fundamental. There is no standard set of "right" project selection guidelines to pull from, given this is a moving target. Guidelines will change based on a number of variables, including management strategy, tactical departmental goals, the competing opportunities in the opportunities backlog, the level of resourcing and funding, and even the level of skills and experience of developers. We will provide a detailed discussion of best practices in Chapter 8 for the selection and prioritization of investment in analytics projects to dramatically increase the chances of success in achieving process control and stability gains and the capture of positive ROI through efficiency savings.

On the flip side, some organizations view enterprise licensing for self-service analytics as a relatively fixed cost, and any incremental effort is self-funded by operators who deem it to either be worthwhile or not, to undertake projects that emerge in their space. In an environment where projects are self-funded, the prioritization and investment governance more generally is performed at the process-level, rather than at the program-level. The downside to the self-funded approach is that opportunities risk not being funneled to and surfaced at the front door of the governance apparatus; there is a higher likelihood that governance is skirted altogether.

In the Chapter 4 section, Self-Service Data Analytics Build Inventory Must be Maintained, we will point to the capture of all builds in an inventory as a foundational step not only to project prioritization but to ensure alignment with organizational strategy, adequately surfacing the risks embedded in the builds for proactive risk response planning, and even identifying replication opportunities for successful innovations across the organization. We recognize some readers may argue that governance should avoid tightening the screws to the degree that innovation and creativity are stifled or stanched. The answer is to optimize the level of governance overhead to achieve risk and investment control, rather than to disregard the governance imperative posthaste. How can organizations justify the fixed cost of licensing, if they are not aware of the benefits driven by the tooling?

While project acceptance criteria and prioritization procedures are critical, organizations must plan for the impact of automation not only on their business processes but on their people. We have already highlighted the control benefits of structuring manual processes in data analytics tooling, but there are other end results from successful automation efforts. In Exhibit 1-1, we illustrated that the efficiency gained through the structuring of routinized processing steps should result in allowing for more time to be spent on meaningful analysis. It is important that organizations consider what this will look like function by function. Successful automation efforts will result in increased capacity, and *excess* capacity must be thoughtfully utilized – or surrendered. In some cases, post-implementation residual processing across multiple operators can now be rebalanced and centralized in fewer heads. Through the efforts of senior sponsors and process owner representatives, governance must provide for how to redeploy personnel resources optimally.

It is worth mentioning that analytics programs benefit from policies that can provide for the rapid redeployment of individuals affected by automation. It is important that the program is viewed by impacted stakeholders as a liberator from low-value-added routine processing steps and as an enabler of more impactful analysis and self-actualization, rather than a sensational movement sowing career disruption in its wake. The most successful programs are able to show this in action and thereby build trust and earn the support of impacted staff in automation efforts. It is important to provide training to equip professionals with technical knowledge and digital skills to pave the way for successful digital transformation, but also to equip impacted individuals who contributed in earnest to project success with the skills they need for the next step in their careers, as capacity is created. *For best results, use a carrot, not a stick.*

An approach to process discovery to uncover processing pain points and manual processes to target for control and efficiency is the central topic of Chapter 7. Discussions of applying project acceptance criteria in light of organization constraints and the prioritization of investment opportunities are presented in Chapter 8. (See sections Project Acceptance Criteria and Organizational Constraints and Automation Heatmap and Prioritization.) Planning and alignment are key not only to project success but to ensuring the right things are done with investment resources, and that the impact of efforts is fully anticipated and managed.

Policies and Procedures

Perhaps the most important goals of governance are aimed at providing for risk transparency and the management of risks introduced by individual builds and the analytics program overall. Self-service data analytics will introduce dependencies, as analytics outputs are consumed pervasively as inputs to further downstream processes across the organization. As analytics becomes deeply embedded in an organization's processing ecosystem, and given the resulting web of dependencies, it is even more critical that outputs are accurate and that failures are limited.

A lack of risk governance to buttress a program touching so many of the organization's processes, systems, and data assets can result in severe and unanticipated consequences of process failures, including interruption to core business processes, economic loss, and even reputational risk. Organizations must develop a robust risk governance program around analytics programs that ensures that the unique risks introduced by the program and its individual components can be captured, assessed, and well understood before the determination is made that the program is in line with its risk appetite. The risk governance framework will oversee the establishment of monitoring capabilities to allow for the swift identification of process failures, and it must encourage the draft of risk responses, such that mitigation steps are at the ready, should exceptions occur. In Chapter 5, we will introduce a robust risk governance framework aimed not only at the risk assessment of individual analytics builds but also providing a portfolio view of risk by department, function, or program.

Development Standards

Governance must specify development standards to address build quality, specify appropriate tooling for specific use cases, and mandate the types of embedded controls that must be put in place across the portfolio. Depending on the composition of project teams and how they are staffed and organized, the development standards must also specify roles, responsibilities, and ownership for project deliverables (such as requirements, benefits cases, effort sizing, and testing evidence) and the handoffs between process owners, developers, and the governance committee. By clarifying expectations, optimal collaboration can be achieved for build development, testing and validation, build maintenance, and internal controls oversight.

The governance committee must invest early in agreeing on a vision of how teams collectively can surface opportunities and develop solutions, in light of organization-specific factors. In the event that opportunities are self-funded, and an operator personally develops a solution to assist in performing their process, the investment governance procedures may be abbreviated. The individual may be responsible for demonstrating that the developed solution works as intended to her direct manager, with a single handoff outside of the team as required project governance artifacts are submitted to memorialize the change, capture benefits, and log the risks for assessment by the governance committee. If instead, a centralized analytics function is established, it may be that process owners raise their hand when they feel pain, and pull in analytics specialists to perform detailed process discovery and to surface opportunities for the backlog, translate problem statements to use cases, produce requirements, and perform prioritization in light of the competing demand pool before developing a solution. Many organizations sit somewhere in the middle. They may have a team of developer specialists, but they may mandate that process owners come to the front door of the demand queue armed with fully fleshed out requirements and with a convincing benefits case preassembled. Of course, there will be later handoffs between developers and process owners during user acceptance testing. The point is that all of these handoffs should be considered so that role profiles are clear and that inputs to their respective processes are well defined.

Testing policies and procedures must be mandated to ensure that analytics builds are fully validated, before promotion to the production environment. Such procedures may include the number of clean test-runs to be completed before sign-off, they may include minimum testing coverage ratios, they may specify the number and variety of test scenarios included in the test plan, and even who must proffer sign-off. The policies may also touch on how test results must be documented and retained for later reference by the governance committee, or to satisfy queries from internal and external auditors.

Finally, development standards may address the internal controls that must be embedded in, or at least accompany, new builds as they are incorporated into the production environment. The need for such controls may be triggered by the outcome of the risk assessment such as the type of deliverable, the anticipated level of scrutiny for the output and the intended audience, or it may be triggered based on the number of dependencies, or any number of factors. What is clear is that controls must be in place to ensure quality inputs and that processing steps have performed as intended – together increasing the likelihood that outputs are accurate and reliable.

A detailed discussion of testing methodologies and the required project artifacts to evidence that the approach to development was sound appear in Chapter 4, in the section Project Development Audit Trail Must Be Captured and Retained. Additionally, we will illustrate development standards at work in the case study featured in Chapter 6.

Conclusion

While mature governance frameworks, regulations, and pronouncements do provide some principles that are applicable to the governance of self-service analytics, a governance gap still exists. In this chapter, we have highlighted pertinent principles selected from the existing body of governance and demonstrated how they may be extended to governing analytics programs – and where they fall short. We will leverage these as the starting point for a more detailed data analytics governance framework to better bridge the gap, as data analytics – assisted processing evolves. In Chapter 4 we will focus on project governance and investment governance, while only touching on risk governance. Chapter 5 will be focused solely on risk governance, and we will provide you with some tools you can leverage at your organization to promote risk transparency, to assess risk, and to protect the value of the analytics function. Chapter 8 will step you through key portions of investment governance as it relates to analytics programs. In developing the purpose-built analytics governance framework in the upcoming chapters, we have considered all the existing guidance and frameworks covered in this chapter.

By weaving together relevant principals borrowed from legacy guidance, regulations, and mature frameworks, we can build solid walls onto the well-trod foundations from the disciplines of data governance, model governance, internal control assurance, and IT governance. As data analytics will soon touch a majority of processes that sit outside of core systems, it is imperative to manage risk and protect the stability of the program, and to ensure that investment dollars and resources are flowing to the right opportunities. That is exactly where we are taking you as we move to Chapter 4, as we begin to outline our governance framework for data analytics that can provide much-needed structure to your analytics program at scale.

Note

1. Allen Sammy, 2018. "Analytic Models Controls and Tests - Auditors can perform numerous tests to provide assurance on analytics controls used in analytic models." Internal Auditor.

Self-Service Data Analytics Project Governance

We have already explained that the hyper-organic growth pattern of self-service data analytics is unlike any other centralized digital transformation change pattern. Once innovators and first-movers adopt tooling, and the success is observed by influencers across the organization, if properly nurtured an eruption of excitement will build around the new capabilities. New users will begin to adopt at feverish pace. As data analytics tooling permeates organizations in every function and at an exponentially increasing rate, it is critical that organizations have strong foundations of governance to keep the ship steadily on course, from early on in their digital journey.

Despite the fact that effective governance *may* be staged around core technology and may operate effectively for core systems-based transformation, in a decentralized user-driven automation environment, the legacy governance structure may be side-stepped. Without the benefit of governance to control and temper the flood of new processing automation, managers can find themselves unaware of the extent to which new procedures have been forged. They may not have clear visibility to the newly created dependencies, which can prevent them from adequately assessing risk, and they may find themselves lacking when asked to demonstrate adequate program control to senior management, auditors, and even regulators. The new decentralized capabilities placed into the hands of end-users with self-service data analytics tools requires a new comprehensive governance framework to be woven from the mature elements of system controls, along with precepts from data governance and model risk governance and extended to the unique profiles, risks, and capabilities of emerging self-service data analytics tooling.

In Chapter 3, we introduced the various existing governance frameworks and revealed the gap in coverage and overlap, permitting many common self-service data analytics use cases and builds to fall through the cracks. In this chapter, we draw upon those frameworks to extract extensible components and weave them into an actionable project governance framework to accommodate the universe of data analytics projects. In addition, we prescribe project governance and investment governance guidelines that must be put in place, in order to prepare for the growth of self-service analytics in your organization.

This framework must be threaded and interconnected throughout the organization by superimposing a strong governance structure. Importantly, it must be sponsored by leadership with adequate seniority, such that the program of transformative analytics technologies does not operate in fragmented pockets or silos. Instead, the queue of opportunities, methods of delivery, governance procedures, and risk management practices must be overseen by senior leadership with enough influence to consider broad swaths of the organization. Only in this way can the full risk context be understood and consistent policies and procedures be formed and adhered to, so that the scope of replication opportunities can be appreciated in full. Given the necessity of having a governance apparatus appropriately staffed and firmly in place, we will lead off the chapter with a section on how best to establish a governing body to ensure control over the portfolio, before moving on to spell out the governance principles and practices that the body will oversee.

Securing Sponsorship and Establishing the Governance Committee

As mentioned in this chapter's introduction, a governance framework must be threaded and interconnected throughout the organization by superimposing a strong governance structure. This starts not with principles and standards, but with people and personalities. We recommend the formation of a data analytics governance committee as the first step in the process of implementing a governing framework. Like all committees, it must be chaired by a sponsor who puts their credibility and influence on the line to ensure that committee goals are achieved. As governance itself is broadly a control function, some believe a governance committee would be best chaired by someone from a control function, say an internal auditor, or a controller from the CFO organization. We take a different view.

We believe that sponsorship should sit with a senior individual in the processing plant. They would stand to gain from the success of data analytics, but also stand to lose, in the event of governance failure. In this way, the sponsor has "skin in the game" and is most likely to promote significant opportunities to digitally advance the organization. Importantly, the committee sponsor must be a leader with adequate seniority to coalesce cross-functional buy-in and support around the program vision and with adequate breadth of remit to ensure that the program amalgamates any fragmented pockets of practice that may have emerged into a unified program spanning the breadth of opportunities, deliveries, governance procedures, and risk management practices. The sponsor will feel the very real benefits of program delivery, and she will be motivated and incentivized to ensure processing integrity and that risks are appropriately managed. It is possible that data analytics tooling will be deployed to streamline processing for the CFO organization, in which case, for different reasons, the sponsor may end up residing in this organization, but not because the governance function, or its sponsorship, must sit within a control function.

After designating an appropriate sponsor to chair the committee, we need to specify the other members who should be represented. The largest portion of the governance body should be composed of senior process owners who, again, both have an interest in the success of data analytics transformation within their organization but also are responsible for process stability and output quality. Other key participants should include one or several core technology liaison(s) who are accountable for replacing limited-life tactical automation with strategic automation over time. They must stand ready to provide updates on the progress of demand items in the backlog and in the various stages of development that will ultimately allow for tactical analytics solutions to be sidelined – or negate the need for them altogether. Increasingly, we believe that internal audit should have a seat at the table, given they are responsible for ensuring adequate process control and must understand focal areas of processing change and significant risks as they emerge. Finally, if the organization has matured to the point that there are data analytics portfolio leads, or if there is a center of excellence function who is tasked with data analytics execution, they should likewise be in the room and accountable for presenting the committee with periodic updates on the portfolio.

Once the committee has been formulated, best practice is for them to memorialize their goals, authority, and objectives in a committee charter. The charter should explain how the committee is composed, how members will interact and work together to meet these objectives, how frequently they will meet, and provide a skeleton agenda to describe the flow of topics to be covered when meetings are convened. Committee objectives should include reference to the following key themes:

- Oversee the implementation of governance controls over the analytics program. Ensure the implementation of policies and procedures that enable sound investment governance, change process governance, project governance, and adequate risk management for data analytics projects.
- Safeguard data and information security through an awareness and active management of emergent cyber risks.
- Perform periodic review of the request pool, demand backlog and delivery portfolio to understand organizational pain points and emergent innovations to redress them.
- Identify applicable replication opportunities for successful innovations, across the landscape.
- Retrospectively review implemented projects to ensure that there has been no reduction of process stability or negative impact to process quality as a result of the automation introduced.
- Review implemented projects to ensure that promised benefits cases have been realized and to understand the relative accuracy of build sizing and cost estimates that informed the prioritization sequence.

- Calculate, consider, and publicize program return on investment (ROI). Consider that some benefits are not directly quantifiable, but must be intuited from prior run rates (i.e., errors, fines, and loss avoidance). Other benefits are qualitative, but must likewise be considered in estimating program value (examples are reputational risk reduction and client satisfaction).
- Ensure that ample funding is made available to adequately scale the program to meet ROI targets and at a velocity that is consistent with stated digital transformation goals and milestones.
- Periodically review adopted third-party tooling against market alternatives and proprietary in-house capabilities to ensure vendor relationship investment is optimized.
- Leverage committee composition and member expertise to act as a control-minded sounding board for junior project teams. Ensure that adequate process controls are embedded in solution workflows, or ensure that the right subject matter experts are engaged to provide the necessary assistance in this pursuit.
- Identify opportunities to streamline and hasten the process of change. The levers at the disposal of the governance committee are varied: project team composition, roles and responsibilities for preparation of required artifacts, required testing rigor, data analytics tooling selection, available workflow tooling, and so on.

Objectives are fluid and should be reviewed with a reasonable periodicity to react to organizational shifts, as well as emerging issues and events. Any number of objectives can be added to ensure that the right work is being done right, that portfolio risk levels are understood and optimized, and that marked progress is made on the digital transformation agenda. Most governance committees meet at least monthly, but depending on the size of the portfolio, the throughput and velocity of analytics development, and any developments inside or outside the organization that require attention, the committee may need to meet more frequently. During times of extreme transformation, they may elect to meet weekly, or even more frequently, as required.

Committee members must be current as trends develop both within and outside of the organization. Within the organization, they must understand processing pain points, emergent innovations, and any new developments in tooling and use cases. Externally, they must be current on evolving governance best practices and any regulatory guidance issued from standard-setting bodies. They must periodically compare company governance standards with competitors' standards, where there is transparency. Further, they must have their ears to the ground on emerging data analytics technologies and capabilities, and the vendors bringing them to market.

As business teams stretch analytics platform capabilities to generate efficiencies in firm processes, innovations emerge that may have broad application across the organization. Organizations should encourage thought leadership, and they should provide a ready means of syndicating innovations rapidly, to maximize the efficiencies generated through organization-wide adoption. The governance committee must therefore serve as a centralized clearinghouse for innovations, so that they are not lost in silos. The committee members must have enough knowledge of the emergent innovations and use cases to understand, at least in a general way, where there may be viable replication opportunities across the plant.

This means that within the ranks of the committee must reside enough influence to be able to gather the right people to the table to consider and explore the efficacy of rolling out a solution more broadly. In this way, individual team innovations can be shared with the entire organization to maximize the multiplier effect (see Chapter 8's section Multiplier Effect of Replication Opportunities on Project Benefits Case for an explanation). Some organizations reward specific innovations and encourage teams to share analytics successes in order to accelerate adoption throughout the firm. The committee will be integral to ensuring that innovations are scaled appropriately and that resulting success stories are broadcast throughout the organization.

There are several governance structure variations that are worth mentioning here.[1] The differences are largely down to whether business units, product lines, and organizational functions are relatively homogenous or whether they are so separate and distinct as to warrant their own governance apparatuses. What we have described above, with a single overarching governance body, is referred to as a "centralized governance model." Here, the governance committee is a central hub responsible for all data analytics governance and infrastructure spanning the breadth of the entire organization. One variation is the "decentralized governance model," which still features a central governance team that works to standardize governance guidelines to the extent possible but allows division-specific, functional, or product line variances to be moderated by separate governance bodies or hubs within these silos. Finally, there is an even looser "federated governance model," which places the power of implementation, infrastructure, and governance in the hands of teams or departments. We are proponents of a strong backbone of centralized governance that best enables the transparent surfacing of risks, the fully informed prioritization of opportunities and allocation of scarce resources, and visibility into replication opportunities for successfully delivered innovations.

Having established the governance body, we will move on to discuss facets of the framework the body must put in place. Below are the prescribed actions that have been highlighted in this section. Throughout the chapter to come, we will call out and underscore the concrete actions as introduced, before they are finally brought together in Exhibit 4-1.

> **Action:** Establish an analytics governance committee sponsored by senior management. Include data analytics portfolio leads (if they exist), key process owners, core technology liaison(s), and internal audit, and such subject matter experts as required to adequately consider and navigate emerging issues.
>
> **Action:** Spell out committee objectives in a governance committee charter. The charter should explain how the committee is composed and how members will interact and work together to meet these objectives, the expected frequency of assembly, with a skeleton agenda frame for such meetings. Committee objectives should include mention of the following:

- Sound investment, change, and risk governance for analytics projects is enforced.
- Data and information security is safeguarded from emergent cyber risks.
- The demand pool and deliveries are reviewed to understand organization-wide pain and solutions.
- Successful projects are reviewed to identify replication opportunities elsewhere.
- Implemented projects are controlled for process stability.
- Implemented projects are controlled for promised benefits and sizing and cost estimates.

- ROI is calculated and publicized. Realized qualitative benefits are also published.
- Adequate funding has been made available to sufficiently scale the program.
- Third-party tooling is reviewed periodically against alternatives and in-house capabilities.
- Committee members act as a sounding board for junior project teams to ensure control.
- Committee identifies opportunities to streamline/hasten the process of change.
- Objectives are reviewed and updated frequently to remain on point.

Extending Governance Precepts from Established Frameworks

Analytics governance should provide for accurate source data inputs, and it must provide policies and practices aimed at the controlled and regimented development of high-quality processing solutions. Further, governance calls for comprehensive documentation of where tooling exists in the organization, evidence of risk assessment, and thoughtful deployment of appropriate tooling throughout project phases. With our new governance committee now in place, we will begin by pulling together fragmented governance principles from the mature existing governance frameworks introduced in Chapter 3, that to date have left a significant portion of analytics builds out of scope. We will reference these frameworks where appropriate, and weave them into a comprehensive and actionable governance framework to be established early in the digital journey to protect organizational strategy, ensure the maximum impact of investment budgets, and to promote build effectiveness and process stability for data analytics transformation programs.

Ensuring Input Integrity

As we introduced in the Data Governance section of Chapter 3, sound processing begins with quality data. We acknowledge that this topic is worthy of far more consideration than we can devote to it within this work. This book is predominantly focused on the governance of data *processing*, rather than data (input) governance itself. In this section, we will discuss some foundational governance steps that should be implemented to ensure that there are practices in place to allow organizations to unlock the value of data assets and to protect their value through the cultivation of high-quality data as a starting point for processing.

In the Data Governance section of Chapter 3, we introduced many of the goals of data governance, including accuracy, completeness, and timeliness. Without input stability, there can be no expectation of quality processing outputs. Companies must manage data assets through the continual measurement, assessment, and improvement of data quality. This begins with the definition of data quality and the identification of data quality exceptions to establish a baseline measure of quality. As categories of exceptions are captured and their root causes addressed, subsequent data quality exception rates should be improved, and you can begin to move the needle on data quality over time.

Of course, the reality is that, in a fluid environment where system flows are built and amended, where new datasets come online with regularity, and where new issues are likely to emerge almost daily, the resolution of a single data quality issue is no cause for breaking out your best bottle of champagne to celebrate. Practitioners find this game to be a lot like whack-a-mole, where one issue is resolved, only to find that another has sprung up elsewhere in its place. Data governance is not a process but a practice that must continually be exercised to maximize the value of enterprise data and to protect this value, as data cascades for further use as processing inputs across the enterprise.

Data Governance Committee

Data governance, much like data analytics process governance, starts by assembling stakeholders and the formation of a purpose-built data governance committee, much like the data analytics governance committee we prescribed in the first section of this chapter. It is likely that committee members would include process owners, data stewards, data producers, and technologists, but their roles and responsibilities may be unique in your own organization. Ascribed roles and the authority commanded by them must be written out in a committee charter, for later reference and to ensure final accountability.

Standard policies and procedures should be established to protect and improve the value of data assets. They should spell out control procedures surrounding the accuracy and completeness of data, specify practices to safeguard data security, and should lay down guardrails on data distribution and usage. Further, organizations must monitor and ensure compliance with the data governance policies and procedures as laid out. What good are policies and procedures if they are not demonstrably followed?

Action: Establish a data governance committee sponsored and chaired by senior management. Include data governance portfolio leads (if they exist), data stewards, key process owners, core technology liaison(s), and such subject matter experts as required to adequately consider and navigate emerging issues.

Action: Spell out data committee objectives in a governance committee charter.

Action: Organizations must monitor compliance with data governance policies and procedures.

Action: Ensure roles and responsibilities are assigned for data stewards, owners, and end-users.

Data Asset Inventory

A prime step in data governance is to produce an inventory of data assets, highlighting such differentiating factors as those containing sensitive private or proprietary information, those that are used for public disclosure and/or regulatory reporting, and other datasets integral to firm value, which may require special care and focus or a customized approach to governance and management. Building an understanding of core datasets – and the processes and outcomes dependent on them – is a starting point for the structure of data governance, inclusive of data and information ownership, data quality procedures, and other internal controls aimed at protecting firm data. Once an inventory is produced, it is more obvious where effort should be spent to protect the assets, and the planning of a suitable, right-sized, and targeted approach to the assessment and control of data quality can commence.

Authoritative golden sources of data should be designated as the single source of truth, in the event that there is significant overlap of arrays or attributes from multiple sources. Doing so prevents the overhead associated with the independent mastering of data and it reduces the opportunity for conflicts to be introduced – and to persist downstream through processing. There are important benefits to this approach. Most important is avoiding the risk of inviting conflicts. If a key premise of data management and governance is ensuring the quality, accuracy, and completeness of data, it follows that organizations should avoid allowing the opportunity for conflict and divergence. If there are multiple data masters, the quality control measures and procedures would necessarily be duplicated. In the later section Data Quality Review Procedures, we will introduce simple reconciliation as the detective control to ensure the agreement of overlapping datasets. However, this introduces an unnecessary complication to data management practices and procedures. By pointing all downstream data consumers to subscribe to the definitive golden source, rather than separately maintaining and controlling data, at least in theory, we can be assured that in every instance where this data is invoked, it has the same quality as in the golden source master.

> **Action:** Produce data asset inventory for assessment, review, and governance/control planning.
> **Action:** Inventory must flag sensitive and proprietary datasets for enhanced control and vigilance.
> **Action:** Inventory must flag data sources for external and regulatory reporting.
> **Action:** Inventory must identify datasets integral to competitive advantage and firm value.
> **Action:** Inventory should identify authoritative golden sources of data for conflict prevention.

Data Lineage

An additional required step is the capture of a clear picture of the data sources and how elements flow to other datasets over time. In data governance terms, this pursuit can be referred to as data lineage, and it is increasingly important for a number of reasons. First, it is important to identify and address data quality issues as far upstream as possible, preferably at source, in order to prevent the persistence of issues down the daisy chain, as data is fed further and further downstream. A set of artifacts in place to allow for the ready tracing of data upstream to source or the tracking of data downstream through the enterprise can assist significantly in pointing data stewards both to the point of origination and any impacted datasets in the event that issues emerge. A second impetus for building a detailed understanding and documentation of data lineage is at least in part driven by regulatory guidelines.

Banks and bank holding companies, for example, are under keen pressure to enhance their architecture to allow for point-in-time retrospection of the status of trades and transactions, account balances, and available capital. The Federal Reserve's annual Comprehensive Capital Analysis and Review (CCAR) assesses whether banks have adequate capital in times of economic stress. To demonstrate that firms meet capital adequacy requirements, they must be able to illustrate data lineage, memorialize data validation procedures, and evidence how data ultimately flows into regulatory deliverables.

In January 2018, Markets in Financial Instruments Directive (MiFID) II went into effect to address the safety and integrity of European markets. The MiFID II regulations are aimed at promoting pricing transparency, market competition, and the prevention of a global financial collapse, in the event of an abrupt market crisis or drastic economic downturn. More specifically and relevant to this section, these regulations effectively enforce the creation of data lineage deliverables. Critically, in order to comply, firms must be equipped for the flexible low-latency capture and retention of data from a large number of internal and even external data sources, to allow for the reconstruction of trades at any point during their life cycle. While only a small subset of the universe of firms (and by extension, our readers) are subject to either MiFID II or CCAR, they are still worth highlighting as regulatory drivers of data lineage programs and deliverables, and to demonstrate the increased focus by regulators on comprehensive data governance practices.

> **Action:** Document the sources, flows, and persistence of data in data lineage artifacts.

Data Quality Review Procedures

Moving on to data quality, a program of control and management of data assets must be built upon measures and assessments. The governance committee and its operators must have a number of review procedures available that can be used for an initial appraisal and the establishment of baseline quality measures. The goal is to improve data quality markedly over time, but this can only be demonstrably accomplished if there are starting point exception metrics upon which to improve. The number of specific tests that can be performed to identify data quality exceptions is limited only by one's imagination, particularly in the increasingly data-rich environment in which we operate.

Procedures generally fall into several key categories. In the following paragraphs, we will discuss three key categories of data quality control and review procedures that can be used to establish baseline quality measurements or to identify data quality issues and anomalies. From there, we can specify procedures for dealing with issues as they are identified. In this way, organizations have a set path for promoting data quality and for the improvement of overall processing integrity, as data is sourced by downstream systems and analytics processing engines.

The first obvious control procedure is basic reconciliation, which compares two datasets to ensure accuracy and completeness. Qualitative attributes can be reconciled to confirm they are complete and in agreement between datasets. Quantitative attributes and values can likewise be compared mathematically to rationalize two datasets. One specific example where this is used is in the unfortunate event that there is a data redundancy between enterprise systems. This situation can emerge from a merger or business combination that results in multiple legacy systems that must be rationalized, or it can emerge from poor planning (see the "consistency" goal of data governance in the Data Governance section of Chapter 3). Whatever the cause, ensuring the complete migration and harmonization of datasets is often accomplished with reconciliation.

A further tool at our disposal to identify data quality issues is analytical review. This is a procedure used to understand movements in quantitative data over time. Those of us that have worked as auditors at some time during our careers have long been familiar with this practice, which, along with tests of details, comprise two main substantive audit testing procedures. Common uses of analytical review in audit include comparing current period financial statements to prior period financials, budgets, or forecasts, to ensure that movements over time are understood and to identify areas where more detailed focus and testing may be required.

The same procedure can also be leveraged to rationalize day-over-day or month-over-month movements of aggregated column sums in quantitative datasets. If on average in your enterprise, daily sales numbers in the Sales table total $10 million and hover between $7 million and $12 million 95% of the time, observing a daily sales figure of $50 million may be a warning sign that an anomaly has occurred. Does your global head of sales appear worse for the wear this morning from celebrations into the wee hours? Is he sporting a new Rolex? If the issue persists and no valid business justification surfaces to explain the spike, you can be relatively confident that data quality may be compromised.

One further procedure that can be performed to test the quality of data is through data integrity and validation procedures. As we introduced for our "conformity" goal of data quality highlighted in the Data Governance section of Chapter 3, many attributes have a predictable format with respect to what is contained in the field. Based on the format requirements, a number of business rules can be established to validate attribute values in a dataset. We cited the example of a telephone number that contains less than 10 digits, or a zip code value which contains other than five (or 9) digits that could be readily identified as data quality exceptions when observed. Other rules can be based on whether field values contain alpha versus numeric characters, whether a particular field is a required field (value must not be null), or for some fields, acceptable values are limited to a finite number – think about how dropdowns force compliance with business rules during data entry.

As business rules are formed to allow for the structured identification of data quality exceptions, they can readily be automated through enlisting data quality tools and platforms that allow users to specify conformity rules to be executed on vast datasets automatically, to be run on demand or by a scheduler. Exceptions identified can be sent to resolution queues for remediation, and data quality key performance indicators (KPIs) can be displayed on interactive dashboards, such that the overall data quality health can be communicated to information guardians and consumers. At the time of writing, Informatica, Cloudingo, Data Ladder, OpenRefine, SAS Data Management, and IBM's InfoSphere QualityStage offer leading platforms and enjoy much of the market share when it comes to the capture of missing or non-conforming data, data duplication, and other data integrity issues that can undermine downstream processing outcomes. Later in this chapter, we will feature an interview with an executive at Informatica, who offers our readers his valuable perspective on how organizations are shifting their mindset to treat data assets as the key strategic innovation engine that must be protected through an effective data management strategy.

Action: Manage data assets through measurement, assessment, and improvement over time.

Action: Employ reconciliation/analytical review/validation procedures to identify DQ anomalies.

Action: Leverage attribute-level business rules to define quality and identify exceptions.

Action: Establish data quality KPIs to assess quality and track progress of improvement efforts.

Action: Display DQ KPIs on an interactive dashboard to communicate overall health and trends.

Action: Baseline quality measures should be recorded to assess the quality of critical datasets.

Resolution Sequence

The above procedures are extremely useful for the identification of data quality issues, but identifying them is simply not enough. The governance program must offer and mandate an action sequence to allow for issue resolution and the continual improvement of data quality over time. To that end, we want to spell out the actions that must take place in order to resolve identified issues. As you might suppose, for each data quality issue that emerges, the first step is to document or log the issue, including when it was observed, who caught it and how it was identified, and the observed impact of the issue. These are important facts to capture, given they will inform the risk and impact assessment, which is the next step in the process.

A list of such data quality issues can then be assessed at the individual level and the portfolio level to understand the risks that are introduced through processing. Such factors as the number of downstream processes that are dependent on the data attribute, what the attributes are used for, whether or not the data appears in accounting or regulatory disclosures, and the potential impact of the quality shortfall should each be considered in assessing severity. Once the assessment is complete, we recommend displaying the list sorted in descending order, from the most severe issues with largest impact at the top, down to the lesser issues with fewer dependencies and risks trailing below. Presentation in this format provides a sense of the relative priority of the issues across the portfolio.

Once the impact severity and the relative priority have been established, the next step is to assign owners and to set reasonable project milestones and timelines. When issues are allocated to owners, they will proceed with the formation of working groups to perform root cause analysis and arrive at proposed solutions. Solutions could involve the overlay of additional control points such as the frequent run of data conformity business rules to identify exceptions; they may involve structuring exception queue workflows, assigning additional roles and responsibilities for stewards and owners; they may involve architecture changes, or even a subscription to a third-party market data service. There are any number of solutions that can be considered, depending on the nature of the gaps noted, the assessed risk they represent, and the many organizational strengths and operational constraints in place across the enterprise.

Once solutions are prioritized, funded, and executed, it is important that stakeholders and end-users agree that the issue has been fully redressed, and this agreement is memorialized with sign-offs at the appropriate levels. This will cement shared responsibility across producers and consumers of data, and it will ultimately encourage confidence in the quality of data that is used as inputs to many processes across the enterprise. Further, given we are now painfully aware that a data shortfall exists, it is imperative that a detective control is devised and implemented to ensure the systematic identification of any future incidents, should the problem persist or re-emerge.

As we have already stated, companies must manage data assets through the continual measurement, assessment, and improvement of data quality. By establishing baseline measures of known data quality issues, and by continually tracking their improvement over time, we can add incrementally to the value of data assets, and we can readily showcase the value of the journey. Comprehensive data governance frameworks involve data lineage analysis of the sources and uses of data, establishing authoritative (golden) sources of data versus supplementary data sources, the production of metadata, data taxonomies and classifications, clear roles and responsibilities across producers, data stewards, technologists, and end-users, and so much more.

In the preceding sections of this chapter, we have introduced and underscored some of the concepts we believe are foundational to implementing a data governance framework, but we have only scratched the surface. In Exhibit 4-1 we will tie together the many actions we have prescribed into a checklist that will help you and your organization to succeed in your own respective governance journey. As you dig in further, you may add any number of discrete action steps that are appropriate, within the context of your organization.

Action: Data quality issues must be logged for risk assessment, prioritization, and resolution.

Action: Risk assessments must consider data uses, user impact, and downstream dependencies.

Action: As solutions are designed and executed, end-users must sign off acceptance.

Action: As issues are identified, detective controls must be devised to identify issue persistence.

Opportunity Capture, Benefits Case, Sizing, and Prioritization

As a fledgling analytics program builds momentum, it will be important to have a means of identifying (or better yet, attracting) opportunities to employ analytics tooling and to implement an efficient means of evaluating opportunities for viability, benefits case, sizing – and priority, relative to other opportunities under consideration. The goal is to build a groomed pipeline of feasible opportunities (project backlog) to pull from, as self-service analytics capabilities grow and mature.

Of course, just because we have a list of opportunities, it does not necessarily follow that all projects will ultimately be taken up.

Any number of a range of shifting project selection criteria will be applied, in consideration of project costs and expected benefits, project complexity, available funding and available development resources, to determine whether individual projects will proceed – and when. It is important that roles and responsibilities for opportunity capture are made clear from the start. If a dedicated project team is in place for process discovery and opportunity capture, then ownership is clear. However, lightly staffed analytics project teams will benefit from decentralizing the responsibility of bringing opportunities to the table with fully developed benefits cases already articulated and logged appropriately at the front door. In most cases, this can be accomplished by level-setting expectations with process owners, making it clear what constitutes a quality opportunity capture, and at what point handoffs to project teams can occur. Irrespective of who has assembled and logged the opportunities, a further check to ensure that solutions are appropriate in light of organizational or functional goals and senior management strategy and constraints must be performed, in advance of pulling backlog items into work in progress (WIP) sprints. All of these rigors are meant to ensure that the organization takes a rational approach to doing the right things at the right time, taking into consideration all risks and benefits in deriving an expected return on investment (ROI).

In Chapter 7, we will introduce an approach to process discovery, and demonstrate, step-by-step, one approach to surveying organizations for processing pain points for detailed study and ultimate redress, with an eye toward the deployment of data analytics tooling in pursuit of operational efficiency. In Chapter 8, we will get you familiar with an opportunity inventory matrix that can be used to log opportunities as they come in the front door. Once captured, we will show you the required steps to flesh out the benefits cases and sizing estimates, to distill problem statements to use cases, and to match appropriate solutions to opportunities. The governance committee must spell out how opportunities are to be captured, centralized, and evaluated for risk, complexity, and expected ROI, from the front door through prioritization and beyond in the development queue.

Action: Governance committee must specify opportunity capture and evaluation procedures.

Action: The front door inputs required for project consideration must be specified.

Action: Clear roles and responsibilities for prerequisite entrance deliverables must be ascribed.

Action: Governance committee must formulate project selection criteria.

Action: Governance committee distills management strategy to set organizational constraints.

Action: Governance committee must ensure organizational constraints inform project selection.

Self-Service Data Analytics Build Inventory Must Be Maintained

As processing teams begin using analytics tools and platforms in production of outputs, an organization must maintain a complete inventory log of all builds in place, for a number of uses. Understanding the increasingly complex process dependencies and how data analytics outputs are consumed by users across the processing landscape is important to understanding the impact of builds on the risk portfolio. Configuration inventory maintenance is imperative for risk governance, and Chapter 5 will be devoted to this topic. However, an inventory is also useful to uncover the number and concentration of tactical tools in place across functions. Where off-the-shelf third-party platforms are in use, understanding the footprint and saturation across the organization can bring visibility to key vendor dependencies. This understanding can inform build/buy decisions and can serve to validate or justify the cost of licensing during the annual investment cycle.

Perhaps just as important, maintaining a record of where tooling has been successfully implemented will prompt thinking about where the work can be leveraged elsewhere in the organization. The first instance where a use case is solutioned may have a far larger benefits case than originally projected, where there are ready replication opportunities to plug in the same developed solutions elsewhere in the organization. See the Chapter 8 section Multiplier Effect of Replication Opportunities on Project Benefits Case for an explanation and illustration of this point.

Building a comprehensive inventory log of builds in production can best be accomplished in two stages, assuming that the door has already been opened to the tools. To catch up retrospectively on any builds that predate governance formation, the committee may call for the widescale distribution of a survey to functional managers, process owners, and operators to allow for the identification and capture of analytics tools in place. Note that when previously delivered tooling is positively identified, the committee will want to understand the impact of self-service analytics on firm deliverables, to evaluate the impact to internal controls of intelligence components, and gather any other information required to evaluate risk. Prospectively, internal auditors can ensure that logging new builds and capturing relevant qualifying attributes describing them to inform risk assessments is critical path, prior to the deployment of a new build. We will focus much of Chapter 5 on risk governance.

Action: Data analytics build inventory must be captured and maintained.
Action: Inventory must name tool developers, process owners (signatories), and operators.
Action: Review vendor concentration and dependencies to ensure in line with strategy.

Self-Service Data Analytics Tooling Is Tactical by Nature

In most organizations, tactical tooling should be viewed as a stopgap until like features and functionality become available in strategic systems, rather than an end-state to live on in perpetuity. The rationale is that strategic core systems should be the home for *all* processing activities. System interoperability should be provided for, such that complementary upstream data sources can be merged into an adequately rich dataset, negating the need for users to perform enrichment activities outside of systems. No longer would users need to open six spreadsheets and use key fields and VLOOKUPs to pull back the data required for a given processing operation. Any calculations or other operations should be embedded in core system functionality, and flexible system reporting should be available to produce outputs in final formats. If system reporting suites were adequately rich and flexible, operators could forego the transformation steps they perform outside of systems to reorder fields or to reformat system outputs. In the perfect world, there would be *no* residual manual processing tail to be performed outside of core systems, which would contain all required features and functionality to encompass all processing steps. Information technology functions make it their mission to develop system processing capabilities to accommodate these fundamental requirements.

However, we understand that this is not always the case, hence why there are use cases for tactical self-service data analytics tooling. It may be that new processing or reporting needs emerge that were not considered at the time that systems were implemented. It may be that requirements were overlooked as specifications were drafted. Perhaps bespoke processing or reporting requirements are required to accommodate new client requests. Any of these scenarios may leave operators with a significant manual tail. Irrespective of the reason that operators are left with manual processing steps, tactical self-service tooling is not a replacement for strategic core technology delivery.

Managers should continue to push the change apparatus in their respective organizations for strategic technology delivery to reduce manual processing steps outside of systems or in spreadsheets. We have already discussed at length that traditional system development and release cycles are often not monthly, but quarterly – and in some cases even annual. Savvy process owners, themselves, increasingly are equipped to take matters into their own hands by employing self-service data analytics tooling to structure their processes tactically, while they await strategic functionality in the core technology platform.

However, a control must be implemented to ensure that all tactical self-service data analytics builds can be cross-referenced back to an enhancement request in the strategic core technology system backlog. Further, for each tactical tool put into place, there should be an assigned retirement date. Finally, the tooling inventory should be kept up-to-date with respect to which builds are live and active versus those that are dormant or retired. By mandating discipline in landing strategic enhancement requests with core technology before a tactical project can be taken up, we can be sure that tactical builds are but a stopgap measure with a limited shelf life, until the strategic solution can be delivered behind it.

Performing a periodic review of the builds approaching expiry can prompt an update from core technology on the progress of the strategic enhancements, in place of which the builds are used. Technology can then either confirm that the features and functionality enhancements will be delivered on time or provide a re-baselined delivery timeline. If the latter outcome occurs, only then should the governance committee consent to moving out the build expiry date. By mandating an assigned retirement date and through requiring this touchpoint with technology, the governance committee can simultaneously advocate the strategic agenda, arm users with practical tools, and ensure that a high-quality data analytics tooling inventory is maintained, in the event of inevitable questions from auditors or regulators.

Tactical builds can pave the way for strategic change by forcing end-users to systematically think through and articulate requirements. The tactical builds can also serve as working proofs of concept (POCs) for requested system enhancements and can be used to demonstrate the required functionality as part of the requirements package handed off to technology. Further, once built, the tactical tool can be run in parallel, as the strategic enhancements are developed and advance to user acceptance testing (UAT) to confirm the test results. If the same test scenarios are run through the tactical tooling in parallel with system test scripts, the results can be compared to confirm that the outputs are consistent, and in this way, substantiate that the system code change under review is operating effectively. Tactical tooling can significantly speed testing cycles and allow for more comprehensive testing and testing coverage by reducing the required manual lift.

With the temporary tactical nature of end-user tooling in mind, as well as the importance to the organization of having an up-to-date tooling inventory for process documentation and risk assessments, it is important that tactical tools do not linger under the radar for an extended period of time. Self-service data analytics tools are widely used to piece together various system outputs (enrichment and interoperability) and to supplement core system functionality not yet in place. However, the goal is to ensure that tactical automation is in place no longer than the features gap in the core technology platform exists. Therefore, organizations are served by establishing shelf-life guidelines and mandating that builds that have been in place longer than this window, or even approaching this window, are reviewed and justified for continuation. At a more basic level, end-users should recertify the efficacy and continued use of builds as part of the inventory maintenance process.

> **Action:** Requesters must evidence core technology referral for demand items to progress.
> **Action:** Data analytics builds must have a fixed shelf-life with a specified end-date.
> **Action:** Builds approaching expiry must escalate to core technology before end dates extended.
> **Action:** All builds must be periodically recertified as "Active" or "Retired."

Project Development Audit Trail Must Be Captured and Retained

Many technology change governance precepts and artifact requirements still remain relevant to end-user data analytics builds and workflows. The production and retention of adequately detailed requirements documents, evidence of UAT testing and sign-offs, post-implementation review outcomes, documents demonstrating any change control procedures – all of which made good sense for larger-scale systems implementations – are required for the very same reasons. The attrition or loss of a key operator who may have performed the process in the past and who over time has structured their operations in a tool could lead to a lapse of knowledge, in the event that adequate documentation is not captured. Further, internal audit and external auditors may demand the production of such artifacts, to evidence that robust internal controls exist surrounding change.

Testing is a key control during implementation of data analytics. The governance committee must prescribe sound development standards to include testing and deployment methodologies as well as controls over them to ensure that analytics builds as introduced are operating effectively. Governance should call for adequate testing and mandate such procedures as the number of testing cycles to run, the adequate number and variety of test scenarios, and even standard testing coverage ratios that must be adhered to. Roles and responsibilities of project teams and process owners must be described, such that there is no vagueness or confusion during development cycles. Further, the governance committee must specify the testing artifacts to be produced and retained that can serve as evidence attesting to adequate consideration of build quality. Finally, the governance committee must specify the signatories – the appropriate organization level of end-users signing off that deliveries meet requirements, so it is clear where the buck stops.

It is imperative that the project development audit trail is captured to avoid such tooling becoming a "black box." This means that the only way that the workings of the build can be intuited is not from a written brief or a review of project artifacts but from loading data inputs to the engine to see what comes out. Auditors do have a "black box" testing approach at hand. They load mocked data as a process input, and based on the processing that is represented to occur, they compare final output to expected output and in this way gain confidence over the "black box" processing. However, this approach is a very specific tool that should be reserved for the rare circumstance when there is no other alternative. For relatively simple data analytics builds, "black box" processing is easily avoidable, through acute discipline surrounding change management documentation.

Let's contrast two approaches to testing build effectiveness to illustrate the point. Imagine an accounting workflow where Alteryx is employed to reformat a subledger input file, before it is loaded to a general ledger system. The system then processes the data through its well-documented engine, as expected, before generating output in the form of a flat-file extract. This flat file is then run back through a second Alteryx workflow for a final enrichment with account mappings/groupings and a quick reformat into a user-defined field order, allowing the grouped and enhanced file to finally be consumed by QlikView or Tableau for dashboard reporting of financials.

On one end of the spectrum, detailed testing of system effectiveness could be performed on the General Ledger *system* through code reviews, where each line of code is tested for the intended outcome and deemed to be adequate or otherwise. As ever, this may be unwieldy for auditors to perform, as it could require technological savvy on par with that of the code developers to decipher. In any case, this approach only provides comfort over the *system* portion of the value chain. As we have already explained, in our example, there are tactical builds both in front of and below the core system. For the rest of the value chain, an external auditor may consider instead using a modular approach, where they identify an ETL use case, then run a mocked-up input file through the "black box" to validate that the output is as expected, based on the inputs. In this way, they can gain comfort that the ETL configuration is working as expected.

Now, let's compare that roundabout approach with the preferred method to gain assurance on build effectiveness. An auditor may simply review build requirements, review the user acceptance testing scripts, procedures, and outputs, and finally ensure there is clear evidence of sign-off at the appropriate level, prior to go-live. After the fact, she may examine the post-implementation review documentation, and finally she may confirm that standard operating procedures (SOPs) have been dutifully updated. In this way, a mosaic can be formed from a number of hard artifacts that taken together point to the fact that the build is operating effectively. Direct testing, supplemented by project artifacts and evidence of governance and controls, can be persuasive.

Hopefully, we have illustrated that adequately detailed requirements must be captured; UAT outputs and sign-off evidence must be retained to satisfy internal and external auditors and to ensure process stability. Evidence of post-implementation review must likewise be retained to demonstrate that the changes in the production environment are operating as intended. All of these disciplines help to give process owners and other internal stakeholders comfort in processing integrity. Further, external auditors must be satisfied that process changes that result from the introduction of data analytics tooling is well considered and disciplined.

As your organization advances along its digital journey, you must strike the right balance between rigorous process and change control and being nimble. Ensuring your organization has quality outputs and robust processes is the main goal of governance, but too, ensuring your organization can withstand later scrutiny is of critical importance. Requirements documentation, proposed solutions, any change control procedures, evidence of testing and sign-offs – all of these rigors are warranted in an environment of self-service data analytics, just as they have been and are still warranted in the systems environment.

Of course, users will balk at being slowed down to satisfy these requirements. They will argue that a key advantage of self-service data analytics tooling is that they have in their hands the capability to streamline processing, without the involvement of the core technology function and the governance overhead that comes with their involvement. It will be down to the influence of governance committee sponsors to convey that the key benefit of the tooling is the relatively short time-to-market it offers in contrast to strategic technology responsiveness. Process owners must be persuaded that these governance controls serve the organization by ensuring effective processing and by safeguarding collective organizational memory. Who was it that said there are only three constants – death, taxes, and governance? We suppose your authors are saying it now. Governance stakeholders, internal auditors, and external auditors have a major influence in determining what governance procedures are adequate. Irrespective on where the debate lands, the prescribed guidelines must be consistently followed across the organization.

There is no doubt that due to the sheer number of configurations that are expected to be administered as the program builds speed, governance artifacts can become tedious to maintain and costly to manage, with decentralization and deep proliferation within an organization at scale. Workflow tooling can be useful to centralizing inbound demand items and discipline around evaluating opportunities, but also as a centralized record of key project artifacts to meet the governance requirements. See Chapter 8's section Workflow Tooling for more detail on what is on offer today, and how even change management and governance processes, themselves, can be bolstered by technology platforms.

Action: Detailed project documentation must be captured and retained.

Action: Project requirements, sizing/benefits estimates must be retained (for later control).

Action: Change control procedures ensure changes to requirements/solutions are documented.

Action: User acceptance testing (UAT) outputs and evidence of sign-off must be retained.

Action: Adequately broad testing scenarios must be included in test plans.

Action: Standardized testing coverage ratios must be specified.

Action: Post-implementation review artifacts must demonstrate changes operate effectively.

Reference End-User Analytics Tooling and Workflows in Process Documentation

Our readers are more than likely well aware of how vital process documentation is to ensuring process consistency and operational resilience throughout normal business cycles. Where new tooling has been introduced, process owners must revisit their SOPs and clearly reference where in the process flow the tool has been inserted and what use case is being solutioned. In most cases, a summary reference to a tool name is not adequate. Here again, processing inputs and transformation steps should be documented, along with how these together combine to yield outputs.

To the extent that data analytics tooling is involved in generating financial information that is relied upon by key internal clients and stakeholders for decision-making, and particularly in cases where such tooling is used to produce financial reporting that external parties and regulators may rely upon, governance is absolutely key to providing documentary evidence that tooling has been introduced in a disciplined and thoughtful way. Even in cases where the tooling is relied upon only for in-house processing applications, there are still practical reasons that documentation must be in place to benefit *internal* stakeholders.

As we introduce change into processes, it is important both that the "as-is" process documentation is retained and that the new "to-be" process is documented as well. The "to-be" process is the new, streamlined, and efficient process that exists with the benefit of the analytics tooling. Instructions must be provided on how to operate the tooling, where the tools enter into the overall process chain, and how to troubleshoot in the event that something goes wrong. The "as-is" process is the longhand process or the legacy process that we are streamlining with our automation tools. Over time, as analytics builds are embedded into the landscape and increasingly relied upon, new staff may not be exposed to the longhand process that is encompassed in the build and they have no recourse to which to resort, in the event that something goes wrong. Therefore, legacy longhand process SOPs must be retained for future reference, in the event that there is a process disruption, and we are required to revert to the manual process. In addition to being a requirement for process stability, turnover risk and key person risk can also be mitigated, when detailed process documentation and SOPs are in place. How better to ensure a smooth transition of process ownership than to have detailed procedure documentation on hand?

As we know, the most frequent cause of process disruption, once data analytics tools are successfully implemented, is a change to the format of inputs. The first time that operators walk in to face a process failure due to input format instability that renders the tool inoperable, they may not be able to reverse engineer the actual processing steps required to generate an output. There may not be adequate collective or organizational memory to understand the processing steps that are being performed behind the scenes. Here again, this could result in the tools being "black boxes," where transformation steps being performed are obscured and difficult to decipher. Up-to-date process documentation, which articulates the full longhand process, shows which of the processing steps have been structured in the tool, and lays out the required initialization steps to run the automation workflow, is key to process stability.

Certain off-the-shelf vendor tools like Alteryx are addressing this need through automated workflow documentation modules. A visual depiction of the enrichments and processing steps is composed by the application in real time. This can provide a shortcut to the generation of conformant process documentation. Review Exhibit 6-4 for an Alteryx workflow document that is created on the fly by the software to memorialize transformation steps. Clearly, such software features can go far toward ensuring that adequate process documentation is put in place and can meaningfully speed its creation. Of course, this must be supplemented and bolstered by written process documentation and SOPs.

Action: Rigorous "As-is" and "To-be" SOPs must be documented and kept up-to-date.

Action: SOPs must instruct users to initialize, maintain, and troubleshoot analytics tools.

Action: Legacy longhand process SOPs must be maintained in the event of tooling failure.

Model Risk Governance

In Chapter 3, we introduced models and described that they are increasingly essential inputs to critical business decisions. In prescribing a single unified governance process for data analytics builds, we must ensure that it can accommodate the distinct governance requirements for models. However, many model governance procedures can be applied to data analytics more generally. Accordingly, we will outline recommended governance procedures to ensure adequate internal controls for models, and where these are applicable to other data analytics builds, we will adopt these as standard governance procedures.

While there are an increasing number of applications for models, there a number of risks that can be posed by models and estimations. In the Model Risk Governance section of Chapter 3, we introduced the Federal Reserve Bank's guidance in SR Letter 11-7 (Supervisory Guidance on Model Risk Management). In this section, we will begin by outlining the major risks represented by models, and then we will leverage SR Letter 11-7 and supplement it, to prescribe sound controls to mitigate each risk, respectively. Following are six main categories of model risk:

1. **Input risk** – Models rely on the integrity of inputs. Input quality must be controlled and monitored, in order to ensure that outputs can be relied upon.
2. **Model methodology risk** – Statistical or mathematical theories employed by models may be unsound or inappropriately applied.
3. **Estimation risk** – Estimations used may be inaccurate, may use unreliable assumptions, or may have been arrived at from extreme or aberrational observations, not representative of prevailing or normal conditions.

4. **Subjective classification risk** – Subjective assumptions fail to consistently classify observations.
5. **Inappropriate use risk** – Models may be employed for an unintended use.
6. **Execution risk** – Even when model theories and logic are valid, they can lead to flawed output when they are not executed appropriately.

Model risk governance is a set of policies and procedures that outline oversight and control over models. Comprehensive model governance should address the identification and mitigation of each of the risks we have listed, as above. For each of the categories of risks introduced above, we will specify applicable governance policies and mitigation steps to manage them and to ensure they are rigorously controlled.

Input risk is shared by all data analytics tools, whether or not they qualify as models by strict definition. For each build, we can only be assured of quality outputs, when input data are of high quality. We discussed this subject in the Inputs and Data Governance sections of Chapter 3, where we introduced COSO IC (2013), COSO ERM (2017), and COBIT 2019, which all address various aspects of data management, to ensure the quality of processing inputs. It was important to cite existing guidance on governing the quality of inputs, but for purposes of this section, we will largely assume that inputs have integrity, as the starting point for processing. Our model governance framework will take over at the point at which inputs are consumed, so we will add a high-level governance action stating only that model inputs must be confirmed and controlled.

Models may have fundamental flaws due to limitations in their methodology. As an example, if we think of regression analysis as a way to identify the factors that can best predict a future outcome, would a model making use of regression precisely predict outcomes 100% of the time? Of course not. Imagine we have a model in use to predict daily ice cream cone sales for a chain of retail stores on Long Island, New York. We have a regression formula that factors in such drivers as the temperature outside and the current month (to adjust for seasonality), the current market price of ice cream (to consider elasticity of demand), and the hours of operation, the day of the week, and even the number of marketing dollars spent and the reach and frequency of the recent advertising campaign. Perhaps a Nobel prize-winning statistician and data scientist has made this her magnum opus, and has fine-tuned this sales prediction tool over the last decade. On a given day, when each of these inputs are plugged in, it is predicted that 16,457 ice cream cones will be sold across locations on Long Island. What do you think the odds are that exactly 16,457 ice cream cones are ultimately sold? It is easy to see that even the best of models may be limited by their ability to take into account all factors that drive outcomes, or in our case, their ability to predict all market factors and the whims of individual behavior.

What controls could be implemented to consider and mitigate model limitations? The limitations of models should be well understood and acknowledged by users, and compensating controls should be implemented as appropriate. Model development, testing, validation, and implementation steps should be thoroughly documented, along with any subsequent modifications to model assumptions, estimations, parameters, or calculations. Finally, models should be independently reviewed prior to use and follow ongoing testing and monitoring requirements, based on materiality. For instance, back testing could be conducted on an ongoing basis to identify additional drivers of sales or to fine-tune the regression formula to allow for better predictions. In this way, the accuracy of models could be increased incrementally over time.

In many cases, models make use of estimations to arrive at outputs. The estimations used may be inaccurate, may use unreliable assumptions, or may have been arrived at from extreme or aberrational observations, not representative of prevailing or normal conditions. In our ice cream sales model, imagine that Saturday is the largest observed sales day in the week, which is assigned a factor of 1.0, followed by Friday and Thursday, which are both assigned a factor of 0.9, or 90% of Saturday sales, followed by Sunday through Wednesday, which are each assigned a sales factor of 0.7, or 70% of Saturday sales. Thursday, however, has an assigned factor of 0.1, or 10% of Saturday sales. In this way, the model bases the sales predictions throughout the week on the preceding Saturday's sales performance. However, what if these factor estimates were set during a week when there happened to be a hurricane on Thursday, accounting for the exceptionally low outlying factor assigned to this day? The model is otherwise sound, but the estimates used may drive an inaccurate projection due to the fact that they were derived during a period of abnormal, erratic, or uncharacteristic observations.

The risk that models are based on flawed estimations can be mitigated through the performance of a detailed initial review during testing ahead of implementation, and periodic review of estimates on an ongoing basis thereafter, to confirm both assumptions and the rationale used to derive estimates. The estimates and assumptions should also be independently reviewed by others within the organization or by third parties, who can act as a sounding board and who must be empowered to challenge any assumptions made, to raise objections, and to call them into question when they are flawed. The hope is that by independently reviewing model estimates prior to use, and by revisiting them over time, model value can be protected.

Some models make use of subjective classifications. The subjectivity introduces the risk of inconsistency over time. One example of this was introduced in the "social listening" contribution made in Chapter 2 by Paul Paris, CEO of Lash Affair. He mentioned that machine learning classification is used to characterize natural language references to the brand as being positive or negative, or somewhere along the continuum in between. Perhaps this is straightforward when an adjective such as "brilliant" is used, which is generally deemed as universally positive, but what if a post is received from someone from Liverpool, UK, who uses "Aces!" or "Blinding!" instead to describe an extremely positive recent service experience. Depending on the interpretation of these exclamations, and perhaps depending on the life experience of the individual preparing training data and performing the initial classification, this observation (and future observations as these adjectives are "learned") could end up in a very different place on the brand sentiment continuum due to the subjective classification relied upon in this model. But what to do about the interpretation risk or the risk that subjective classification is not consistent or is incorrect? The same procedures must be relied upon as above; extensive documentation of model methodology, assumptions, any subjective classification employed, extensive testing and back testing, and independent review – all of these rigors can increase the likelihood of model success and positive outcomes.

Models may also introduce risks if they are inappropriately used, outside the scope for which they were conceived, designed, and tested. If our ice cream sales predictor was used to make sales predictions for snow shovels (a stretch, we know), the seasonality coefficient may be inverted or the temperature factor may be misinterpreted. This is an obvious example of using a model for unintended purposes, but what if with some modification, the model was used to predict Italian ices or snow cone consumption in the London metropolitan area? At least these are somewhat related commodities that people may seek out as alternatives to ice cream. But the fact remains, our Nobel laureate tested, designed, and implemented the model for a specific purpose – to predict ice cream sales in a specific market. Repurposing or misapplying the model can lead to excessive risk and low-quality outcomes.

This risk is quite easy to mitigate. The application for which the model was devised should be spelled out concretely in the model documentation. Product details, any assumptions used, the markets for which use was intended, all of this should be crystal clear with disclaimers and warnings written across the top of the page in bold red font: "Beware. Use at Your Own Peril." We are being facetious here, but the point is that the documentary step becomes extremely important in explaining the intended purposes for models, and the employment of models for any other use must trigger disciplined and well-considered redesign, any required modifications, and of course regimented testing, as was done by our Nobel laureate prior to implementing her original model.

A final risk that models introduce is execution risk. There could be flaws in the execution of otherwise sound and robust model logic. We will take a roundabout approach to highlighting this risk. Some time ago, one of your authors sat for the CFA Level I exam. During the intense preparation leading up to the big day, he committed to memory a number of important formulas that the review course and the study materials pointed to as essential and indispensable. Among them were formulae for variance and standard deviation, holding period return, Z-Scores, risk premium, and the Sharpe Ratio. Great! Step one is done. Check! Armed with an HP-12c (Hewlett Packard financial calculator), and the required formulas memorized by rote, the author worked through many sample exams and ultimately demonstrated proficiency with the exam topics.

However, the Friday night before the Saturday exam, in making last-minute preparations, a quick check of the calculator battery revealed that the HP was out of commission! Off to the local drugstore for batteries, but no luck. Then to the office supplies center, but no luck. As a final resort, the increasingly anxious author checked the website and learned that an alternate calculator, the Texas Instruments BA II Plus, was also on the approved list for use on the exam. Three phone calls and a four-avenue, cross-town dash later, and the author was the proud owner of the TI BA II Plus. Back at home, having wrested the item from the heavy gauge clear (and unbelievably sharp when cut with scissors) plastic, and having quickly scanned the keyboard functions, the implications of execution risk became quite clear. No matter how exceptional the planning, how sound the theory, and how vigorous the practice, if the author was not in command of the calculator functions, he would be unlikely to execute the standard deviation calculation successfully!

In the same way, as models are carefully planned and conceived, they will only be as good as the ultimate execution of what began as sterling statistical theories and magical mathematical brilliance, as theories are put into practice. Errors or flaws introduced during model implementation can result in failures of the same magnitude as those that result from flawed logic. Scrupulous and dogged testing procedures are the best available detective control to identify execution errors for redress. Multiple iterations of a wide and varied set of testing scenarios are in order to confirm that models have been built to operate as intended.

While many similarities exist between models and data analytics and automation workflows, the distinguishing characteristics of models is that they contain estimates, assumptions, probabilities, mathematical computations, algorithms, and/or quantitative theories. Many, if not most, of the data analytics and automation builds deployed across finance, accounting, and operations functions perform simple extract, transform, and load (ETL) or automate routine accounting work such as reconciliations, aggregations, and selections, rather than the more complex analytical applications that invoke models to answer "what-ifs" or to predict outcomes. However, whether or not ETL or processing builds qualify as models, they may represent their own complexities, given the span and breadth of processing steps they have been scoped to include.

For this reason, model governance precepts are very much applicable to data analytics builds. Many of the practices that have been codified and integrated to model governance are applicable, even to analytics builds not meeting the strict definition of models. While model methodology risk, estimation risk, and subjective classification are unique to models, whether or not an analytics workflow meets the definition, they may exhibit input risk, inappropriate use risk, and of course, execution risk. Ensuring a configuration inventory is maintained, ensuring the performance of input verification, rigorous testing, and the maintenance of project documentation surrounding the development, testing and modifications of builds – all of these requirements prescribed for model governance are best practices for analytics builds beyond models.

> **Action:** Model input integrity must be confirmed and controlled.
> **Action:** All models and qualitative models (QMs) are be logged in firm-wide model inventories for risk management.
> **Action:** All models and QMs should be independently reviewed prior to use.
> **Action:** All models and QMs must follow ongoing testing and monitoring requirements.
> **Action:** Model development, testing, validation, and implementation must be documented.
> **Action:** Modifications to assumptions, estimations, or calculations must be documented.
> **Action:** Users should understand the limitations of the models and QMs.
> **Action:** Compensating controls to supplement model limitations must be invoked, if needed.
> **Action:** Roles and responsibilities are specified for model operators, executors, and managers.

Organizational and Functional Goal Alignment

Digital transformation projects must universally be linked to overall functional goals. In Chapter 3, we introduced the COBIT framework, which explains the need to ensure alignment between functional goals and digital transformation opportunities. Any number of functional goals may be crystalized by senior management, which can relate to value-added to clients, internal efficiency goals, control objectives or any other objective; in all cases, the projects selected to progress into the prioritization queue must support the goals and objectives established and handed down by senior executives. It must be ensured that projects taken up do not operate counter to organizational strategy, irrespective of the analytics tooling that is invoked. To ensure this is the case, we recommend the further step of requiring the documentation of the organization's goals that are supported by the build, in advance of project selection.

For instance, imagine that senior management has arrived at a strategy to build solutions in-house, over the use of vendor software. In this case, as projects are evaluated to ensure they align with organization objectives, we must be careful to heed the constraint and to reject any projects which build further dependence on our vendor relationships. See Chapter 5's section Alignment of Finance Function Goals with Digital Transformation Capabilities for more on establishing a critical path control point, where builds are evaluated against organizational goals and constraints.

As another example, imagine that recently, a given department has been the subject of an internal audit, where several action points were raised to management concerning the number of end-user computing tools (EUCs). One action given to management was to reduce the number of high-risk EUCs by 15%. In response to this action, an organizational constraint was put in place to give preference to those projects that structure EUCs through the employ of self-service data analytics tooling. On this basis, product managers (those that are tasked with assigning priority to demand items in the backlog) must give deference and priority to builds that advance this goal.

Remember, your organization may have additional or varied goals, but a control point must be put in place to allow only projects that support them to move forward. See section Project Acceptance Criteria and Organizational Constraints in Chapter 8 for a discussion of this topic and examples. While there are many tools and transformation technologies under the data analytics umbrella, the most preferred in finance, accounting, and operations functions are those that align with functional goals. See Exhibit 5-2 for a matrix illustrating sample stated functional goals.

Action: Prior to project acceptance, evaluate solutions against organizational constraints.

Action: Each build must demonstrably support functional goals and management objectives.

Action: Specific organizational/functional goals supported by build are captured and retained.

Adequate Training for Developers and End-Users

As introduced in Chapter 3, one thread that can be borrowed from the AICPA's Committee on Auditing Procedures is the need to ensure those on whom reliance is placed to develop and introduce data analytics tools to processing workflows must be well trained and qualified with the tools. Further, end-users who will operate and rely on the tooling must likewise be trained on tooling use. SAS No. 1, Section 210 of *The General Standards* is highly relevant, as it states that "The examination is to be performed by a person or persons having adequate technical training and proficiency as an auditor." In paragraph 2, the standard goes a step further to recognize that just because individuals are qualified in other areas of business and finance, they do not meet the requirements of auditing standards, without proper education and experience in the field of auditing. Finally, in paragraph 4, the standard reminds us that the independent auditor's education and professional experience are complementary and should be weighed in assessing competency.

On the topic of internal controls for analytics programs, we also considered Allen Sammy's article as published in *Internal Auditor* magazine.[2] No matter how sophisticated and user-friendly a tool may be, for obvious reasons, we cannot expect developers to serendipitously employ it to drive control and efficiency without adequate training. Perhaps it is useful to consider the risks that the organization may face in an extreme example, were there are no guidelines in place to mandate that developers and end-users of data analytics tooling are adequately trained.

If NASA put its full suite of rocket engines in your authors' hands, we would be unlikely to harness these extreme technological capabilities to choreograph an interplanetary landing in an afternoon. Even were NASA to seat us at a futuristic console and instruct us to simply "Push the big red button to launch the rocket and it will automatically land on Saturn," we would find ourselves at a distinct disadvantage, absent the *Rocket Science 101* training seminar. We may not be able to detect any anomalies in the flight path in the event that something goes wrong. Nor would we be equipped to troubleshoot or correct any disparities. In much the same way, developers and users of data analytics tooling are on the back foot when it comes to ensuring robust processing without the benefits of adequate education, process familiarity, and training with the tools.

A fetching example to be sure, but you get the point. Just as an external auditor must have adequate technical training and proficiency to perform an audit, however capable she may be in other fields (SAS No. 1, Section 210), so in practice must the end-user be technically trained in order to develop and deploy configurations into her daily workflow, in place of longhand procedures. The level of training and competence required should be commensurate with the degree of complexity assessed to the build. End-users, for their part, must be able to articulate the use case they seek to solution, specify processing inputs, iterate transformation steps in the "as-is" process, and document how these together combine to yield outputs.

Your organization must decide what training is appropriate and available to meet the training requirements, and you must determine how best to gauge process familiarity, but it is important that there are rules in place to spell out minimum qualifications required to develop and introduce data analytics, and even who should be operating tooling on an ongoing basis.

> **Action:** Executors who develop data analytics must be trained and qualified with the toolset.
> **Action:** End-users must certify they are trained on inputs, expected outputs, and processing steps.
> **Action:** End-users must certify they are trained to initialize, operate, and troubleshoot builds.

Establishment of Risk Assessment Criteria

There are many factors that contribute to the riskiness of introducing data analytics tools into process flows and to the builds themselves. How many downstream processes will be dependent on configuration outputs? Who is the intended audience for the output? Is it intended for senior management or other internal stakeholders? Will the outputs be submitted to external consumers such as clients and customers, or even regulatory agencies? Is the build extremely complex? Does the workflow contain a significant number of transformational steps? Any assumptions made may likewise weigh into overall risk (such as probabilities versus discreet observations). All of these factors can lead to specific builds representing more risk than others. We can easily see why considerable time and resources should not be spent managing the relatively little risk introduced by a build with low complexity, no key dependencies, that is relied upon by a single user, and promises few consequences of failure. Conversely, a highly complex build, upstream of many other dependent processes, whose outputs are heavily relied upon by senior management, external clients, and tax authorities or other regulators, may warrant a high level of focus and careful consideration.

Risk drivers and risk-assessment criteria must be established by the governance committee, after thoughtful consideration of which factors could increase risk within the organization. Documentation must be maintained to reflect how individual analytics tools are contributing to operational deliverables and to financial, regulatory, or management reporting in the organization. Each build must then be scored according to these criteria to allow for a ready stratification of builds into risk categories.

Further, the impact of failure should be adequately considered. Is there a regulatory impact, in the event of misstatement? Could failure result in a direct financial loss? Could errors result in restatement of financial statements and therefore fall under SOX 404 or other regulatory pronouncements? If the firm acts as a risk-taking intermediary for its client-base, could it be held liable, in the event of error or process failure? The impact of failure must be assessed for each build.

The risks represented by the builds in and of themselves as identified in the risk scoring, complemented by the impact assessment, can allow for the identification of builds that require more care and due diligence prior to introduction. Risk mitigation strategies, or risk responses, should be documented and retained to ensure there is a ready plan on hand to reduce the *risk* of failure to a palatable level, and to reduce the *impact* of failure, should it occur. The governance committee should put guardrails in place to ensure that risk responses and crisis runbooks are at hand to draw from, in the event of failure. Chapter 5 will cover risk governance steps in detail, but a mention of them is warranted here.

Action: Risk assessment criteria must be established for data analytics projects.

Action: Risks must be weighed against risk assessment criteria for each data analytics project.

Action: Portfolio-level risk must be assessed in aggregate by the governance committee.

Action: Risk responses are drafted to specify ways to reduce likelihood or impact of failure.

EXHIBIT 4-1 Data Analytics Governance Checklist

Sponsorship Is Secured and Data Analytics Governance Committee Is Established:	____
Committee Objectives Are Documented in a Committee Charter	____
Sound investment, change, and risk governance for analytics projects is enforced	____
Data and information security is safeguarded from emergent cyber risks	____
The demand pool and deliveries are reviewed to understand organization-wide pain and solutions	____
Successful projects are reviewed to identify replication opportunities elsewhere	____
Implemented projects are controlled for process stability	____
Implemented projects are controlled for promised benefits and sizing and cost estimates	____
ROI is calculated and publicized. Realized qualitative benefits are also published.	____
Adequate funding has been made available to sufficiently scale the program	____
Third-party tooling is reviewed periodically against alternatives and in-house capabilities	____
Committee members act as a sounding board for junior project teams to ensure control	____
Committee identifies opportunities to streamline/hasten the process of change	____
Objectives are reviewed and updated frequently to remain on point	____
Ensuring Input Integrity	____
Data Governance Committee	____
Establish a data governance committee sponsored and chaired by senior management	____
Spell out data committee objectives in a governance committee charter	____

(continued)

EXHIBIT 4-1 Data Analytics Governance Checklist *(continued)*

Organizations must monitor compliance with data governance policies and procedures	____
Ensure roles and responsibilities are assigned for data stewards, owners, and end-users	____
Data Asset Inventory	____
Produce data asset inventory for assessment, review, and governance/control planning	____
Inventory must flag sensitive and proprietary datasets for enhanced control and vigilance	____
Inventory must flag data sources for external and regulatory reporting	____
Inventory must identify datasets integral to competitive advantage and firm value	____
Inventory should identify authoritative golden sources of data for conflict prevention	____
Data Lineage	
Document the sources, flows, and persistence of data in data lineage artifacts	
Data Quality Review Procedures	
Manage data assets through measurement, assessment, and improvement over time	____
Employ reconciliation/analytical review/validation procedures to identify DQ anomalies	____
Implement attribute-level business rules to define quality and identify exceptions	____
Establish data quality KPIs to assess quality and track progress of improvement efforts	____
Display DQ KPIs on interactive dashboard to communicate overall health and trends	____
Baseline quality measures should be recorded to assess the quality of critical datasets	____
Resolution Sequence	____

(continued)

EXHIBIT 4-1 Data Analytics Governance Checklist *(continued)*

Data quality issues are logged for risk assessment, prioritization, and resolution	____
Risk assessments consider data uses, user impact, and downstream dependencies	____
As solutions are designed and executed, end-users sign off acceptance	
As issues are identified, detective controls are devised to identify issue persistence	____
Opportunity Capture, Benefits Case, Sizing, and Prioritization	____
Governance committee specifies opportunity capture and evaluation procedures	____
The front door inputs required for project consideration are specified	____
Clear roles and responsibilities for prerequisite entrance deliverables are ascribed	____
Governance committee translates management strategy to organizational constraints	____
Organizational constraints inform project selection	
Governance committee formulates project selection criteria	____
Self-Service Data Analytics Build Inventory Is Maintained	
Data analytics build inventory is captured and maintained	____
Inventory explicitly names tool developers, process owners (signatories), and operators	____
Vendor concentrations and dependencies are reviewed to ensure they are in line with strategy	____
Self-Service Data Analytics Tooling Is Tactical by Nature	____
Evidence of core technology referral is required for tactical demand items to progress	
Data analytics builds have a fixed shelf life, with a specified end-date	____

(continued)

EXHIBIT 4-1   Data Analytics Governance Checklist *(continued)*

All builds must be periodically recertified as "Active" or "Retired"	____
Builds nearing expiry are escalated to core technology, before expiry dates extended	____
Project Development Audit Trail	____
Detailed project documentation must be captured and retained	____
Detailed requirements and sizing/benefits estimates are retained for later control	____
Change control procedures ensure changes in requirements/ solutions are documented	____
Adequately broad testing scenarios are included in testing approach	____
Standardized testing coverage ratios have been specified	____
User acceptance testing (UAT) outputs and evidence of appropriate sign-off is retained	____
Post-implementation review artifacts demonstrate that changes operate effectively	____
Process Documentation References Analytics Tooling and Workflows	____
Rigorous "As-is" and "To-be" Process SOPs are documented and kept up-to-date	____
Process SOPs instruct users on how to initialize, maintain, and troubleshoot analytics tools	____
Legacy longhand process SOPs are maintained in the event of tooling failure	____
Model Risk Governance	____
Model input integrity is confirmed and controlled	____
All models and QMs are logged in firm-wide model inventories	____
All models and QMs are independently reviewed, prior to use	____
All models and QMs follow ongoing testing and monitoring requirements	____

(continued)

EXHIBIT 4-1 Data Analytics Governance Checklist *(continued)*

Model development, testing, validation, and implementation is thoroughly documented	____
Modifications to assumptions, estimations, parameters or calculations are fully documented	____
Limitations of the models and QMs are understood by users	____
Compensating controls to supplement model limitations are invoked, as needed	
Roles and responsibilities are specified for developers, executors, and managers of models	____
Organizational and Functional Goal Alignment	____
Solutions are evaluated against organizational constraints at project acceptance	____
Each build demonstrably supports functional goals and management objectives	____
Specific organizational/functional goals supported by each build are captured and retained	____
Adequate Training for Developers and End-Users	____
Executors who develop data analytics tools are trained and qualified with the toolset	____
End-users certify they are trained on the inputs, expected outputs, and processing steps	____
End-users certify they are trained to initialize, operate, and troubleshoot builds	____
Risk Assessment Criteria	____
Risk assessment criteria have been established for data analytics projects	____
Risks are evaluated against risk assessment criteria for each data analytics project	____
Portfolio-level risk is assessed in aggregate by the governance committee	____
Risk responses are in place to specify ways of reducing the likelihood/impact of failure	____

Discussion with Jitesh Ghai, Chief Product Officer at Informatica

"How must organizations change their thinking to adapt to the sheer magnitude of data they are faced with today?" Organizations need to change their thinking in terms of people, process, and technology in order to adapt to the exponential growth in data, new types of data, and number of data consumers. From a people and process perspective, it's not just about adding more manpower to get through the massive backlog of IT requests which means you'll need greater process automation that eliminates thousands of manual tasks. Organizations will likely need to hire or up-skill their current workforce to manage, govern, and analyze massive amounts of data. Furthermore, enterprises can no longer afford to have data reside in departmental silos because there are more data consumers that need broader access to enterprise data so they can answer more complex questions having greater business impact – in other words, data must be democratized and shared and this means data must be available 24x7 in a self-service fashion, trusted, governed, and protected.

To address these challenges organizations are choosing to deploy an intelligent cloud-native data management platform powered by AI and machine learning (AI/ML). Only through AI/ML can a data management platform automate the thousands of tasks data analysts, data engineers, data stewards, and other data professionals must perform daily as relates to data integration, data quality, data governance, master data governance, customer 360, and much more.

"Is data quality a foundational pillar for analytics?"
Data quality is without question a foundational pillar of analytics. There are numerous studies showing poor data leads to bad decision-making and misguides AI/ML models with unintentional bias and poor predictive power resulting in significant costs or missed opportunities. It is therefore disconcerting that 67% of executives lack trust in their data according to a recent Accenture survey of 190 executives, Data is the New Capital.[3] This is indicative of a systemic problem at many companies – how to ensure

policies that govern data quality are implemented consistently for all data across the enterprise.

Today, advanced analytics is fueled by large volumes of more types of data from multiple departments that must be consistent, complete, accurate, and impute missing values through inference. This requires a tight linkage among data quality, data governance, and data cataloging. For example, data quality policies are defined for business-critical data through data governance workstreams and related to business terms. These business terms and policies can then be automatically mapped to actual enterprise data under management within a data catalog by applying AI/ML. Once this is achieved, AI/ML and NLP can automatically generate the data quality rules associated with the policies and automatically apply these rules to the data under governance.

Through this level of integration, intelligence, and automation, data quality is ensured to be consistent, complete, and accurate for all enterprise data whether it be for analytics or any other data-driven business initiative. Furthermore, we've found that this is best achieved when data quality, data governance, and data-cataloging software all share a common metadata foundation and are part of an AI-powered platform.

"How is Informatica bringing emerging data analytics technologies to their customer base?"
Companies are using data analytics to improve productivity, increase operational efficiency, and drive profitable outcomes by discovering business insights within their enterprise data. To achieve these goals, our customers have embarked on three journeys: 1) cloud data warehouse and data lake modernization; 2) data governance and privacy; 3) 360 views of their business for customers, products, suppliers, and finance.

Informatica delivers solutions for all three of these journeys with an integrated and intelligent cloud-native data platform powered by AI and machine learning. Firstly, business data is growing exponentially and distributed across the enterprise in hundreds of data silos – Informatica enables data engineers to rapidly build and easily maintain data pipelines that ingest, integrate and cleanse data at any latency and scale for cloud data warehouses and data lakes. Secondly, data scientists and analysts need to quickly find the right data and know whether they can trust it while protecting sensitive data – Informatica delivers end-to-end collaborative data governance that includes an "Amazon-like" data marketplace such that data consumers can easily "shop" for data while adherence to corporate policies (e.g., data quality) and industry regulations (e.g., GDPR, CCPA) are assured. Lastly, customers struggle to get a complete view of their business in order to address the key and more complex business initiatives such as improving omni-channel customer experience and opti-mizing supply chains while avoiding disruptions – Informatica provides business 360 applications for customers, products, sup-pliers, and finance along with multi-domain master data man-agement that deliver AI-powered business insights that leverage powerful matching capabilities.

"What is the mission of Informatica?"
Our mission at Informatica is to empower companies to accel-erate data-driven digital transformations that are changing the world. Our passion, inventiveness, and investments have created wave after wave of innovation, helping businesses unleash the power of their data for over 25 years. As the leader in enterprise cloud data management, we are arming companies to take their businesses to new heights, fueling their innovation, even disrupt-ing industries – intelligently. Informatica has helped over 9,700 customers (85 of the Fortune 100) worldwide integrate, govern, master, and manage all their enterprise data with the industry's most advanced intelligent cloud-native data management plat-form powered by AI/ML. Informatica pioneered the use of AI/ML in data management – we call our AI/ML engine CLAIRE. CLAIRE provides intelligence for contextual automation by using advanced AI/ML models, algorithms, and supervised and unsu-pervised training methods leveraging all types of metadata (e.g., business, technical, operational, etc.). Consistent with our mis-sion, CLAIRE empowers data-driven organizations with enterprise scalability and automation across the entire platform portfolio. We've internalized this mission through our culture and values we call DATA: Do good, Act as one team, Think customer-first,

Aspire to the future. Through our mission and values, Informatica has achieved many industry firsts:

- The only independent cloud data management vendor with industry leading best-of-breed cloud-native capabilities
- The #1 cloud data management (i.e., iPaaS, DI, DE, DQ/Governance, MM) rated by Gartner as the industry's best for "VISION" and "EXECUTION"
- The most comprehensive cloud data management solution providing cloud-native data integration, data quality and governance, and metadata management
- The most scalable cloud data management solution processing 15T+ transactions/month across all major ecosystems, doubling by quarter
- The only cloud data management vendor with #1 in customer loyalty 13 years in a row
- Industry's First Catalog of Catalogs, Intelligent & Automated Governed Data Marketplace to Drive Data Value

Jitesh Ghai, Chief Product Officer at Informatica
www.informatica.com

Conclusion

We predict that self-service tooling will permeate almost every major organization to a degree never seen before in the coming years. In this chapter, we referenced a number of governance frameworks that largely did not consider self-service data analytics tools. We have attempted to weave them into a comprehensive and actionable governance framework that can be established early in the digital journey to protect organizational strategy, ensure the maximum impact of investment budgets, promote build effectiveness and process stability, and finally to prescribe a high-quality audit trail standard for data analytics transformation programs.

We admit that this is only the start of an important conversation for organizations beginning their digital journey, or for those speedily advancing on their course. The coordination of a governance committee, comprised of subject matter experts, core technologists, analytics tooling developers, and even internal auditors, as valued business partners, can help to pave the way for control by getting ahead of this trend. Through advising on sound data governance practices and procedures and through framing solid build governance, the governance committee must prevent the inevitable formation of a spaghetti-knot that must be unwound down the road.

While this chapter has been focused on developing a governance framework for self-service data transformation and enrichment tooling, rather than the many other artificial intelligence utilities that have recently emerged, many of the same tenets of governance are directly applicable to the portfolio of predictive machine learning, robotics, or other processing and decision-making tooling that were not the focus. Though self-service tooling is most often employed to structure manual processes and to capture efficiencies for end-users in their daily processing tasks, rather than targeting a fundamental edge or competitive advantage that predictive tooling can offer, when one considers the newfound prevalence across large organizations, this subset warrants keen consideration and vigorous governance.

Further, organizations must be prepared with tools to enable the all-important risk assessments that inform the substantive portion of external audits. Due to the sheer number of builds that can be expected to emerge across digitally charged organizations, the traditional procedures used to evaluate the control and effectiveness of systems and processes must be rethought. In Chapter 5, we will advance the governance guidelines and procedures we have developed to include risk governance procedures.

Notes

1. Loreal Jiles, 2020. "Govern Your Bots!." Strategic Finance.
2. Allen Sammy, 2018. "Analytic Models Controls and Tests – Auditors can perform numerous tests to provide assurance on analytics controls used in analytic models." Internal Auditor.
3. Shail Jain, 2019. https://www.accenture.com/_acnmedia/PDF-129/Accenture-Data-is-the-New-Capital-POV.pdf

CHAPTER 5

Self-Service Data Analytics Risk Governance

In this chapter, we will introduce and develop a comprehensive risk-governance framework that is fit-for-purpose for data analytics and automation programs in the accounting, finance, and operations functional settings. We explore the critical need for governance in anticipation of widespread adoption of data analytics tools and capabilities across medium-to-large enterprises. The marked pace of change as development capability is put into the hands of end-users leads to a far more complex risk environment. We will begin this chapter with a discussion of how organizational risk appetite must be reevaluated, as new channels of processing risks are introduced through the adoption of analytics. We will discuss how to draw a cross-functional and inclusive governance framework around IT, process owners, project teams, internal audit, and control stakeholders to ensure the required knowledge and perspective exists to provide adequate oversight. We will highlight the key risks introduced to the processing environment by data analytics and introduce methods for the assessment, measurement, and monitoring of such risks – and provide an approach to mitigate and manage them with risk response capabilities.

In the past, the control environment which safeguarded an enterprise from processing risk was centered around the core technology stack. The advent of self-service data analytics tools has dramatically shifted an enterprise's technology risk environment by decentralizing development patterns, giving end-users the capacity to perform such actions as importing data, analyzing it, structuring processing steps, and exporting outputs. As a result, the robust governance that was built around systems has been side-stepped by decentralized end-user data analytics processing, necessitating a commensurate adaptation of controls. It follows that in the resulting decentralized processing environment, a risk-mitigation framework is needed to address the re-allocation of control risk to the end-user.

Since process owners, themselves, oversee many facets of solution design and project delivery – and in effect develop code – it is no longer possible to relegate controls oversight to technology, alone. Users are changing the processing landscape at a feverish pace, but are no longer funneled to the controlled, IT-administered domain. As such, enterprise system architecture (and the governance apparatus structured around it) no longer serves as the guardian and gatekeeper of risk controls, in an environment of decentralized processing. In place of system governance alone, a framework must be developed to pull together the mature elements of system controls and marry them with the unique profiles, risks, and capabilities of emerging self-service data analytics. This framework must be threaded and interconnected throughout the firm and sponsored by firm leadership. As discussed in Chapter 3, the most applicable frameworks that can be drawn from to develop a risk governance framework for the automation environment are the Enterprise Risk Management (ERM) – Integrated Framework (COSO ERM) and the Model Risk Framework, which provide guidance on the development of risk management procedures throughout the enterprise. In this chapter, we will build upon the COSO's ERM-Integrated Framework, as well as the Model Risk Framework, to develop a robust risk governance framework for data analytics programs in the finance, accounting, and operations settings.

Setting Risk Appetite in an Environment of Changing Performance Expectations

To better understand the risk environment in core enterprise systems and connect risk to performance, let's examine the performance expectations of accounting systems. Previously, the performance expectations from accounting systems and the CFO organization had been to provide reliable information that is timely and free of error, in a relatively static format, for management stakeholders. Now, expectations on the function overall have shifted significantly. Not only must reporting integrity be preserved, but there is an increased emphasis on capturing efficiency from the acceleration of routine processes to allow for the recapture of bandwidth and more strategic deployment of people resources. The discovered bandwidth is subsequently rededicated to unlocking further value from data and for enhanced decision-making, leading to innovative new deliverables, and further processing evolution. The processing chains drift to produce more valuable outputs and evolve to produce them more efficiently and methodically – in a continuous cycle, growing ever more valuable and efficient with each revolution. This represents a powerful shift for accounting professionals, as those previously viewed as value *stewards* are now driving value *creation*. Accordingly, with the widespread adoption of data analytics in furtherance of this goal, the implications of heightened functional performance expectations must be reflected in an adapted risk governance strategy.

The changing performance expectations for enterprise functions are likely to impact the balance of component risks within the organizational risk profile. To demonstrate, let's examine the embedded risk appetite within the systems environment. We take it as a given that some likelihood of processing error may be acceptable (though not desirable), in a given system or the system environment, as a whole. Note that companies have three levers at their disposal to reduce the risk introduced by systems: money, time, and development resources (see Exhibit 5-1 regarding Risk and Value tradeoff considerations). Assuming thoughtful management consideration,

EXHIBIT 5-1 Risk and Value Considerations as Relates to Analytics and Automation

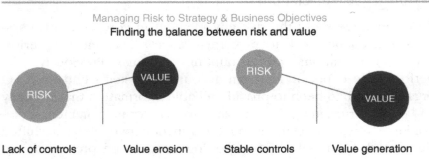

that such systems persist and live on, in spite of the risks introduced by them, implies that the level of risk is acceptable and in line with enterprise risk appetite.

With the rise in analytics, the risk appetite embedded in enterprise systems must be reassessed as new tools, new processes, and new expectations have fundamentally changed the risk environment. In the new environment, data analytics is an additive source of risk not previously considered when the risk tolerance was initially assessed. Organizations must therefore evaluate the incremental risk embedded in the data analytics environment and compare the findings with the organizational ability to manage it. This exercise serves to inform enterprise risk tolerance and allows for thoughtful and effective risk optimization. That said, perhaps the greatest danger posed by an emergent risk in the business environment is for it to emerge undetected. Lack of awareness can cause misalignment in understanding of the risk environment among managers, executives, and the board of directors. Particularly for organizations that are rapidly scaling up their analytics capabilities, it is imperative to take careful stock of both the risks inherent in the legacy systems environment and the risks introduced by data analytics. Once the full picture of systems and analytics processing risk is properly understood, risk appetite and risk tolerances can be thoughtfully updated. As a final measure, governance constraints can be dialed in to meet organizational risk tolerances, and the data analytics portfolio risk can be reined in within optimal bounds.

Action: Embedded risks in data analytics portfolio must be compared to the organization's ability to manage them.

Action: Risk appetite must be determined to balance time, money, and resource tradeoffs.

Action: Risks must be understood to reduce likelihood that failures exceed risk appetite.

Data Analytics Risk Governance Enhances Value Creation

A firm must manage its risk to strategy and business objectives in consideration of its risk appetite. In the data analytics governance domain, this means that the risk embedded in the data analytics environment must be managed in parallel with the value that the data analytics program is generating; risk mitigation efforts must be focused on enhancing and safeguarding value creation.

The value created by data analytics capabilities are manifold, such as rebuilding resource capacity through automation, increased reporting reliability through reduced human error, and the introduction of predictive decision-making to increase competitive advantage. However, in the pursuit of value and performance through the deployment of enhanced analytics, an organization must establish controls to protect against the erosion of the very value they create. The risks introduced through analytics deployment can be more closely controlled and managed by formulating standardized tooling-specific risk mitigation procedures, thereby facilitating the harmonization of risk mitigation measures throughout the organization. The frequent and persistent performance of risk assessments, the continual testing of the analytics portfolio to observe and quantify output variability, and devising and implementing tool-specific risk response strategies (outlined later in this chapter) are the foundations of strategic risk management and value preservation.

Action: Risk appetite must inform business strategy and tactical objectives.

Action: Controls must be built around data analytics portfolios to protect the value they are creating.

Action: Risk mitigation strategies are formulated at tool-specific level to harmonize responses.

Data Analytics Tool Selection Drives the Level of Partnership with IT

The availability of technology and tooling is ever-expanding, as we enter the age of analytics and automation. While the focus of this book is largely on self-service analytics and automation technologies, in Chapter 2 we introduced various other analytics technologies such as robotic process automation (RPA), machine learning, optical character recognition/intelligent character recognition (OCR/ICR), and natural language processing (NLP). While *self-service* analytics tools and technologies require little-to-no partnering with the technology function and apparatus, these more complex technologies require a medium or even a high-level of partnership with core technology. For more complex data analytics technologies where a significant level of partnership with technology is required, the governance should likewise encompass and overarch the technology function. Given that these advanced analytics tools and technologies fall into a distinct subset of analytics tooling, we recommend using a purpose-built analytics governance function, as described at the open of Chapter 4, rather than shoehorning this into the existing enterprise IT governance apparatus.

While IT has its own *systems* governance schema that utilizes various controls and legacy IT governance frameworks (as highlighted in Chapter 3), the most prevalent and widely subscribed uses for data analytics are *small automation*[1] deployments. Small automation efforts target one process or a portion of the process that can be streamlined through the deployment of a specific solution. The best available analytics tool is then deployed to automate only that portion of the process chain. Small automation can be considered in contrast to the larger, more front-to-back process automation efforts, and even strategic system implementations, where a far wider portion of the value chain is within scope and targeted for uplift. While certain processes may require the sophisticated analytics tools (e.g., machine learning), the governance of such tools requires the involvement of multidisciplinary teams that understand both the target business process(es) and the tools and technologies enlisted for solutioning – and that collectively are qualified to shape procedures to promote stability and control around automated processes. Accordingly, the IT governance apparatus may lack the necessary process knowledge to effectively administer a control framework for small automation efforts.

In Chapter 3, we recommended the establishment of a data analytics governance body chaired by a senior management sponsor, with the representation of process owners, data analytics practitioners and project teams, internal audit, and representatives from IT. This recommendation is echoed by the Deloitte and Internal Audit Foundation *Analytics and Automation for Internal Auditors Report*, where they refer to the recommended governance apparatus as the Automation Center of Excellence.[2] Irrespective of the name given to the governance body, it is clear that a broad cross-section of functions must be involved to ensure that project execution is successful in meeting business requirements, that process stability is safeguarded, and that the risks introduced are well understood, actively managed, and carefully mitigated. We will further develop a risk-scoring and risk-prioritization methodology to assist in identifying, assessing, and addressing the risks introduced by the various analytics solutions and tools presented in this chapter.

> **Action:** The amount of IT involvement in analytics governance is matched appropriately with tool selection.
> **Action:** Governance committee members must understand tooling *and* processes.
> **Action:** Governance framework must span functions or silos to harmonize standards.

Alignment of Finance Function Goals with Digital Transformation Capabilities

While there are many analytics tools and technologies available for use in automation and digital transformation efforts, the most preferred in finance, accounting, and operations functions are those that align with functional goals. In Exhibit 5-2, we present hypothetical functional goals communicated by leadership, along with short descriptions in the second column. We will discuss each in turn in the following section. Later, we will assess analytics tools and capabilities, to understand which categories of tools support these goals and identify those solutions that may conflict.

EXHIBIT 5-2 Digital Transformation Alignment with Finance Function Goals

Model transparency	Models need to be understood and validated by internal auditors.
Process assurance capability	Processes demonstrate a seamless compatibility with assurance tools that can reveal output variability and process failures.
Quality inputs	Inputs must be consistent, of high quality, and presented in a clean and standardized format.
Process stability	The process needs to be easily repeatable and generally error-free.
Automated control testing	The testing of the controls around the process are automatable and efficient in ensuring control and stability.
Minimum standards of process memorialization	Process documentation must adequately record processing steps executed in the analytics build, from input to output. Process memorialization provides the audit trail to support process assurance.
Resource optimization or efficiency	Ensuring the automation and analytics deployments produce sufficient return on investment. Assessments of the impact of automation projects on resource optimization must be performed, tracked, and recorded for management review and prioritization.

Since the finance functional outputs are highly scrutinized not only by company management but by active and potential investors and regulators, auditors will insist upon a minimum level of transparency, so that they can "lift the hood" to ensure process effectiveness and that processing outputs are accurate and comply with International Financial Reporting Standards (IFRS) or Generally Accepted Accounting Principles in the United States (GAAP). A set of processing steps involving nebulous AI algorithms, with no documentation of their internal workings or how the final result was reached, is considered a "black box" and would not meet the first finance objective in Exhibit 5-2, Model Transparency. If a black box algorithm was deployed by an organization to assist in making *marketing* decisions, auditors may be less concerned, as the downside of failure is likely to be suffered only by the company itself, perhaps by making poor advertising investment decisions or by diverting focus from products with the highest demand. However, as *finance* functional outputs are likely to effect financial reporting and to impact stakeholders extending beyond company management to the markets and even to regulators, transparency is especially critical. Black box processing steps may pose significant challenges for auditors who are charged with ensuring that outputs are correct and that there are functioning controls around the process, and they would be in conflict with a stated functional goal, in this particular case.

Model transparency as discussed above can be supported by another goal shown further down the list. Process memorialization supports model transparency, as it provides for a clear documentation of the process from start to finish. Such documentation should clearly detail the specific transformation steps automated by an analytics deployment, it should contain pre-automation standard operating procedures (SOPs), as well as post-automation SOPs detailing how the process is performed with the assistance of analytic tools. In the event of failure, it is not uncommon for a temporary reversion to legacy manual processing to be required, while the failure points are addressed. This can be made more difficult with turnover and attrition, as new joiners may have never performed the manual processes as was done in the past. Having clear documentation can assist in providing an understanding to operators who must step in, should a failure occur. Of course, such documentation goes far to providing auditors with a better understanding of deployed tools and can prevent builds from being deemed black boxes.

Looking at the other functional goals, we see that the process assurance capability goal requires that any tooling implemented can readily be integrated with assurance tools to highlight failures and significant output variability. Active risk mitigation requires the prompt awareness of process failures in order to ensure failures can be addressed and to prevent impacts from cascading downstream through a web of dependencies. This goal is closely related to the automated control testing goal. Increasingly, digital tooling can be used to continually test build effectiveness, and dashboards may be used to monitor performance and failures. The functional goal as stated requires that builds deployed must be seamlessly integrated with process assurance capabilities to support risk management. Automated control testing is fundamental to placing reliance on certain of the analytics tools, when introduced into the processing chain.

While quality inputs are listed third on the list, this concern is arguably the first concern for all processing efforts, whether or not aided by data analytics and automation tools. Not only must inputs be accurate and free of error, for many analytics technologies, even a minor change in column order could prevent successful processing. Bots in particular are trained to look only at a specific address in a data array. Even the subtlest source file change can often result in a process breakdown. A perfectly performed process based on faulty data results in the same outcome as would a faulty process performed on perfect data – abject failure. In our example, the finance functional management has recognized this, and they have elected to make input quality a stated functional objective.

Additional challenges arise with outsourced automation technologies, such as RPA, where a knowledge gap can emerge. A detailed understanding of the solutions deployed and the risks they introduce may be obscured from process owners and internal control teams. As outsourcing is common, supplemental procedures may need to be performed to guarantee that the third party has adequate controls and risk mitigation procedures in place to identify process failures promptly, if and when they occur.

As a final point, we will turn our attention to the stated resource optimization and efficiency goal. In large organizations today, this goal is likely to be paramount in virtually any function, rather than in finance alone. As we have emphasized throughout this book, one of the reasons that the emergent technology can be implemented with an attractive and immediate return on investment (ROI) is the efficiency that can be gained from automation. This goal is more related to *investment* governance than it is to *risk* governance, but it appears here in the sample listing of functional goals. In our example, when considering the viability of solutions, preference and prioritization would be given to those that best support this management goal.

In this section, we have presented an example set of functional goals that may be appropriate in an organization. Of course, these goals may vary depending on management and organizational strategy, the maturity of the function, and possibly even the personalities and personal goals of leaders in the function. Your authors had a secondary goal in mind in presenting these specific functional goals: we wished to discuss key risk governance precepts for data analytics portfolios. These goals are fundamental to ensuring process quality, process stability, minimum standards of documentation and transparency, and active risk management to protect the value of data analytics implementations.

In Exhibit 5-3, we identify the tools and technologies that best align with the stated finance function goals that were laid out in Exhibit 5-2. We can see that machine learning does not promote the goal of model transparency and may not therefore be an appropriate solution, given it is counter to stated functional goals. Similarly, NLP and OCR do not readily allow for process assurance and automated

EXHIBIT 5-3 Alignment of Digital Transformation Tooling with Stated Functional Goals

	RPA	Self-Service Analytics & Automation	Tableau and Dashboards	Machine Learning and AI	NLP and OCR
Model transparency	X	X	X		
Process assurance capability	X	X	X		
Quality inputs	X	X	X	X	X
Automated control testing	X	X	X		
Process stability	X	X	X	X	X
Minimum standards of process memorialization	X	X	X		X
Resource optimization or efficiency	X	X	X	X	X

control testing; therefore, solutions making use of these technologies may not be viable in light of functional goals. We have enlisted this exhibit to help readers contrast the enabling analytics technologies and to show that function-specific constraints may rule out their usage.

Action: Projects and the tooling they employ must align to functional goals.

Action: Models must be understood and validated by internal auditors.

Action: Processes must be compatible with assurance tools to reveal output failures/variability.

Action: Inputs must be in a standardized format of consistent high quality.

Action: Post-implementation, analytics processes must be easily repeatable and error-free.

Action: Process controls testing should be automatable and efficient in ensuring control/stability.

Action: Process memorialization artifacts must comprehensively record build processing steps.

Action: Resource optimization/time savings projections should inform project prioritization.

Data Analytics Risk Governance

While banking institutions are adept at using model governance for mathematical models, and banking regulators have begun fleshing out guidelines for adequate model governance, non-banking institutions and non-banking regulators are not as far along in mandating governance and providing compliance recommendations. With the rapid deployment of self-service analytics, users at organizations are now operating model-like self-service data analytics tools in day-to-day business activities across processing functions. Prior research has linked this use and its implications to the control environment[3] and indicate that model governance is applicable to self-service analytics tools. We similarly linked them in Chapter 4, for data analytics builds, which qualify as models (see the section Model Risk Governance).

As we described in the Model Risk Governance section, model governance by definition is applicable only where mathematical operations, probabilities, or assumptions exist within a model setting, while many applications of data analytics do not involve mathematical operations – and therefore do not qualify as models. Increasingly, a vast proportion of data analytics builds used in process automation are used for extract, transform, and load and data abstraction operations, to better organize, abstract, and transform data for further processing. With this distinction in mind, we can distill principles from model governance literature, and extend them in developing a comprehensive data analytics governance framework that aligns with COSO ERM – Integrated Framework (2017) for outputs that *do not* impact financial reporting, and with COSO – Internal Control Framework (2013), when the outputs *do* impact financial reporting. With the shift in the control environment as analytics technology is widely adopted in a decentralized manner by end-users, new risks must be identified, new assessment capabilities developed, and new risk responses must be devised to mitigate the risks introduced – and protect the value created from data analytics at scale.

The risks that are introduced with the rapid rise of data analytics are new, not always recognized, and rarely understood. The democratization of data and broad distribution of tooling to individual operators puts advanced capabilities in the hands of users who may not be adequately trained to consider and mitigate inherent risks. The relatively new appearance of data analytics tools in organizations that have not yet developed capabilities to recognize, assess, and respond to these new risks means that companies must respond – and quickly. The key risks in the data analytics environment often depend on the risk profile of the tools being used, the outputs generated, and the audience consuming them. In the following section, we will provide tools to allow for thoughtful risk assessment of individual analytics builds, as well as the portfolio as a whole.

Assessing Risks in the Analytics and Automation Environment

In this section, we will discuss how best to assess the risk of data analytics builds by category-type in accordance with the COSO ERM Framework – Assess severity of risk. To create a risk assessment for data analytics governance, the dimensions or drivers of risk must be agreed. Then each analytics build or model must be assessed, based on each risk factor. The projected impact of the risk must be considered, along with the likelihood of the risk impact (or event) materializing. When the risk score has been captured across all risk dimensions, taken together, they can inform the risk ratings for each build and ultimately allow for a ready comparison and risk stratification of the entire data analytics stack.

In the increasingly interconnected data analytics environment, there are outputs that serve as inputs to other processes. As such, process dependency documentation must be developed to fully document how one build's outputs and performance affect the inputs of others. Furthermore, the stakeholders and consumers of each model output must be understood and documented. Model outputs used for financial reporting or that may be published to external regulators for further scrutiny may warrant more testing, documentation, and risk management overall than do internal models serving one operator's individual needs. Since organizations may have hundreds or even thousands of analytics builds deployed concurrently, the builds can also be assessed based on category type or a risk profile that is developed for each analytics tool invoked. Assessing the builds collectively will promote increased risk awareness and can enable the development of standardized risk responses. Once the risks of the builds have been assessed both at the individual level and at the collective level, their impact must be examined and understood at the department level, business unit level, and the functional level to ensure they are in line with organizational risk tolerances and goals. The firm-wide view provides visibility into which risks pose the highest threat to business objectives and to the organization, overall. Risk responses can be designed accordingly, with risk-prioritization in mind, and with the appropriate materiality and scope thresholds set.

There are seven categories of risk[2] that are highly relevant to data analytics and automation that we will consider in the following section. Understanding these risk categories is fundamental to robust data analytics risk governance.

Action: Risk dimensions and drivers must be agreed.
Action: Number of dependencies, the users, and the uses must be considered as risk drivers.
Action: Each build or model must be evaluated across each risk dimension.

Action: Degree of impact and likelihood of occurrence must be used to evaluating risk drivers.

Action: Final quantitative risk scores can be compared for risk stratification and categorization.

Action: Portfolio-level risk should be considered to ensure it is in line with firm risk appetite.

Action: Portfolio-level risk can be assessed at department, business unit, and functional levels.

Seven Relevant Risks to Data Analytics

1. Operational Risk: Operational errors could occur due to failures in the automation environment. Without proper monitoring and timely identification, operational errors could result in cascading processing failures throughout the organization.
2. Financial Risk: Errors in the automation environment could result in financial losses. Financial risk is also introduced through investments in automation that do not produce ROI.
3. Strategic Risk: Analytics-related projects may lead to business objective failures by failing to produce reliable metrics or by slowing down business objectives tied to digital transformation goals.
4. Compliance Risk: Analytics process failures could result in non-compliance with federal, state, or local regulations, due to errors or omissions in outputs.
5. IT Risk: Technology risk exists in the development and testing of the automation builds, as failure to maintain proper IT infrastructure to support the automation environment could result in technology risk, and in some cases even vulnerability to cyber-attack.
6. Black Box Risk: Black box risk refers to a lack of transparency to the inner workings of processing solutions. Without clear documentation of the processing steps performed and methodology employed to solution, auditors will find it difficult to conclude that the process is operating effectively or that adequate controls exist. Other risks in this category include the possibility that algorithms are incorrectly trained or have embedded bias that impacts the decision-making processes.

7. Reputational Risk: Reputational risk in the analytics environment relates to the potential for processing failures to cause reputational damage to the organization. In this category are errors that cause financial restatement or regulatory sanctions, errors impacting flagship clients, or those that attract negative media coverage. Reputational damage can be severe and long-lasting.

These key risks will be referenced in the sections to follow. The next step in our governance strategy will be to assess each risk according to several applicable metrics and dimensions. We will weigh these risks based on several scales[4] that will ultimately consider each risk along four dimensions:

1. Impact scale
2. Likelihood scale
3. Vulnerability scale
4. Speed of Onset scale

Action: Assess risks:
Operational/Economic/Strategic/Compliance/IT/Black box/
Reputational.
Action: Rate seven risks for Impact, Likelihood, Vulnerability, and Speed of Onset.

Impact Scale for the Analytics Risk Environment

The impact scale as presented in Exhibit 5-4 is subjective and must be catered to the scale and risk appetite of an organization. The scale uses both qualitative and quantitative factors to allow for the stratification and assessment of impact severity, on a scale ranging from extreme to incidental. The purpose of this scale is to provide criteria against which to assess and stratify risks with a high expected severity of failure. For each specific risk introduced to the portfolio, we must understand the severity of impact should failure occur. Further, we can construct an aggregate view of potential impact of failure, from each of the seven risks.

Action: Use subjective Impact Scale to categorize the risk impacts from incidental to extreme.

EXHIBIT 5-4 Impact Severity Category Descriptions

Rating	Descriptor	Definition
5	Extreme	Financial loss of $1 million or more ■ Reputational loss to due regulatory compliance issues that get reported widely in the media ■ Significant financial loss due to errors or analytics process failures ■ Significant compliance issues due to errors, failures, or analytics process breakdowns, including issues with regulatory examination findings
4	Major	Financial loss of $500,000 up to $1 million ■ Report to regulator or internal stakeholders requiring major corrective action ■ Limited financial and reputational damages realized due to analytics process failures ■ Limited compliance issues due to regulators examining erroneous analytics outputs
3	Moderate	Financial loss of $100,000 up to $500,000 ■ Breach reported to regulator and immediate action required ■ Minor financial and reputational damages realized due to analytics process failures ■ Minor compliance issues due to regulators examining erroneous analytics outputs
2	Minor	Financial loss of $25,000 up to $100,000 ■ Local reputational damage ■ Reportable incident to regulator, no follow-up ■ Immaterial and narrow-scope financial damage realized due to analytics process failures ■ Immaterial and narrow-scope compliance issues due to regulators examining erroneous analytics outputs
1	Incidental	■ Financial loss up to $25,000 ■ No financial and reputational damages due to one-off analytics process failure ■ No compliance issues due to regulators examining erroneous analytics outputs

Likelihood Scale for the Analytics Risk Environment

The likelihood scale indicates the likelihood of a risk materializing based on probability of occurrence and expected frequency of recurrence, ranging from frequent to rare. The purpose of the scale, as presented in Exhibit 5-5, is to categorize the likelihood of a risk materializing, taking into account the past observed failure run-rate (if the risk existed previously) or projecting the expected frequency of future failures (if the risk is introduced due to a process change). This exercise establishes expectations regarding the likelihood of

EXHIBIT 5-5 Risk Likelihood Scale

	Annual Frequency		Probability	
Rating	Descriptor	Definition	Descriptor	Definition
5	Frequent	Up to once in a one-week period	Frequent	90% or greater chance of occurrence over life of the analytics build
4	Likely	From one occurrence per week to one occurrence per month	Likely	65% up to 90% chance of occurrence over life of the analytics build
3	Possible	One occurrence per month to once per quarter	Possible	35% up to 65% chance of occurrence over life of the analytics build
2	Unlikely	One occurrence in a 6-month period to one occurrence per year	Unlikely	10% up to 35% chance of occurrence over life of the analytics build
1	Rare	One occurrence in 24 months or less	Rare	10% chance of occurrence over life of the analytics build

issues materializing, for each of the seven analytics risks introduced earlier in the chapter. Note that in most cases, a reduced likelihood of failure is anticipated post-implementation, as manual processes are structured in tools.

Action: Use Likelihood Scale to categorize expected exception frequency from rare to frequent.

Vulnerability Scale for the Automation and Analytics Risk Environment

The vulnerability scale is used to assess and document the degree of risk vulnerability in a range spanning from very high to very low. Some risks may be more vulnerable than others to exceptions, output variability, or other process failures. To document the degree of vulnerability, we will use the scale presented in Exhibit 5-6, to highlight the risks to which the portfolio is most vulnerable. Once vulnerability

EXHIBIT 5-6 Risk Vulnerability Scale

Rating	Descriptor	Definition
5	Very High	■ Individual analytics builds not assessed based on a risk-scoring methodology ■ Lack of process-level capabilities to address analytics environment risks ■ Risk responses not implemented ■ No contingency or crisis management plans in place
4	High	■ Risk scoring for key analytics risks and builds is performed ■ Low process-level capabilities to address analytics environment risks ■ Responses only partially implemented or not fully achieving control objectives ■ Some contingency or crisis management plans in place

(continued)

EXHIBIT 5-6 Risk Vulnerability Scale *(continued)*

Rating	Descriptor	Definition
3	Medium	▪ Risk scoring for most analytics risks and builds is performed ▪ Medium process-level capabilities to address analytics environment risks ▪ Most contingency and crisis management plans in place
2	Low	▪ Risk scoring for all analytics risks and builds performed ▪ High process-level capabilities to address automation and analytics environment risks ▪ Responses implemented and regularly achieve objectives except under extreme conditions ▪ Contingency and crisis management plans in place, some rehearsals
1	Very Low	▪ High process-level capabilities to address analytics environment risks, with automated controls implemented and monitored on a continuous basis ▪ Redundant response mechanisms in place and regularly tested for analytics risks ▪ Contingency and crisis management plans in place and rehearsed regularly

has been assessed for each risk, root causes of vulnerability can be identified to further understand, document, and mitigate the underlying drivers. Identifying vulnerabilities by risk category will also allow management to prioritize risk responses and to address the most acute vulnerabilities in the environment.

Action: Use the Vulnerability Scale to highlight the risks to which builds are most vulnerable.

Action: Evaluate risks to assign a vulnerability rating ranging from very low to very high.

Action: For risks to which the portfolio is most vulnerable, perform root cause analysis.

Action: Root causes to be understood, documented, managed, and mitigated with risk responses.

EXHIBIT 5-7 Speed of Onset Scale

Rating	Descriptor	Definition
5	Very High	▪ Very rapid onset or instantaneous onset, with little or no warning
4	High	▪ Onset occurs in a matter of days
3	Medium	▪ Onset occurs over one to several week(s)
2	Low	▪ Onset occurs over one to several month(s)
1	Very Low	▪ Very slow onset, occurs over a year or more

Speed of Onset Scale for the Automation and Analytics Risk Environment

The Speed of Onset Scale presented in Exhibit 5-7 provides criteria allowing the discernment of the speed with which failures become acute and cause cascading issues throughout the organization. Risks vary in how fast they become acute when processing failures occur, and to assess sensitivity to speed of onset, we will assign a rating to each risk for speed of onset, ranging from very high to very low. By categorizing risks in this way, management can prioritize controls and governance measures to ensure that risks with a very high speed of onset have robust controls built around them, are monitored closely, and are frequently tested to ensure that if failures do occur, they do not permeate throughout the organization.

> **Action:** Use Speed of Onset Scale to highlight risks where failures quickly cause cascading issues.
> **Action:** For risks with high speed of onset, prioritize controls and governance steps to mitigate.

Developing the Portfolio View of Risk

In the next phase of our risk management exercise, we will perform risk assessment by rating each of the unique risks according to the Impact, Likelihood, Vulnerability, and Speed of Onset scales, where the Total Risk assigned to each individual risk is the product of the Impact, Likelihood, Vulnerability, and Speed of Onset ratings in the preceding columns. Once completed, the list of risks is sorted in

EXHIBIT 5-8 Portfolio View of Risk

Risk	Impact	Likelihood	Vulnerability	Speed of Onset	Total Risk
Regulatory	3	4	5	4	240
Operational	4	5	3	3	180
Financial	3	4	2	2	48
Strategic	2	2	4	3	48
IT and Cyber	2	1	3	4	24
Black Box	1	4	1	5	20
Organizational	1	1	2	5	10

descending order, such that the risks in the portfolio with the highest Total Risk score are presented at the top. The portfolio view of risk as illustrated in Exhibit 5-8 can clarify which of the seven analytics risks pose the most concern to the organization, and risk responses can be prioritized accordingly.

In Exhibit 5-9 we present a visualization which contains a representation of each of the risks in a horizontal stacked bar chart. This format allows us to see the relative weightings of the Impact rating, Likelihood rating, Vulnerability rating, and Speed of Onset

EXHIBIT 5-9 Risk Assessment and Prioritization

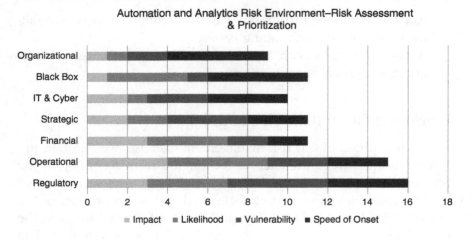

EXHIBIT 5-10 Total Risk by Category

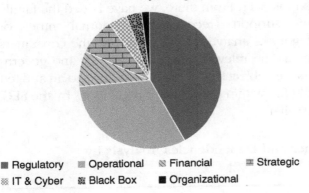

Automation and Analytics Risk Environment -
Total Risk by Category

■ Regulatory   ▧ Operational   ▧ Financial   ▦ Strategic
▨ IT & Cyber   ▨ Black Box   ■ Organizational

ratings that are stacked and graphed on the chart for each of the seven risks. In this example we can see that operational and regulatory risks emerge as the key risks to manage, according to the scales.

Exhibit 5-10 is a visual representation of the Total Risk column in Exhibit 5-8, which again is the product of the four risk dimension assessments in the preceding columns. It is obvious from this representation that the very same two risks stand out as the largest risks in the portfolio, as they did in Exhibit 5-9: Operational risk and regulatory risk.

> **Action:** Use Impact, Likelihood, Vulnerability, and Speed of Onset scores to derive Total Risk.
> **Action:** Total Risk is the product of Impact, Likelihood, Vulnerability, and Speed of Onset scores.
> **Action:** Sort risks by Total Risk in descending order to create a portfolio-level view of risk.
> **Action:** Use portfolio-level view to manage and mitigate risks with highest Total Risk scores.

We will now assess the risk of specific builds that are embedded in an organization's operations, accounting, and finance infrastructure.

Let's suppose that an organization has deployed a wide assortment of the data analytics technologies (introduced in Chapter 2) to automate their functional processes. We have dropped this hypothetical list into the first column of Exhibit 5-11. From there, we have added the family of processes the build supports (reconciliations, journal entries, or dashboards), the category of analytics tools deployed, the consumers of the output, as well as the relevant regulatory agency and governance to which outputs are subject (i.e., if the output flows to an audited annual report, it would fall within the scope of regulations by the SEC, US GAAP, and/or SOX 404).

EXHIBIT 5-11 Consumer and Dependencies Analysis by Risk Category

Automation and Analytics Process	Process Family	Analytics Tool	Output Consumer	External Regulator / Compliance Rules
Bank Reconciliations	Reconciliations	RPA	Operations	SEC; USGAAP and SOX 404
Credit Card Reconciliations	Reconciliations	RPA	Operations	SEC; USGAAP and SOX 404
Prepaid Account Reconciliations	Reconciliations	Self-Service Analytics	Operations	SEC; USGAAP and SOX 404
Accounts Payable Reconciliations	Reconciliations	Self-Service Analytics	Accounting	SEC; USGAAP and SOX 404
Accounts Receivable Reconciliations	Reconciliations	Self-Service Analytics	Accounting	SEC; USGAAP and SOX 404
Fixed Asset Reconciliations	Reconciliations	Self-Service Analytics	Accounting	SEC; USGAAP and SOX 404
Revenue & cost allocations	Journal entry	Self-Service Analytics	Finance	SEC; USGAAP and SOX 404
Tax Calculations & Accruals	Journal entry	Self-Service Analytics	Finance	SEC; USGAAP and SOX 404

(continued)

EXHIBIT 5-11 Consumer and Dependencies Analysis by Risk Category *(continued)*

Automation and Analytics Process	Process Family	Analytics Tool	Output Consumer	External Regulator / Compliance Rules
Amortizations	Journal entry	Self-Service Analytics	Finance	SEC; USGAAP and SOX 404
Matched Items Within Threshold	Journal entry	RPA	Finance	SEC; USGAAP and SOX 404
Intercompany Loans/Interest Entries	Journal entry	RPA	Finance	SEC; USGAAP and SOX 404
KPI Dashboard	Visualization	Dashboard	Finance	None noted
Risk Metric Dashboard	Visualization	Dashboard	Management	None noted
Loan Reserve Loss Calculation	AI / Machine learning	Machine Learning	Management	SEC; USGAAP and SOX 404

Action: Group builds into families and log the internal external consumers of build outputs.

Action: Log regulatory bodies and guidelines to which families are subject.

While, ultimately, we would like to present risk in the context of the seven risks discussed above, we must go further. We must recognize that each of the builds is different – not only because they automate unique processes but also because they use different inputs, a variety of analytics solutions, and unique processing steps to derive outputs. In order to create true risk transparency per the seven risks discussed above, we must assess each individual build along these dimensions. While there are no prevailing or widely subscribed governance recommendations that prescribe metrics for risk-scoring

EXHIBIT 5-12 Analytics and Automation Build Risk Scoring Methodology Metrics

Degree of complexity (Complexity)	If the automation build is more complex, encompasses a wider scope of processing steps, or is customized in a way that renders testing more difficult, a higher complexity assessment is warranted.
Exposure to economic loss	Increased level of precision is required when failure could result in an explicit or direct economic loss to the firm.
Ultimate consumer (Regulatory, Internal Consumer or High-Value Client)	If build outputs are scrutinized by regulators and auditors, then regulatory risk will be higher than in cases where builds are consumed solely by internal users.
Past failures build (Variability)	As part of the control process, observed output variances are measured and recorded on a continuous basis. Those builds that produce higher degrees of observed output variability will be considered as higher risk than others that consistently produce optimal outputs.
Build dependency (Dependency)	When analytics builds produce outputs that serve as inputs to other processes, build dependency is higher, as errors will cascade to other processes. Builds with fewer or no dependencies will be assessed as lower risk in this dimension.

individual automation builds, we have derived a risk-scoring methodology, which is extended from the model governance literature[3] as presented in Exhibit 5-12.

Action: Assess each build for complexity, risk of loss, consumer, variability, and dependencies.

Based on the above risk-scoring metrics, we have assigned a rating to each build. Exhibit 5-13 displays a summary of the builds with the ratings, as assigned. You will find that each build was

EXHIBIT 5-13 Risk Scoring Categories Example

ID	Automation process	Complexity	Ultimate consumer	Variability	Dependency	Economic Loss
1	Bank Reconciliations	Low	Medium	Medium	High	Low
2	Credit Card Reconciliations	Low	Medium	Medium	High	Low
3	Prepaid Account Reconciliations	Low	Medium	Medium	High	Low
4	Accounts Payable Reconciliations	Low	Medium	Medium	High	Low
5	Accounts Receivable Reconciliations	Low	Medium	Low	High	Low
6	Fixed Asset Reconciliations	Low	Medium	Low	Medium	Low
7	Revenue and Cost Allocations	Low	Medium	Low	Medium	Low
8	Tax Calculations and Accruals	Low	Medium	Low	Medium	Low
9	Amortizations	Low	Medium	Medium	Medium	Low
10	Matched Items Within Threshold	Low	Medium	Medium	Medium	Low
11	Intercompany Loans/Interest Entries	Low	Medium	Medium	Medium	Low
12	KPI Dashboard	Medium	Low	Low	High	Medium
13	Risk Metric Dashboard	Medium	Low	Low	High	Medium
14	Loan Reserve Loss Calculation	High	High	Low	High	High

EXHIBIT 5-14 Illustrative Risk Dashboard

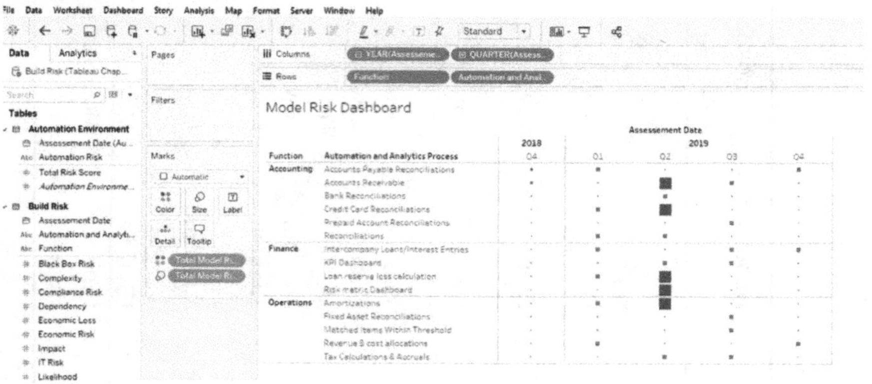

evaluated and assessed to assign a low, medium, or high rating for the five analytics governance risk metrics shown in Exhibit 5-12 (complexity, ultimate consumer, variability, dependency, and economic loss).

In the dashboard presented in Exhibit 5-14, we track the assessment results over time for the full analytics portfolio, where each individual build is evaluated, based on the above methodology. Using this dashboard allows for the effective monitoring and management of the portfolio-level risk, according to the risk metrics developed above.

Action: Use dashboard to visually depict portfolio based on individual build risk assessments.

Developing Risk Responses and Controls in the Analytics and Automation Environment

Using the portfolio view developed in an interactive dashboard provides the capability to drill down by department (operations, finance, accounting), by ultimate consumer of the output, by specific core process (journal entries, reconciliation), by balance sheet account (such as accounts receivables), by tools (such as RPA), or by any of the tags captured through the exercises in preceding sections of the chapter. Risk stratification across these dimensions provides for visibility of risk throughout the organization and can inform the prioritization of risk responses. Importantly, it gives clarity to how the portfolio is performing and it provides key insight into expected variability by precise area of operation. As the automation and analytics program is scaled up, frequent performance testing must be conducted and closely monitored. Where possible, automated controls should be engineered to test and confirm that each analytics run was performant and operated as intended.

Should a failure occur, organizations benefit from automated controls to help identify the failure point. Failure events should be logged for each build, and root causes should be investigated and redressed. Failure rates over time should be maintained and monitored to ensure they are within an acceptable range, based on the organization's risk appetite. A robotics build with limited downstream dependencies that performs data entry to a little-subscribed redundant system might warrant a reasonably high risk-tolerance. In this case, the higher risk-tolerance is appropriate, as the build is relied on only by a single internal user for a low-priority process. In contrast, in the case of an automated process to produce regulatory filings, the risk appetite would be extremely low. Irrespective of the consumer, failure rates exceeding agreed limits of risk tolerance must be urgently addressed.

The performance of the builds can be tracked and monitored using a command center. A command center is a digital monitoring dashboard that can track the performance of builds in place across the organization. In the case of the 15 builds shown in Exhibit 5-14 the command center dashboard shows the current performance and past failure rates for active builds in real time. Automated controls can be engineered to identify failure events for display on the command center dashboard. Such controls must be customized and thoughtfully incorporated into sensitive analytics builds to enable continuous process assurance and to complete the feedback loop to confirm the success or failure of each run.

The controls around each automation build must also be specific and customized such that when a failure does occur, detective controls can identify the failure point and can provide insight into the cause of the exception. Such controls can be tested for effectiveness by feeding mocked data with known defects and variability into builds to observe whether designated control builds flag the output as expected. By feeding a spectrum of test data that provides for a variety of test scenarios, rigorous testing can be performed to examine whether the builds operate as designed in a stable and repeatable fashion. By conducting frequent testing and by consistently documenting success and failure rates, automated controls themselves can be adequately tested, and any appropriate remediation action can be taken. By decision of the governance committee, control testing may be performed by the internal audit function to ensure the creation of a robust and properly documented control environment that can withstand external audit scrutiny and form the basis for the SOX 404 assessment of controls.

We will now turn our attention back to our hypothetical example of the analytics portfolio featuring 15 builds. To more fully understand the risks introduced by component builds within the portfolio, we will end the chapter by examining how each contributes to the seven major categories of analytics risk. Exhibit 5-15 presents a list of the builds in the portfolio and indicates the risks that are represented by each, respectively. We have sorted the listing such that those builds representing the highest number of the seven identified risks are positioned at the top. This exercise helps to identify the risk contribution of each build to the overall risk environment. Such analysis is critical once analytics programs begin to scale up in size and complexity to prompt the right level of attention to those builds that contribute significantly to the risk equation. Risk assessments performed with this methodology can be of help in prioritizing the formulation of risk responses. For example, were management to target one specific risk of the seven for reduction, it becomes a simple exercise to identify the automation builds that drive the risk in the specific target dimension.

Action: Use risk dashboard to scrutinize risk at department/account/consumer/process level.

Action: Conduct performance testing frequently to assess and monitor portfolio.

EXHIBIT 5-15 Example of Individual Contribution of Builds to the Seven Risks

Analytics and Automation Process	Operational	Economic	IT	Strategic	Reputational	Compliance	Black Box
Bank reconciliations	X	X	X	X	X	X	X
Credit card reconciliations	X	X	X	X	X		
Prepaid account reconciliations	X	X	X	X			
Accounts payable reconciliations	X	X	X	X			
Accounts receivable reconciliations	X	X	X				
Fixed asset reconciliations	X	X	X				
Revenue and cost allocations	X	X	X				
Tax calculations and accruals	X	X	X				
Amortizations	X	X	X				
Matched items within threshold	X	X	X				
Intercompany loans/interest entries	X	X	X				
KPI dashboard	X	X					
Risk metric dashboard	X	X					
Loan reserve loss calculation	X	X					

Action: Implement automated controls to test that builds operate successfully as intended.

Action: Automated controls must be designed to provide insight and highlight failure points.

Action: Mock data can be used to test that automated controls flag exceptions as expected.

Action: When failures/exceptions occur, they must be logged and analyzed for root cause.

Action: Failures rates must be tracked and monitored to ensure they are within accepted levels.

Action: Impact of failure, build purpose, and audience inform "Acceptable" failure rate ranges.

Action: Command Center dashboards should be used to monitor performance and failure rates.

Action: Use Individual Contribution matrix to display risks each build contributes to overall risk.

Interview with Two Big Four Audit Executives

"How has the accounting profession evolved to embrace the emergence of data analytics technologies?"

As clients are using data analytics and automation technologies to improve the efficacy of their accounting and finance departments, the need for accounting firms to actively develop adaptive approaches to validating the accuracy and completeness of clients' financial information through the use of data analytics and automation tools is paramount.

There is a recognition for the need to innovate and scale emerging data analytics capabilities. We believe while it's important to invest in enterprise-wide solutions, it is also imperative to enable innovation and automation at the individual level. Therefore, accounting firms are partnering with several software vendors to provide professionals access to both desktop and cloud-based data analytics and automation solutions. For example, Alteryx Designer is a flexible tool that allows for individual-level automation when the need surfaces for a versatile tool that can enhance productivity and quality of outputs. At the enterprise level, a number of solutions are being developed that allow for automated transmission of client data that is processed using data analytics solutions, to create standardized auditable outputs. These outputs can be used to replicate client records and review exceptions and differences with a few clicks of a button. Additionally, data analytics tools further enhance the quality of analytical review audit procedures.

Account correlation analysis, as an example, enables accounting professionals to analyze the relationships between related accounts in a class of transactions (such as the sales process, which typically involves the revenue, accounts receivable, and cash accounts). When the debit and credit activity do not have a high-level of correlation, it is oftentimes because of areas of heighted audit scrutiny, such as sales discounts, bad debts, or potential fictitious sales. This is one of many ways that data analytics can be used for targeted risk-based sampling and analysis of large volumes of data that was not possible until recently.

"How are large accounting firms adapting their people agenda to pave the way for digital transformation?"
The focus on digital literacy is being reinforced at all levels of the organizations, as professionals need to be knowledgeable, prepared, and the best equipped to respond to the changing needs of our clients. Many larger accounting firms are adapting their learning curriculum to include the application of data analytics, and this in turn impacts the recruitment, training, and development of professionals. Now more than ever, we are seeking graduate professionals with proficiencies beyond traditional accounting and finance disciplines – those demonstrating digital proficiency in data analytics and automation tools are stronger candidates and stand out amongst their peers, during the recruitment process.

"Is governance of data analytics crucial to creating an environment of strong internal controls?"
Governance plays an important role in ensuring that the solutions developed and utilized are reliable and achieve the desired productivity gains while maintaining quality of the outputs generated. The establishment of risk governance and investment

governance frameworks is therefore critical. The existing governance frameworks such as COSO are still relevant, as they are principles-based, rather than rules-based. However, they must be adapted to emerging data analytics technologies. This requires bringing together all relevant stakeholders ranging from risk management leaders, business leaders, technology leaders, and project teams under a common governance structure.

Likely, public companies will be first movers in forging strong governance, due to SOX 404, and the expectations of external regulators and investors. For the smooth functioning of the capital markets it is essential to ensure the financial information produced by organizations is reliable and that the chances of introducing error are minimized. As such, due to the breadth and scale of adoption, larger public entities will find governance to be an imperative, and smaller non-public organizations will be better able to preserve the value realized from data analytics portfolios, by developing governance frameworks to mitigate risk and cultivate process quality. It is possible that in the future, guidance may be issued to codify and crystallize required data analytics governance, but organizations should not wait.

"Is understanding risk key to audit planning?"

Now and always, risk assessments are essential for audit planning. When we consider the high volume of data points that must be considered, in order to opine on the effectiveness of controls and to conduct an effective audit, a risk-based approach is key to achieving the right level of focus on material and higher-risk portions of audit engagements. As an example, high-frequency funds and broker dealers execute a high volume of trades and execute millions of transactions daily. Given these volumes, use of data analytics to audit the relevant assertions of completeness and measurement is imperative. Data analytics solutions allow us to scale our substantive testing approaches from individual transaction-level testing of a few transactions on one end of the spectrum to broad-based correlations analysis focused on the identification of unusual patterns and trends at the other end, thus allowing for widespread testing coverage to uncover potential errors or misappropriation.

Conclusion

With the increasing capabilities of data analytics technologies, organizations are equipping users with tools to automate manual processing steps. While the introduction of tooling, such as RPA, ML, and self-service data analytics offerings, undeniably enables the capture of substantial control and efficiency benefits by improving process stability and by freeing up resources, these tools open the door to new risks. A new governance structure must be established to control and mitigate them. While many organizations have built up robust *system* governance, these tools are being built outside of systems. In many cases, end-users are structuring their spreadsheet processing in tools independently, without the involvement of systems or IT, given increased access to (democratized) data, new tools, and increased power at their fingertips to perform value-added analysis. As core systems are no longer critical path for users, a new control structure must be established to govern self-service data analytics and "small automation" efforts.

In Chapter 4, we introduced *project* governance and *investment* governance precepts, which form a necessary part of the story. In this chapter, we have added the complementary *risk* governance framework that must be deployed to manage the risks inherent in the new analytics and automation environment. We introduced seven relevant risks to analytics programs: operational risk, financial risk, strategic risk, compliance risk, IT risk, black box risk, and reputation risk, all of which must be assessed for each build and in aggregate for the portfolio as a whole. While process owners tend to be focused on operational risks introduced by build failures, any combination of the other risks can threaten the health of the enterprise. Regulators and auditors may be most concerned with compliance and black box risks that obscure their ability to test and validate that analytics solutions are operating effectively in the production of financial information. Management must concern themselves with each respective risk in order to safeguard the value created by the digital transformation program.

To fully get their arms around the risks that a scaling automation and analytics program poses, an organization must risk score the individual analytics and process automation builds. Using the risk-scoring approach provided in this chapter, an organization can not only risk score individual builds but also develop a comprehensive view of the risk embedded in the entire portfolio by aggregating the individual build risk scores. Once the aggregated portfolio view of risk is assembled, the next step is to prioritize risk responses to effectively mitigate risks in a way that optimizes the total risk to the entire analytics program. Risk governance adds incrementally to the project governance and investment governance framework introduced in Chapter 4. Taken together, we present you with the promised comprehensive framework that is customized and purpose-built for data analytics governance.

In order to fully harness the capabilities of automation and analytics capabilities, organizations must deploy a comprehensive risk governance framework alongside their analytics programs to ensure process stability and to safeguard the value of the program. Risk governance is key to scaling the analytics and automation programs in a stable, controlled, and sustainable manner. Throughout the chapter, we have underscored the key actions we have prescribed for risk governance, as was done in Chapter 4. We will end the chapter with a summary of these actions (see Exhibit 5-16), which we have framed as a Data Analytics Risk Governance Action Checklist. We hope you will find this artifact useful, as you implement risk governance at your respective organizations.

EXHIBIT 5-16 Data Analytics Risk Governance Action Checklist

Setting Risk Appetite in Environment of Changing Performance Expectations	
Risks embedded in the data analytics portfolio are compared to the ability to manage them	_____
Risk appetite is determined considering time, money, and resource tradeoffs	_____
Risks are identified and understood to reduce likelihood of failures exceeding risk appetite	_____
Data Analytics Governance Enhances Value Creation	
Risk appetite informs business strategy and tactical objectives	_____

(continued)

EXHIBIT 5-16 Data Analytics Risk Governance Action Checklist *(continued)*

Controls have been built around data analytics to protect the value they are creating	_____
Risk mitigation strategies are formulated at a tooling-specific level to harmonize responses	_____
Data Analytics Tool Selection Drives the Level of Partnership with IT	
The amount of IT involvement in analytics governance is matched to tool selection	_____
Governance committees consist of members who understand the tooling *and* processes	_____
An overarching governance framework spans functions and silos to harmonize standards	_____
Alignment of Finance Function Goals with Digital Transformation Capabilities	
Projects and the tooling they employ are aligned to functional goals	_____
Models are understood and validated by internal auditors	_____
Processes are compatible with assurance tools that reveal output failures and variability	_____
Standardized format of consistent high-quality is enforced for process inputs	_____
Post implementation, analytics processes must be easily repeatable and error-free	_____
Testing of process controls is automatable and efficient in ensuring control and stability	_____
Process memorialization documents comprehensively record build processing steps	_____
Resource optimization/time savings projections inform project prioritization	_____
Assessing Risks in the Analytics and Automation Environment	
Risk dimensions and drivers have been agreed by the governance committee	_____

(continued)

EXHIBIT 5-16 Data Analytics Risk Governance Action Checklist *(continued)*

The number of dependencies, the users, and build uses are considered in risk assessments	____
Each build or model has been evaluated across each risk dimension	____
In evaluating risk drivers, the degree of impact and likelihood of occurrence are considered	____
Final quantitative risk scores are compared to allow for risk stratification and categorization	____
Portfolio-level risk is considered to ensure it is in line with firm risk appetite	____
Portfolio-level risk is assessed at the department, business unit, and functional-level	____
Seven Relevant Risk to Data Analytics	
Operational/Economic/Strategic/Compliance/IT/Black box/ Reputational risks are assessed	____
Each risk rated across four dimensions: Impact/Likelihood/ Vulnerability/Speed of Onset	____
Impact scale for the analytics risk environment	
Subjective Impact Scale is used to categorize the risk impacts from incidental to extreme	____
Likelihood scale for the analytics risk environment	
Likelihood Scale used to categorize expected frequency of occurrence from rare to frequent	____
Vulnerability scale for the automation and analytics risk environment	
Vulnerability Scale is used to highlight the risks to which builds are most vulnerable	____
Risks are evaluated and assigned a vulnerability rating ranging from very low to very high	____
For risks to which the portfolio is most vulnerable, root cause analysis is performed	____
Root causes are understood, documented, managed, and mitigated with risk responses	____

(continued)

EXHIBIT 5-16 Data Analytics Risk Governance Action
Checklist *(continued)*

Speed of onset scale for the automation and analytics risk environment	
Speed of Onset Scale is used to flag risks where failures quickly cause cascading issues	____
Controls and governance steps are prioritized to mitigate risks with high speed of Onset	____
Developing the Portfolio View of Risk	
Total Risk is derived from individual Impact/Likelihood/ Vulnerability/Speed of Onset ratings	____
Total risk defined as the product of Impact/Likelihood/ Vulnerability/Speed of Onset scores	____
Portfolio-level view is used to manage risks with the highest assessed Total Risk scores	____
Portfolio-level view shows build families, with users and regulatory guidelines logged	____
All builds are assessed for complexity/risk of loss/consumer/ variability/dependencies	____
Dashboard is used to visually depict portfolio risk assessment based on individual build risk assessments	____
Developing Risk Responses and Controls in the Analytics and Automation Environment	
A dashboard is used to scrutinize risk at department/ account/consumer/process-level	____
Performance testing is conducted frequently to assess and monitor portfolio	____
Automated controls are implemented to test that builds operate successfully as intended	____
Automated controls are designed to provide insight and highlight failure points	____
Mock data is used to test that automated controls provide expected exception data	____
As failures/exceptions occur, they are logged and analyzed for root cause	____

(continued)

EXHIBIT 5-16 Data Analytics Risk Governance Action
Checklist *(continued)*

Failure rates are tracked and monitored to ensure they are within accepted levels	____
Impact of failure, build purpose, and audience inform the "Acceptable" failure rate range	____
Command Center dashboards are used to monitor build performance and failure rates	____
The Individual Contribution matrix highlights the risks each build contributes to overall risk	____

Notes

1. Dan Priest, Kumar Krishnamurthy, and Alex Blanter, 2018. "The New Automation Is Smart, Fast, and Small. Emerging digital tools and techniques are reinventing large-scale IT initiatives, one process at a time." Strategy + Business.

2. Internal Audit Foundation & Deloitte, 2020. "Moving Internal Audit Deeper into the Digital Age – Part II." Internal Audit Foundation.

3. Kelley Ellis, 2018. "Model Governance, Where to Begin? Internal Audit should periodically review governance structure and related sub-process responsibilities." Internal Auditor.

4. Patchin Curtis and Mark Carey, 2012. "Risk Assessment in Practice." Deloitte & Touche LLP.

CHAPTER 6

Self-Service Data Analytics Capabilities in Action with Alteryx

In each of the previous chapters, we have referenced self-service data analytics tools and touted their benefits at every turn. We have mentioned the capabilities they offer to better understand past events and their drivers, to uncover relationships between attributes, and to structure manual processing steps into automated, stable, auditable, and repeatable workflows. In contrast to core systems development, which requires annual investment planning, prioritization, and the involvement of the oversubscribed IT function, process owners can circumvent the backlog, roll up their sleeves, and accomplish much the same end results, armed only with detailed process knowledge and a willingness to embrace the tools.

Alteryx has emerged as a leading analytics platform, which is becoming a must-have for finance, accounting, and operations professionals who seek to accelerate digital transformation and to automate routine processes with analytic process automation (APA). In areas of the organization where spreadsheet processing outside of systems is the norm, Alteryx offers flexible low-code/no-code capabilities to interrogate vast datasets to answer business questions and unlock value from data. Perhaps just as important to managers in medium- to large-size organizations are the features that can be enlisted to replace manual processing steps as done today in spreadsheets in transparent, documented, and auditable workflows. It is important that this book be grounded in representative illustrations and examples, rather than offering only theory and opinions. Accordingly, we will demonstrate Alteryx in action in a step-by-step case study to give readers a sense of the capabilities on offer.

We have structured this particular case study to begin with posing five questions for answer through the interrogation of a sample data array and demonstrating the enabling Alteryx features that can be pieced together in a workflow to reveal insights relevant to the questions posed. We have chosen this format as it does two things: it allows us to highlight very basic analytic capabilities that can be enlisted to discover relationships and trends within large datasets, which is valuable and exciting, but perhaps more important to our audience of resource-starved and risk-averse finance, accounting, and operations managers, we can demonstrate opportunities for Alteryx workflows to replace the processing steps your teams are performing manually in spreadsheets day in and day out. By reducing the manual processing performed in Excel, managers can stabilize and lock down spreadsheet-driven processes into more repeatable, structured, and time-efficient workflows. By minimizing both process variance and time spent performing routinized processing steps, spreadsheet-based jobs of the past will evolve to remove the most manual and least value-added steps in the processing chain.

Readers are aware that the costs of employees are often the most significant expense on the income statement for many service organizations. Each hour of captured efficiency means that teams can process more with fewer people and focus their attentions on true value-added pursuits. Once familiar with the tooling, savvy process owners find it worthwhile to build a workflow to automate routinized process steps that may take only a half-hour to perform. Perhaps that is not a startling benefit, but when time savings realized from several "small automation" efforts sum to more than eight hours per day, it is easy to see that there is a headcount avoidance benefit that can easily be measured in dollars. The incremental efficiency benefits, when considered alongside significant control benefits that result as processes are structured in stable and repeatable workflows, can more than offset the licensing costs in a matter of weeks, providing an extremely attractive ROI. As you follow the examples, keep an eye out for where the features highlighted can be applied to automate routine processes performed in your own organizations to reduce risk and capture efficiency through automation.

In this case study, we examine a financial dataset that includes accounting balance sheet and income statement account data for the 500 companies in the S&P 500 Index for the period of 2014 to 2018. Together, we will analyze the data at several levels to reveal key insights: we will examine the dataset to see what can be uncovered about the S&P 500 Index as a whole, we will analyze component industries represented within the index and top performers within them, and finally, we will examine single names, or specific companies included in the index, that draw our attention as outliers. By building a stabilized workflow in Alteryx to structure the analysis steps, we effectively create an analysis tool that can be refreshed quarterly to provide market insights and discover trends on a continuous and autonomous basis.

What can we find out about the index, its component industries, or even individual constituent companies through analysis of this dataset? We will limit the scope of our analysis for the moment to these five questions:

1. Provide a visualization of the five-year trend for total S&P 500 (Whole Index) revenues, earnings, and book assets (total assets). Do the observed trends appear rational, in light of market performance in the US economy over the period (2014–2018)?
2. Which industries in the S&P 500 are leaders in earnings, profit margin, and return on equity for the period (2014–2018)?
3. What are the five-year sales and earnings trends for the information technology industry?
4. Who are the top performers in the IT industry by earnings and sales?
5. What are the five-year sales and earnings trends for Apple Inc.?

Before directly answering these questions, there are several preliminary steps we need to perform to familiarize ourselves with the data and to prepare it for analysis, namely ensuring that the file is clear of errors and missing values and the enrichment of the file with additional fields. After we complete these foundational steps, we will proceed to data analysis and visualization steps to answer the five questions above.

Alteryx Functionality

Understanding the Data

The first step in any data analytics project is to gain an exceptionally detailed understanding of the underlying dataset upon which the analysis is based. To fully understand our data, we need to know what is represented in the array, and we must ensure that it is accurate and complete. In the case of our S&P 500 data file, the file displays 2,525 observations, meaning that there are 2,526 rows in the data file (with the first row containing column headings). As shown in Exhibit 6-1, each row represents income statement and balance sheet data for one year for one company, where there are a total of 500 companies and five years' worth of data. There are five companies that have two classes of shares, and therefore we have an additional 25 (5*5) observations added to the 2,500 (500*5) rows. Each column in the file represents individual income statement and balance sheet accounts that can be used or combined to compute net income, total assets, total liabilities, and total equity for each company in the index. This computation was done in Excel prior to the import and can be reperformed in Alteryx to ensure the accuracy of these important data points. Now that we are familiar with the data contained in the source file, understand the number of data observations, and have surveyed the additional computed fields, we proceed to importing the source file into Alteryx.

Importing the Data

One of the major trends driving the growth of data analytics applications is the democratization of data, but what is data democratization? In the context of self-service analytics, democratization refers to the broad provision of enterprise data access to users throughout the organization. Finance, accounting, and operations users can take advantage of increased access to firm data by designing analytics and automation process flows to increase productivity, without the

EXHIBIT 6-1 The S&P 500 Five Years of Balance Sheet and Income Statement Data

No	Ticker	Company Name	Company Industry	Year	Sales (Net)	Cost of Goods Sold	R&D Expense	SG&A Expense	Depreciation & Amortization	Interest Expense
2	MMM	3M Company	Industrials	2014	31,821,000	(15,039,000)	(1,770,000)	(6,469,000)	(1,408,000)	(109,000)
3	MMM	3M Company	Industrials	2015	30,274,000	(13,908,000)	(1,751,000)	(6,167,000)	(1,435,000)	(123,000)
4	MMM	3M Company	Industrials	2016	30,109,000	(13,644,000)	(1,764,000)	(6,115,000)	(1,474,000)	(170,000)
5	MMM	3M Company	Industrials	2017	31,657,000	(14,632,000)	(1,862,000)	(6,493,000)	(1,337,000)	(272,000)
6	MMM	3M Company	Industrials	2018	32,765,000	(15,167,000)	(1,816,000)	(7,424,000)	(1,488,000)	(280,000)
7	AOS	A.O. Smith Corp	Industrials	2014	2,356,000	(1,436,900)	0	(572,100)	(59,800)	(5,700)
8	AOS	A.O. Smith Corp	Industrials	2015	2,536,500	(1,463,700)	0	(610,700)	(63,000)	(7,400)
9	AOS	A.O. Smith Corp	Industrials	2016	2,685,900	(1,506,600)	0	(653,800)	(65,100)	(7,300)
10	AOS	A.O. Smith Corp	Industrials	2017	2,996,700	(1,694,200)	0	(711,900)	(70,100)	(10,100)
11	AOS	A.O. Smith Corp	Industrials	2018	3,187,900	(1,810,500)	0	(743,100)	(71,900)	(8,400)
12	ABT	Abbott Laboratories	Health Care	2014	20,247,000	(8,237,000)	(1,285,000)	(6,327,000)	(1,509,000)	(73,000)
13	ABT	Abbott Laboratories	Health Care	2015	20,405,000	(7,903,000)	(1,371,000)	(6,742,000)	(1,427,000)	(58,000)
14	ABT	Abbott Laboratories	Health Care	2016	20,853,000	(8,284,000)	(1,442,000)	(6,558,000)	(1,351,000)	(332,000)
15	ABT	Abbott Laboratories	Health Care	2017	27,390,000	(10,446,000)	(2,183,000)	(8,804,000)	(3,019,000)	(780,000)
16	ABT	Abbott Laboratories	Health Care	2018	30,578,000	(11,559,000)	(2,288,000)	(9,531,000)	(3,278,000)	(721,000)
17	ABBV	AbbVie Inc.	Health Care	2014	19,960,000	(3,603,000)	(3,297,000)	(6,774,000)	(786,000)	(391,000)
18	ABBV	AbbVie Inc.	Health Care	2015	22,859,000	(3,403,000)	(4,101,000)	(5,663,000)	(836,000)	(686,000)
19	ABBV	AbbVie Inc.	Health Care	2016	25,638,000	(4,604,000)	(4,385,000)	(5,837,000)	(1,189,000)	(965,000)
20	ABBV	AbbVie Inc.	Health Care	2017	28,216,000	(5,187,000)	(5,007,000)	(5,878,000)	(1,501,000)	(1,004,000)
21	ABBV	AbbVie Inc.	Health Care	2018	32,753,000	(5,953,000)	(5,259,000)	(7,865,000)	(1,765,000)	(1,144,000)
22	ACN	Accenture plc	Information Technology	2014	30,002,394	(19,697,185)	0	(5,401,969)	(620,743)	12,749
23	ACN	Accenture plc	Information Technology	2015	31,047,931	(20,827,754)	0	(5,308,988)	(410,938)	19,413
24	ACN	Accenture plc	Information Technology	2016	32,882,723	(22,159,678)	0	(5,466,982)	(445,618)	14,226
25	ACN	Accenture plc	Information Technology	2017	34,850,182	(23,307,456)	0	(5,888,090)	(512,234)	22,395
26	ACN	Accenture plc	Information Technology	2018	39,573,450	(26,536,879)	0	(6,601,872)	(593,658)	36,798

involvement of IT. While data democratization has fostered innovation and the rapid adoption of emerging capabilities, one significant impediment in the past has been the difficulty of consolidating various source arrays into one adequately rich data source that can be mined with data analytics tools and techniques.

Companies traditionally have multiple caches of stored systems data that may reside on servers, on local machines, in the cloud, or often some combination of the above. To integrate diverse datasets into one place often requires data consolidation procedures. As shown in Exhibit 6-2, Alteryx is able to draw data from single source files (such as Excel), enterprise databases, private servers, public and private cloud platforms, and the wide range of locations where data is located to perform the desired analysis.

One of the biggest strengths of self-service analytics tooling is the ease with which data from varied sources can be assembled and consolidated for analysis. While the consolidation process may seem obvious or rudimentary, it can be the most challenging step, in light

EXHIBIT 6-2 Data Import Options in Alteryx Include Various Data Storage Options

	Frequently used data sources		
Recent			
Saved	Oracle	Quick connect | OCI | ODBC | OleDB	
Files	Microsoft SQL Server	Quick connect | ODBC | OleDB	
Data sources			
Gallery	**All data sources**		
	Adobe Analytics	IBM DB2	MySQL
	Quick connect	ODBC | OleDB	ODBC
	Amazon Athena	IBM Netezza	NetSuite
	ODBC	ODBC	ODBC
	Amazon Aurora	Impala	Oracle
	ODBC	ODBC	Quick connect | OCI | ODBC | OleDB
	Amazon Redshift	Marketo	Pivotal Greenplum
	ODBC	Quick connect	ODBC
	Amazon Redshift Spectrum	Microsoft Analytics Platform System	PostgreSQL
	ODBC	ODBC | OleDB	ODBC
	Amazon S3	Microsoft Azure Data Lake Store	Salesforce
	Quick connect	Quick connect	Quick connect
	Cassandra	Microsoft Azure SQL Data Warehouse	SAP Hana
	ODBC	ODBC | OleDB	ODBC
	Databricks	Microsoft Azure SQL Database	Snowflake
	ODBC	ODBC | OleDB	ODBC
	ESRI GeoDatabase	Microsoft Cognitive Services	Spark
	Quick connect	Quick connect	ODBC

of the increasing number of internal and external data sources that must be sourced and consumed to build adequately rich arrays – even before analysis can begin. Once the various data sources have been imported and transformed to a consistent format, they may require cleansing and further enrichment, before being normalized to arrive at a clean, rich, standardized data array.

In our example, we will pull in a locally stored file. As shown in Exhibit 6-3, the Alteryx data import features are available from the *Input Tool*. Once the *Input Tool* is dropped into the workflow, we can select the file option and browse locally for the Excel source file containing our S&P 500 index source data. After the Excel file has been selected, the specific sheet where the target data resides must be specified to establish the data connection. Once the connection is established, we have accomplished the task of creating a "link" to the data within Alteryx, and from this point forward our data will always be connected to our workflow. While we can add additional datasets into the workflow, we will not need to re-import a previously linked data file. The *Input Tool* preview pane shown at the bottom left in Exhibit 6-3 shows our linked data, including all columns and rows, has successfully been included in the Alteryx view and in the intended format. In addition to verifying that the data visually appears correctly, we must also ensure that individual attributes have the correct

EXHIBIT 6-3 The Input Tool and the Data Input Preview Screen

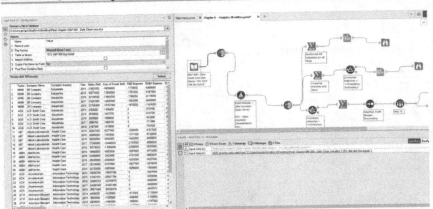

formats assigned. If, for example, a numeric data attribute was mistakenly imported in text format, future issues may arise during enrichment further down the processing stream. We can future-proof the array by checking each column to ensure that the format has been assigned appropriately and as intended.

Cleansing the Data

Data cleansing is the next step to prepare the data for analysis. In our sample file, there are several records that include incomplete data, with values missing from some of the columns. When files contain incomplete records, errors may result when computations are attempted at a later point. In our example, when we compute net income by netting sales and expenses, errors arise as certain of the company observations have missing data in expense fields. (Think of the #DIV/0! error that results when the attempt is made to divide an integer value by zero or a null value in Excel.) To resolve the issue and prevent this error in the future, we can perform data cleansing using the *Data Cleansing Tool* in Alteryx. As shown in Exhibit 6-4, the *Data Cleansing Tool* can be used to replace null values with zeros, allowing the net income computation to successfully complete.

EXHIBIT 6-4 Data Cleansing Tool and the Data Cleansing Tool Option Screen

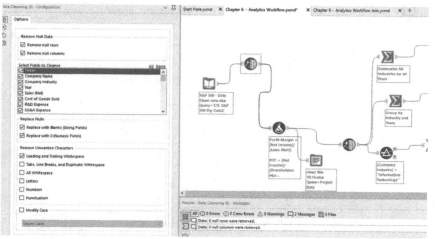

The Select Fields to Clean drop-down menu allows us to specify which column(s) we wish to cleanse. We can select all, none, or individual columns from our file. For the S&P 500 Excel input file, we will select *all* columns. The additional features of the *Data Cleansing Tool* provide for the removal of null values from rows and columns, as well as the removal of unwanted characters and white spaces. The data cleansing features assist users in improving integrity of inputs and will ultimately enable future sorting, blending, sampling, and analysis steps to complete as expected.

Blending and Joining

As we have described, data must frequently be assembled and consolidated from multiple sources. Another defining feature of Alteryx is that it provides the ability not only to capture and import source data, but to readily blend data from separate source arrays with the *Join Tool*. Consider an example where accounting data is sourced from one file, while each company's industry is stored in another file, and company names are stored in a third file. To bring this data

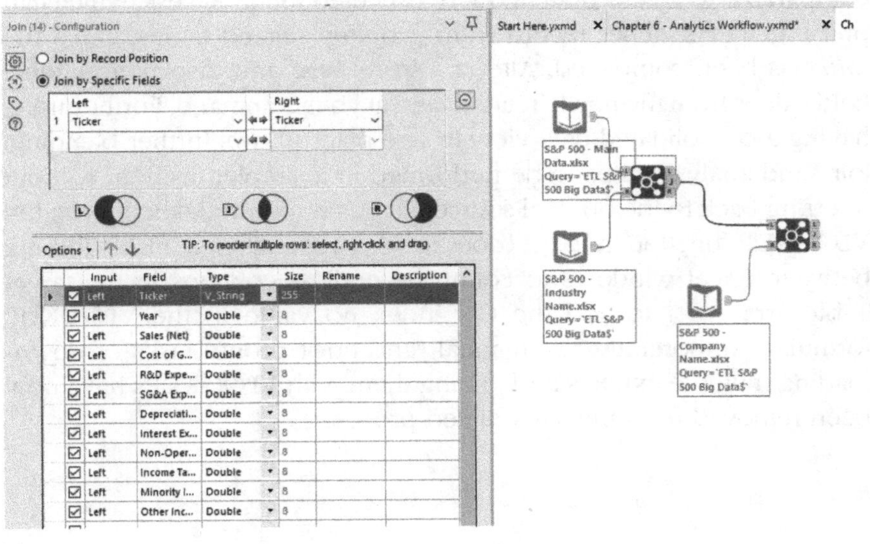

EXHIBIT 6-5 Data Joining Tool is Used to Blend Data from Different Sources

together from all three sources, we must use relational database principals to join the company's name, industry, and accounting data into one single row or record based on primary or secondary keys before we progress to our next analysis steps, where we will compute and analyze key performance metrics and group component companies by industry.

With the *Join Tool*, we can look up the company industry from the file containing Company Industry, before displaying it in an added column in our view. We specify that we would like to *Join* the two datasets (based on the ticker identifier) and an enriched view is produced that includes the company industry, added to the company accounting data. We perform a further *Join* to add "Company Name" to the view in the same fashion, using the ticker as the unique identifiers (keys), allowing for the relation of records across the disparate source files.

Does this operation seem familiar to you? This is effectively the same operation that so many accounting and finance professionals perform with VLOOKUPs in Excel, to bring two different datasets together for analysis, comparisons, or further processing. The benefit of a *Join* operation over a VLOOKUP is that after the VLOOKUP in Excel, the two datasets continue to be separate and distinct but ever-growing and dynamic as they are blended and joined. Alteryx offers a quantum leap forward to allow the instant on-demand display of a fully integrated enriched view, built from the legacy datasets – more comparable to a Select-detail query executed in MS Access, which can pull together a richer record from properly related tables. Once the *Join* has been completed, Alteryx can retrieve and display additional field values from the newly related files, at your command. Furthermore, having a consolidated data view in one place allows further blending, join, and analysis steps to be performed in a simpler fashion, without referring back to the original source files, as is required when using the VLOOKUP function in Excel (does anyone remember Control+Tab-ing between Excel windows to count the endless columns in the target Table_array, just to add the Col_index_no value to the VLOOKUP formula?). Importantly, the manual (and error prone) tasks of downloading multiple extracts and joining them with VLOOKUPs have now been removed from the streamlined process.

Enriching Data

Now that we have completed the steps to import, cleanse, and blend the data, it is finally ready for enrichment. Enriching data means that from the data already captured in our view, we can create more attributes from values in the fields already displayed. Recall the first of our five case study questions at the outset of the chapter, where we set out to prepare a visualization of the aggregate index financial ratios versus the market as a whole from 2014–2018. To begin, we will build on the accounting data we have assembled by inserting a computation of four key financial ratios for the 2,525 company/year observations using the *Formula Tool*. This functionality is much like inserting a new column in Excel and populating it with a formula referencing other columns for calculation and display in the newly added column.

In this case, we specify the new column name for each of the financial ratios that we intend to compute and select the "double" output format. Selecting the "double" format ensures that the calculated output is in the number format, such that we can perform mathematical computations further down the processing stream with this field. As later, we will be aggregating individual company financial ratios in these calculated fields using the "average" function, it is essential that the "double" format is assigned to each field. To complete our financial ratio computation, we add the required formulas in four new columns to compute the ratios as follows:

Profit Margin (New Column) = Net Income / Sales (Net)

Return on Equity (ROE) = Net Income / Shareholders Equity

Asset Turnover = Sales / Total Assets

Leverage Ratio = Total Assets / Total Liabilities

The preview pane provides us with the resulting financial ratio computation for the first row of the dataset. Upon entering the

EXHIBIT 6-6 Formula Tool Used to Enrich the Data File by Computing and Adding Fields that Include Financial Ratios for All 2,525 Observations

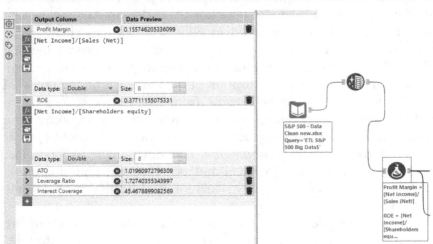

formula for profit margin, we can see that the resulting calculated profit margin for the first row in the dataset is 0.155 (15.5%). Continuing with the remaining columns, we will specify the computation of ROE, Asset Turnover, and Leverage Ratio in the same manner. Once completed, we have accomplished our goal of enriching our view with valuable additional datapoints that can help us in analyzing whole market, industry, and individual company trends using the financial ratios we have calculated. While we have successfully derived the additional company/year data needed to perform the analysis, with the help of the Alteryx data transformation tools, we must further group and order the data to answer the five questions included within the scope of the case study.

Data Transformation

After enriching the data view, we can proceed to the first stage of data analysis. The primary goal in this case study is to examine time-series financial ratio data to uncover trends, whether across the entire S&P 500, specific component industries represented in the index or for specific companies within them. As shown in Exhibit 6-7, the

EXHIBIT 6-7 The Summarize Tool is a Data Transformation Tool

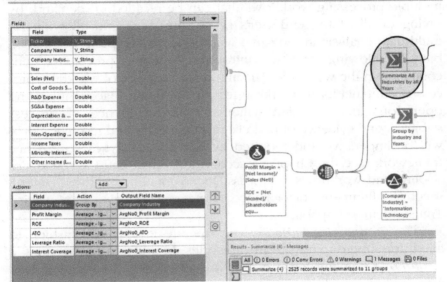

Summarize Function allows us to group the dataset by Company Industry and compute the average of the calculated ratios for all company/year observations in each industry. Performing this step allows us to determine the average profit margin, return on equity, asset turnover, and leverage ratio for each of the industries in the S&P 500.

The *Summarize Function* is one of the key advancements in Alteryx enabling users to select, manipulate, or abstract data without writing code. In the past, such data selections would require lines and lines of SQL, but the *Summarize Function* allows the end-user to perform customized data selections and aggregations "drag and drop" with a few clicks of the mouse. While this functionality compares to the Excel Pivot table functionality, the Alteryx *Summarize Function* adds significantly by memorializing each distinct processing step in an analytics workflow. The creation and retention of workflows allows for the data selection process to be more structured, easily accessed, and invoked repeatedly. Furthermore, users may easily recall previously structured workflows to use as a starting template to alter or customize to accommodate slight process amendments and variations. Alteryx allows for the ready capture of multiple processing workflows that can be recalled on demand. By saving of all of the end-user's processing steps and allowing for multi-path analysis in the same workflow, Alteryx promotes auditability by allowing for easy control and review of processing steps contained in the workflow. The automated capture of workflow process documentation is a critical feature for finance, accounting, and operations analytics deployments, where evidence of process stability – and evidence of periodic process review and recertification – will be imperative and required by our own analytics governance framework (see the Chapter 4 section Reference End-User Analytics Tooling and Workflows in Process Documentation and the Chapter 5 section Alignment of Finance Functional Goals with Digital Transformation Capabilities).

The *Summarize Function* can operate in a nested fashion to allow for subgrouping within categories. In addition to executing a *Group by* Company Industry, we will add a nested *Group by* Year. This nested *Group by* data transformation results in a dataset that includes the financial ratio averages for all industries, as well as calculated yearly averages of the ratios for each industry. Subgrouping by year is necessary for us to later perform time series analysis of financial ratios further down the processing chain. It is worthwhile to note that a number of mathematical, statistical, and financial calculations, in addition to Average, can be performed with the Summarize Function, including Sum, Standard Deviation, Median, Mode, NPV, and IRR.

The *Filter*, *Sample*, and *Sort* Functions allow for further manipulation and shaping of the data. Now that the financial ratio calculations have been completed, to examine the trends for a specific industry over time we need to use the *Filter Function* to filter for a specific industry. This operation provides us with the dataset limited to financial ratios for one industry over five years, as is required for the next step of visualization and to analyze the trend. While the *Filter Function* allows us to reduce a dataset to exactly what we need by limiting the values displayed in one or several fields, the *Sample Function* allows us to draw out a portion of the dataset based on certain characteristics. Using the *Sample Function*, we can limit the dataset to the first 10 rows to highlight the top results. In the example shown in Exhibit 6-8 we can specifically target the top 10 most profitable companies in the Information Technology industry for display. After limiting our dataset to include only the Information Technology Industry using the *Filter Function* (Exhibit 6-8), we will sort the Profit Margin column in descending order using the *Sort Function* (Exhibit 6-9), resulting in a view which displays information technology companies arranged in descending order, based on the values of the profit margin ratio. We now select a sample of the first 10 using the *Sample Function* (Exhibit 6-10), which narrows the view even further to include *only* the 10 companies in the Information Technology industry with the highest profit margin, sorted in descending order.

EXHIBIT 6-8 The Filter Tool is a Data Transformation Tool Used to Enhance Dataset Selection to Transform the Data for Analysis

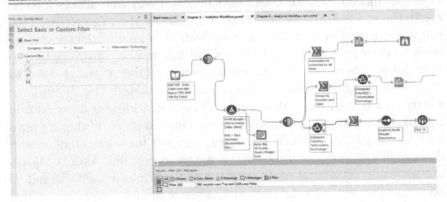

EXHIBIT 6-9 The Sort Tool is a Data Transformation Tool Used to Enhance Dataset Selection to Transform the Data for Analysis

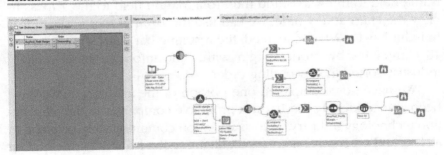

EXHIBIT 6-10 The Sample Tool is a Data Transformation Tool Used to Enhance Dataset Selection to Transform the Data for Analysis

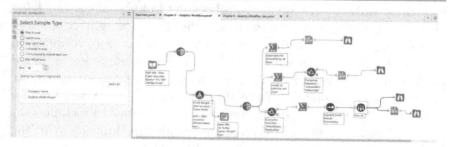

Data Visualization

The final step in our processing chain is to present the data that we have assembled, cleansed, and enriched in a way that allows it to be easily interpreted. For this purpose, we will use the *Interactive Chart* reporting function to create a visualization from the data view we wish to display. Exhibit 6-11 shows the *Interactive Chart* configuration pane, where we can assign attributes to the X and Y axes to allow values to be plotted and visually depicted. The *Interactive Chart Tool* features the ability to add layers. Adding a layer simply means adding an additional plot to the chart to show multiple views and relationships. For our purposes, we will limit the chart to the display of a single plot, though it is worth noting that Alteryx allows the inclusion of several plots into one chart. While we will default to bar charts to visualize ratio trends, Alteryx flexibly supports scatter plots, line graphs, pie charts, and box and whisker plots, which may better suit other data types. To set up the chart, we will begin by adding a blank layer to our chart shell, and we will assign the Company Name field to the X axis and the Profit Margin field to the Y axis. To view the chart at any time, we can use the *Browse Tool* as illustrated in Exhibit 6-12. When executed, the resulting bar chart shows the top 10 companies by profit margin within the information technology industry, sorted in descending order.

We have now completed one portion of the analysis, as we have been able to identify the 10 most profitable companies in the information technology industry. The visualization communicates the result in a clear and persuasive manner, highlighting the leaders in descending

EXHIBIT 6-11 The Interactive Chart is Part of the Reporting Set of Functions and is Used to Visualize Data

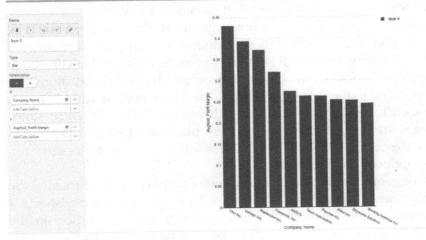

order of profitability. The question of which companies have the highest profit margin in the information technology industry and the data interrogations aimed at answering it may lead to tangential questions and further analysis, and further value can be iteratively unlocked from the data. Operators or analysts could readily amend the workflow to display the profitability trend for these companies over the

EXHIBIT 6-12 The Browse Tool Allows for Viewing the Chart Created Through the Interactive Chart Tool

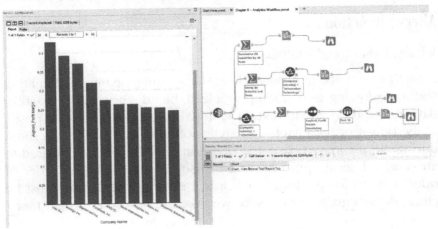

past five years. They could examine which company has the steepest upward sloping profitability trend within represented industries in the S&P 500 or in the index overall. It would be interesting to relate the financial ratios to share price observations over the same period. With the import and blend functions demonstrated in prior sections, this would be only a matter of sourcing the market data and relating company names before enriching the records with price observations corresponding to the ratio observation dates. Your authors would be very pleased to be armed with a data-driven prediction of which single names are most likely to outperform the index in future years. It is easy to see that Alteryx offers limitless self-service capabilities to interrogate and analyze rich datasets.

Beyond the inherent value such analysis could provide, the advantage of performing the analysis in Alteryx over spreadsheets is that process design must be performed only once. From then on, the analysis steps have been structured and retained in the workflow, such that they are both highly reliable and easily repeatable for ready use in the future. As new data becomes available, the workflow as previously designed and structured can be invoked to roll forward the analysis nearly instantly, without requiring users to manually copy down formulas, add VLOOKUPs, or change selection ranges for pivot tables and charts, as would be required to accomplish the same outcomes in spreadsheets. Importantly, by negating the need to manually manipulate data in Excel, we avoid introducing risk to the process and reduce the opportunity for error.

Alteryx in Action

Whole Market Trend Analysis

Now that we have introduced key Alteryx functionality, highlighting features allowing users to import, clean, blend, enrich, and visualize data, it is appropriate to revisit the initial case study questions posed at the outset of the chapter. Analytics often begins with a question; during the planning phase, the question must be well considered to arrive at a logical approach and course of action and the order of operations to follow. In other words, before we begin, we must be clear on the end goal to ensure we take the best route to get there.

Newly armed with the capability to build customized analytics work-flows, let us return to the first question:

Question 1: Provide a visualization of the five-year trend for total S&P 500 (Whole Index) revenues, earnings, and book assets (total assets). Do the observed trends appear rational, in light of market performance in the US economy over the period (2014–2018)?

To answer this question using Alteryx, we begin building the workflow with the import and preparation phase. Once completed, we move on to the enrichment steps to add more fields to our data view. We see from the language in the question that we must refer to the blending and joining steps illustrated above to source the required attributes, including total assets, total equity, net income, and sales. Once we have loaded, cleaned, and enriched the data, how would we go about getting the information required to answer the above question? To acquire data that can be analyze for whole market analysis, we need to group our data by year using the *Summarize Tool*, as shown in Exhibit 6-13.

Using the *Group by* functionality, we group the file by year, so that we can capture a time-series trend to analyze the data over the

EXHIBIT 6-13 Summarize Tool Utilized to Group Data for Whole Market Trend Analysis

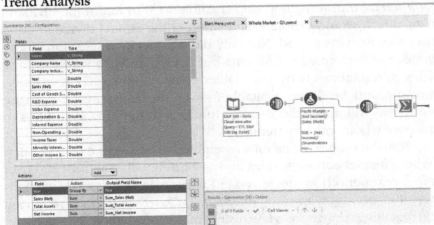

five-year period, but further attributes are required. Of course, we must source the fields specifically referenced in the question (and whatever else you may find interesting). For now, we will add three fields: Net Income (earnings), Sales (Net), and Total Assets. We also must pick a mathematical operator in order to complete our grouping. Since we would like to see total sales, earnings, and assets by year, we will select the *Sum by* operator to aggregate earnings, sales, and assets by year.

Data transformation using the *Summarize Tool* gives us the functionality to transform the original dataset into a summarized, transformed, or enriched view that can be used to answer business questions. By grouping the original file to aggregate earnings, sales, and assets by year, we have transformed the original data to an enriched view that will better enable us to answer the question and to proceed with further analysis. In Exhibit 6-14 we see the dataset resulting from the execution of the transformation step, as set up in Exhibit 6-13. We can view the grouped results of our *Summarize Tool* transformation step by linking the *Browse Tool,* as shown in Exhibit 6-14. A quick review confirms that the resulting data file provides everything needed; it shows the sum total for the three fields specified in the data transformation step (Sales (Net), Net Income, and Total Assets). Of course, any other fields of interest that could be useful for further analysis could quite easily be pulled into the view.

For example, if we wanted to examine the dividend trend for the entire market, we could simply add an additional column in the *Summarize* transformation step (Exhibit 6-13) to return the dividend data, which would enable examination of the annual dividend trend over the five-year period. Not only did we specify a selection of columns, we performed a mathematical computation to sum earnings, sales, and total assets by year. Other computations such as *average, median,* and *mode* are available as well. In later parts of the case study, we will apply the *average* function to key financial ratios to uncover whole industry trends.

With the required data fully assembled to answer the first question (whole market earnings, sales and asset trends for the S&P 500 over a five-year period) as previewed in Exhibit 6-14, we proceed to charting the trends with the *Interactive Chart Tool* and retrieving the resulting charts for view using the *Browse Tool,* as shown in Exhibit 6-15 for earnings, Exhibit 6-16 for sales, and Exhibit 6-17 for

EXHIBIT 6-14 Data Transformation Using the Summarize Tool to Transform the Original Data File into a Data Set Suitable for Whole Market Analysis

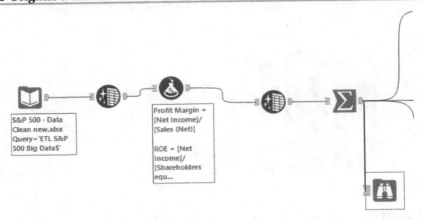

Record	Year	Sum_Sales (Net)	Sum_Total Assets	Sum_Net Income
1	2014	10352834224.32	31795586965.9	914480026.04
2	2015	10072147185.7	32286762898.76	881896185.99
3	2016	10321835279.55	33813540332.28	934118952.95
4	2017	11094824459.46	35284779780.75	1025318270.96
5	2018	12081742935.09	36038153663.97	1197102477.76

EXHIBIT 6-15 S&P 500 Total Earnings Five-Year Trend

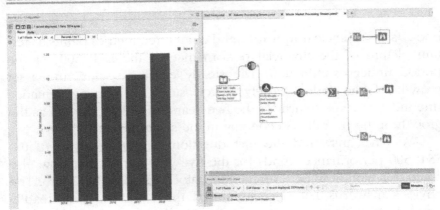

EXHIBIT 6-16 S&P 500 Total Sales Five-Year Trend

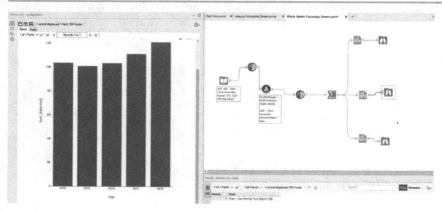

EXHIBIT 6-17 S&P 500 Total Assets Five-Year Trend

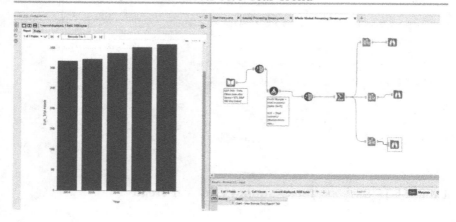

book assets. The clear upward trend in all three metrics paints a sterling picture of the financial performance of the S&P 500 for the period under examination. The steady earnings, sales, and asset growth of the index closely match stock market performance (the index average return for the five years was 8.9%), as well as the growth of the overall US economy in the same period.

We have answered the first question through analysis of the S&P 500 performance trends for the five-year period, but how else could this workflow be leveraged to unlock value in the future? The obvious answer is that, once structured, this workflow could readily be updated with more current data without the need to repeat the design and setup steps. Further, the workflow could be used as a starting point template and leveraged to analyze other datasets. For instance, if source data was acquired for other European or Asian indices, with only minor amendments, we could analyze trends and performance in global markets using the same processing steps and visualizations. Such analysis may be useful as an investor considers global market alternatives. The point is that, unlike spreadsheet processing, the structured analysis workflow designed in Alteryx persists, is available for reuse and repurposing, and is consistently stable and performant, when designed correctly. *Rinse and Repeat.*

Our work to uncover S&P 500 financial performance trends gives rise to other interesting questions. What region, industry, or specific company should we consider for investment? Building on the analysis of the S&P 500, it would be interesting to discover the industries contributing most to the growth in earnings during the period. In the following section, we will narrow our focus from the whole market to the industries represented in the index. We will compare performance across industries and identify industry-specific trends to highlight those performing best during the period examined.

Industries: Comparative Performance

Thus far, we have analyzed the S&P 500 as a whole market, and our analysis demonstrated that for the period spanning 2014 to 2018, there was consistent growth in earnings, sales, and total assets – all pointing to a strong economy and solid market performance. In the next stage of our analysis, we will address the second question posed on the relative financial performance of industries within the S&P 500.

> **Question 2:** Which industries in the S&P 500 are leaders in earnings, profit margin, and return on equity for the period (2014–2018)?

We must now build out the workflow to accommodate this slightly different question. When analyzing the whole market, we grouped the data by year, but we will turn our attention to component industry data. As was done previously, we must first import and cleanse our dataset, and then we will need to add the enrichment processing step, as the question involves financial ratios not contained in the raw source file. As illustrated in Exhibit 6-6, we can repeat the needed enrichment step to calculate the financial ratios, before transforming the data using the *Summarize Tool*.

Using the *Summarize Tool*, as shown in Exhibit 6-18, we first *Group by* Company Industry and then add the fields required for analysis: Profit Margin, Return on Equity (ROE), and Net Income. To get at the heart of the question, we must devise an approach to analyzing each field appropriately. To identify earnings-leading industries, our approach will be to simply sum earnings (Net Income) by industry over the full five-year period and compare the results. In contrast, an average would be a more logical operator to allow us to assess profit margin and ROE, as they are ratios rather than values. As we execute the transformation step using the *Summarize Tool*, we can confirm that the transformation steps executed properly, by linking the *Browse Tool* to the *Summarize Tool*, as shown in Exhibit 6-19. We see that the transformation step in fact resulted in aggregated and meaningful data by industry.

At this stage, we have the capability to add more attributes that may provide more color on performance by industry. Analysts love rich datasets, as available data enables and often drives the level of analysis performed. The converse is also true; analysts are very often limited by the data they do not have. We could examine revenues, total assets, total dividends, or financial ratios such as asset turnover, the leverage ratio, or the interest coverage ratio. To do so, we could

EXHIBIT 6-18 Grouping the Data by Company Industry to Include Industry Profit Margin, Return on Equity, and Earnings

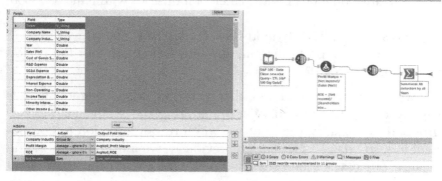

EXHIBIT 6-19 Resulting Data File from the Summarize Tool and Grouping by Company Industry

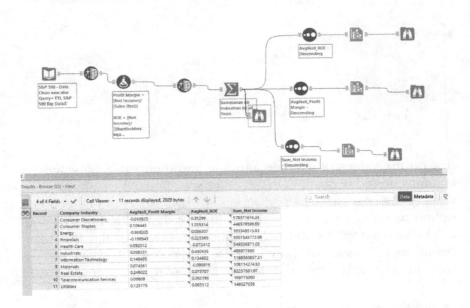

Record	Company Industry	AvgNo0_Profit Margin	AvgNo0_ROE	Sum_Net Income
1	Consumer Discretionary	-0.010925	0.35299	578371614.24
2	Consumer Staples	0.106443	1.035314	446579698.69
3	Energy	-0.868205	0.036307	161549515.83
4	Financials	-0.198943	0.223369	1051545772.08
5	Health Care	0.092012	-0.072412	549356871.05
6	Industrials	0.098331	0.440435	488977890
7	Information Technology	0.140495	0.134602	1168360657.31
8	Materials	0.074561	-0.090815	108114274.53
9	Real Estate	0.248022	0.073707	82257681.97
10	Telecommunication Services	0.08809	0.262196	169775000
11	Utilities	0.125176	0.065512	148027038

pull them in and apply either a sum to aggregate them over the period (for values such as revenues or dividends) or an average (leverage ratio, interest coverage ratio, and asset turnover ratio) to rank each industry's performance in these dimensions. For the moment, we will include only earnings, profit margin, and return on equity to answer the question at hand.

Now that the view has been adequately enriched, we can proceed to evaluating performance, based on the given criteria. First, we will compare the industries based on total earnings over the five-year period. While we have the data needed, we will sort the aggregated earnings data in descending order, such that higher-performing industries are at the top of the list (see Exhibit 6-20). Later, when we plot the sorted industry datapoints in a bar chart, the visualization will be better-ordered and far easier to interpret.

Exhibit 6-20 shows the functionality of the *Sort Tool*. The *Sort Tool*, much like the sort function in Excel, provides the ability to arrange the selected records in ascending or descending order, based

EXHIBIT 6-20 The Sort Processing Step Transforming the Data in the Last Transformation Step before Visualization

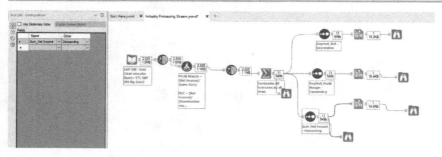

first on the values of a single attribute and then value by values in columns nested beneath it, in the order specified. As we are eager to identify the best earnings performers, we will select the descending option to show industries with the highest aggregated net income values at the top. Exhibit 6-21 shows a preview of the final data before visualization. Not only have we transformed the data, but we have arranged it in a logical order. We are now ready to move forward

EXHIBIT 6-21 The Resulting Transformed Data After the Sort Processing Step Resulting in the Earnings Data Being Sorted in Descending Order by Industry

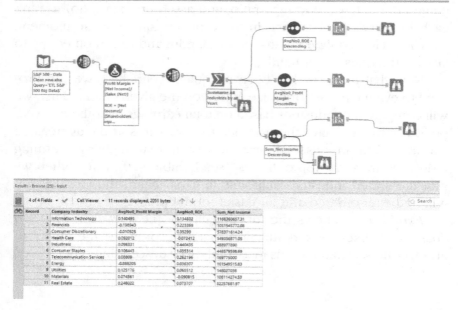

Record	Company Industry	AvgNo0_Profit Margin	AvgNo0_ROE	Sum_Net Income
1	Information Technology	0.140495	0.134602	1168360657.31
2	Financials	-0.198943	0.223369	1051545772.88
3	Consumer Discretionary	-0.010925	0.35299	578371614.24
4	Health Care	0.092012	-0.072412	549356871.05
5	Industrials	0.098331	0.440435	488977890
6	Consumer Staples	0.106443	1.085314	448579598.69
7	Telecommunication Services	0.08809	0.262196	169775000
8	Energy	-0.888205	0.036307	161549515.83
9	Utilities	0.125176	0.065512	148027098
10	Materials	0.074561	-0.090815	108114427.59
11	Real Estate	0.248022	0.073707	82257681.97

to the last step of visualizing our data. Note that to similarly identify top performers for average profit margin and average return on equity, we need only sort descending on those columns, respectively, as we have done for earnings.

To finalize our Net Income analysis, we move forward to the last processing step. Using the reporting tool *Interactive Chart* and the *Browse Tool*, we can plot and visually display the earnings data in a bar chart, as illustrated in Exhibit 6-22. The resulting graph shows that two specific industries, Information Technology and Financials, are leading the S&P 500 in total earnings by industry, while Consumer Discretionary, Healthcare, Industrials, and Consumer Staples are firmly in the middle of the pack. The remaining industries lag the index in earnings.

To perform the industry comparison based on average profit margin and average return on equity, we simply create two more processing streams containing the same steps, with a slight varia-tion at the *sort* processing step, where we will change the target field to sort descending by profit margin or by ROE, respectively. The resulting processing streams and visualizations are shown in Exhibit 6-23 for the industry comparison by profit margin and in Exhibit 6-24 for the industry comparison by return on equity. Looking first at Exhibit 6-23, it is clear that the leading industries in terms of margins include Real Estate, Information Technology, and Utilities, while Energy stands out as an outlier in last place with a negative average profit margin. Moving on to ROE (Exhibit 6-24),

EXHIBIT 6-22 Industry Comparison Based on Companies' Total Earnings for the Period of 2014–2018

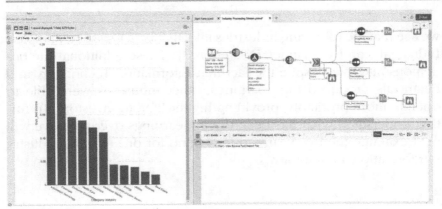

EXHIBIT 6-23 Comparative Industry Analysis by Profit Margin of Industries in the S&P 500

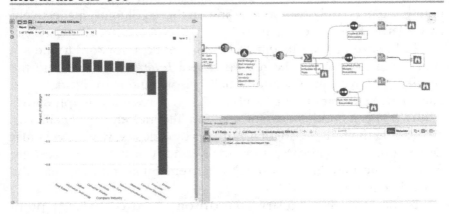

EXHIBIT 6-24 Comparative Industry Analysis by Return on Equity of Industries in the S&P 500

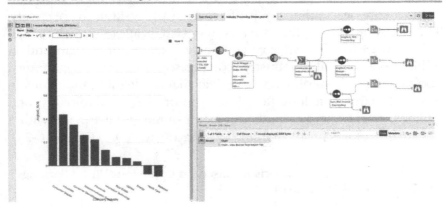

we see that the following industries take the lead: Consumer Staples, Industrials, and Consumer Discretionary. These additional metrics demonstrate that despite the fact that Information Technology and Financials produced high earnings, other industries were able to operate more profitably, providing higher ROE to investors. To further understand what has been driving earnings over time, we will next examine the five-year earnings trend for one specific industry – Information Technology.

Information Technology: Trend Analysis Over Five Years

We began by analyzing the entire S&P 500 index over five years and noted positive increases in earnings, sales, and assets. We further examined the data by industry, revealing that Financials and Information Technology made an exceptionally large contribution to total S&P earnings during the period examined. We will now drill in further to the information technology industry, as it has emerged a leading industry, based on the comparison criteria in the second question posed. To examine whether information technology represents a lucrative investment opportunity, we will take a closer look at the five-year trend of earnings and sales in the industry.

Question 3: What are the five-year sales and earnings trends for the information technology industry?

To answer this question, we start with the *Summarize Tool* to perform the transformation step in our workflow. As shown in Exhibit 6-25, we group the data by Company Industry and by Year. Of course, we can see from the question that we must add the Net Income and Sales (Net) fields to our view.

EXHIBIT 6-25 Summarize Tool Functionality in Transforming Data for Analysis for Information Technology Trend in Five-Year Period

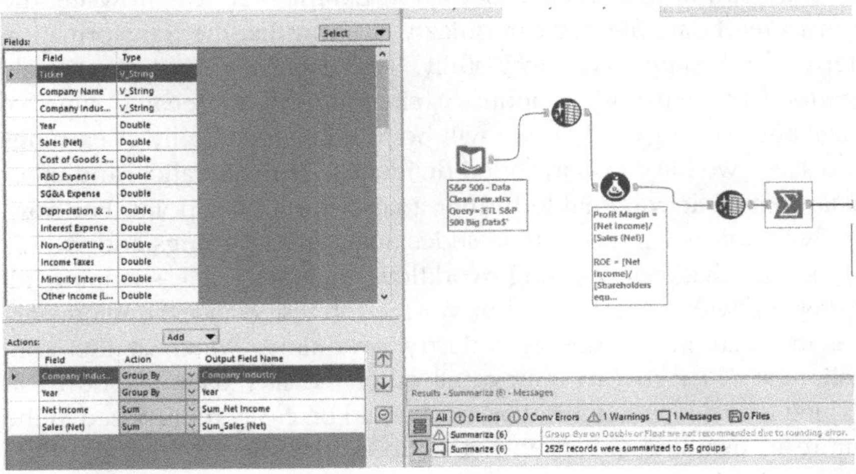

EXHIBIT 6-26 Browsing the Transformed Data to Examine the Resulting Transformed Dataset

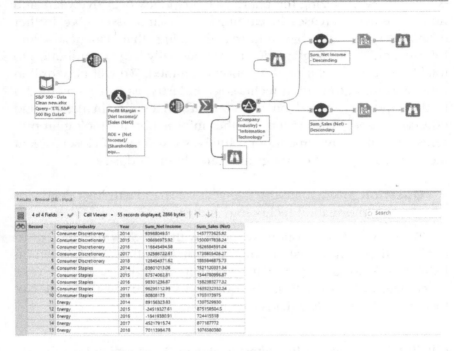

The resulting output can be previewed by linking the *Browse Tool* after the *Summarize Tool*, as shown in Exhibit 6-26. By browsing the transformed data file, we can quickly confirm that the transformation steps were completed successfully. The data is now appropriately grouped by year and by industry, showing the aggregated sums of sales and earnings. While we will be looking specifically at earnings and sales, we have also included dividends, financial ratios, and other datapoints that will enable further analysis at a later point. For now, we will limit our industry time-series analysis to earnings and sales.

Recall that our existing workflow includes data spanning all industries within the index, but we are interested in examining only the information technology industry over time. We must therefore enlist the *Filter Tool* to remove all other industry data, as shown in Exhibit 6-27. Note that this workflow could be easily repurposed in the future to examine any of the other industries by changing the filter parameters in this step. The workflow allows for dynamic analysis of any industry, once the *Transform Tool* steps have been completed.

EXHIBIT 6-27 Filter Tool Function is Used to Further Transform the Data

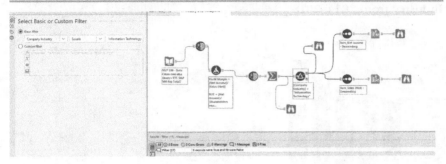

EXHIBIT 6-28 Five-Year Earnings Trend for the Information Technology in Industry from 2014–2018

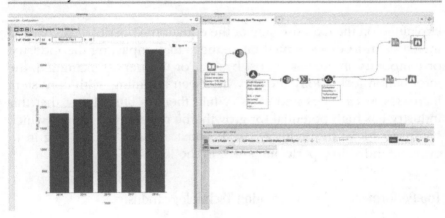

Now that we have removed the extraneous industries, our view features precisely (and only) what is required to analyze the earnings and sales trends for the information technology industry. The next step is to run the *Interactive Chart Tool* and the *Browse Tool* to view the chart. Exhibit 6-28 shows the earnings trend, while Exhibit 6-29 displays the five-year sales trend for the industry. The earning trend reveals a consistent increase over the five years with the exception of 2017, which appears as an outlier compared to the positive growth observed in the remaining four years. The sales trend shows a consistent annual increase for the five-year period, indicating that the 2017 earnings reduction did not result from a dip in industry sales for the same year. Rather, the lackluster earnings would more likely be

EXHIBIT 6-29 Five-Year Sales Trend for the Information Technology in Industry from 2014–2018

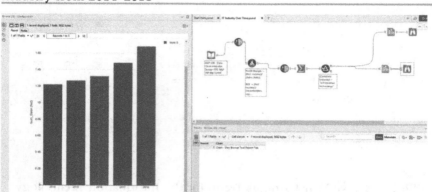

explained on the expense side of the equation – possibly tax charges, increases in reserves, structural changes that impacting the industry, or temporary increases in cost bases. For the period examined, the information technology industry has been booming, with consistent increases in earnings and sales. While there is little doubt that this industry has high potential for growth, the question remains – which companies lead the industry? In the next section, we will dig in to evaluate individual performers within the industry.

Top Performers in the Information Technology Industry

In the previous section, we examined the performance of the information technology industry and revealed that it has achieved very strong sales and earnings growth in the five years observed. In this section, we deepen our analysis by looking within the industry to determine which companies are top performers based on sales and earnings.

Question 4: Identify the top performers in the information technology industry in terms of earnings and sales?

By now, you likely are aware of the next step, which is to enlist the *Summarize Tool* to group the data by Company Name and Company Industry to allow us to directly answer the question posed.

EXHIBIT 6-30 Summarize Tool Used to Transform Data to Prepare the Data for Analysis of Top Performers in the IT Industry

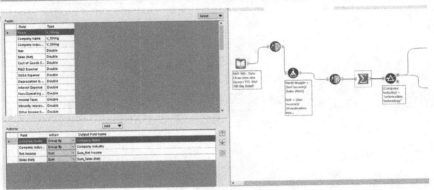

As shown in Exhibit 6-30, the sum operator must be applied to both earnings (Net Income) and sales (Sales (Net)), as was done previously. To view whether the transformation step executed properly, we run the workflow and add the *Browse Tool* after the *Summarize Tool*, as shown in Exhibit 6-31. A quick review of the output confirms that we have correctly captured individual company sales and earnings performance. However, we can see that all industries are represented.

To limit the view to display only information technology companies, we must filter by Company Industry and specify presentation of information technology companies, as shown in Exhibit 6-32. This filter could easily be changed to allow for the identification of sales and earnings leaders in other industries, should they be of interest at a later point. After applying the filter, we use the *Sort* and *Sample* tools to sort the data file in descending order and to select the top eight rows. Exhibit 6-33 shows the top eight *earners* in the industry, while Exhibit 6-34 shows the eight top-performing companies in terms of *sales.* The resulting leaderboard features familiar names such as Apple, Google, Microsoft, Intel, IBM, and Facebook. Apple stands out not only as the leader in five-year sales, but it is a clear powerhouse for five-year earnings. Apple shines as a clear industry leader in performance over the period, but it would be useful to see how sales and earnings performance is trending – within the period. Are its best days ahead, or has performance leveled off? In the next section, we will analyze Apple's performance trends over the five-year period.

EXHIBIT 6-31 Browse Tool Functionality Displays the Transformed Data
File to Ensure Transformation Step Executed Properly

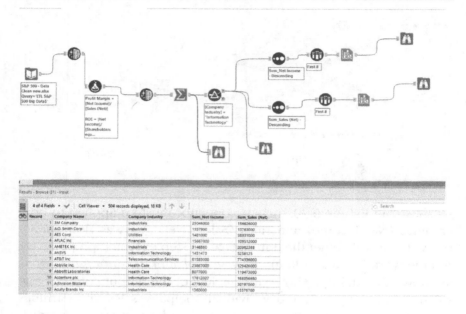

EXHIBIT 6-32 The Filter Tool is Used to Transform the Data into Include
Only Companies in the IT Industry

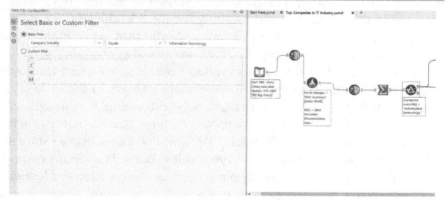

EXHIBIT 6-33 Information Technology Top 8 Performers to by Total Earnings for the Period 2014–2018

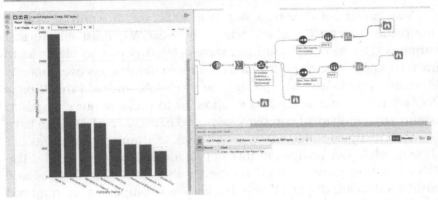

EXHIBIT 6-34 Information Technology Top 8 Performers to by Total Sales for the Period 2014–2018

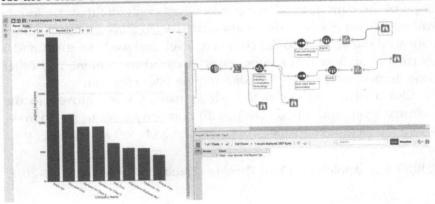

Apple Inc.: Sales and Earnings Trend Analysis

In the previous section, our analysis pointed to Apple as a sales and earnings leader within the information technology industry, when five-year company figures were *aggregated* and compared. In this section, we analyze Apple's annual performance to arrive at a *five*-year trend, giving us a clearer indication of how the company is tracking relative to recent years, and perhaps more importantly how they are poised for the road ahead.

Question 5: What are the five-year sales and earnings trends for Apple Inc.?

You guessed it! The next step is to enlist the *Summarize Tool* to group the data by Company Name and Year. We must ensure that earnings (Net Income) and sales (Sales (Net)) persist to allow us to track annual company performance for these dimensions over time. As illustrated previously, we can run the workflow and add the *Browse Tool* after the *Summarize Tool* to allow us to preview our changes to confirm that individual company sales and earnings performance have been correctly captured. As we would expect, many companies are shown, while our analysis in this step is focused only on Apple. The *Filter* function must be used to specify that only Apple's sales and earnings data are displayed and that all other companies are removed from the view. The resulting five-year trends for earnings (as shown in Exhibit 6-35) and for sales (as shown in Exhibit 6-36) reveal that Apple is on an uptick tear across both dimensions. Based on the upward slope of the current trend, we can be more confident that Apple Inc. will put big numbers on the board next year. In this exercise, we have narrowed our analysis to the company level, and we have structured a dynamic workflow that can be easily tweaked to examine any other company's trends, merely by adjusting the filter criterion.

Our analysis started at the whole market level, moved to the industry level, and has resolved with company-level trend analysis. While the path taken was to examine the S&P 500 as a whole, then

EXHIBIT 6-35 Apple's Five-Year Earnings Trend for the Period 2014–2018

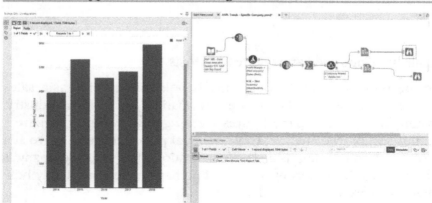

EXHIBIT 6-36 Apple's Five-Year Sales Trend for the Period 2014–2018

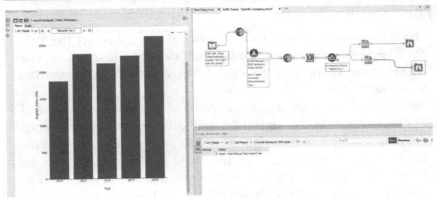

drill into the information technology industry, before turning our attention to Apple Inc., there are nearly infinite possibilities for analysis, assuming availability of data. If data was available to us from other indices such as the Hang Seng, the FTSE Italia All-Share, or the DAX, in addition to the S&P, we might have analyzed and compared global markets. We could have then narrowed our focus to the market that appeared most promising based on key performance measures and then drilled in further to compare industries within the indices, as was done for the S&P.

Interview with Dean Stoecker, Co-Founder and Executive Chairman, Alteryx, Inc.

"How is Alteryx being taken up across industries to reduce manual processing and thereby increase control and efficiency?"

We are seeing a broad variety of clients across industries grappling with control and efficiency demands, in a way never before seen. Couple those with the need to sort through the ever-increasing body of data and the requirement to mine critical information for decision-making, and it is clear why Analytic Process Automation (APA) is becoming increasingly indispensable for information workers across enterprises, spanning from investment banking to healthcare. Currently, we are serving more than 37% of the Global 2000 in driving change and more intelligent outcomes.

"Has data democratization increased the demand for self-service data analytics tools and capabilities? How can Alteryx be employed to enable business transformation at scale?"

Data must be accessible and available to end-users on demand. Those users must be upskilled and prepared to capitalize on the increased volume of data available from an increasing number of sources. Alteryx places advanced tooling directly into the hands of end-users that can help them digest the vast body of data they have at their fingertips, to understand relationships and trends, and to streamline their data processing. We routinely speak to clients who need help getting started transforming their organizations to deal with the new reality, and we are uniquely positioned at the apex of emerging technology, amassing and democratized data, and unique organizational demands. Our approach is to provide a flexible single unified platform bringing together analytics, data science, and process automation into one place. When operators have the right data, the right skills, and the right tools, transformation can happen at lightning speed. At the heart of digital transformation is creating a culture of analytics that allows for innovation and ultimately solving bigger and more complex problems that organizations face.

"What feedback has been provided from users that have adopted Alteryx? How quickly can users move to adopt and deploy Alteryx capabilities?"

Alteryx offers an extremely approachable and user-friendly user interface (UI) that allows users to get up to speed very quickly. In fact, we have heard many reports from users that within hours they were able to transform a tedious and manual process into a structured workflow enabling tight control, efficiency, and auditability. We also hear from users that as their routine processes are made more efficient through Analytics Process Automation (APA), they can recapture scarce capacity to perform more complex analysis – and unlock further value from organizational data.

"What training avenues are available to new users of Alteryx?"

The Alteryx company website features user guides and videos demonstrating Alteryx features and functionality. Additionally, the Finance Function Tool pack features many workflow demonstrations that serve to open users' eyes to the power of the tools. This additional download is targeted toward Finance, Accounting, and Tax users, and it provides case studies directly applicable to use cases frequently encountered in the Finance Function. Our organization has also begun the Alteryx for Good program that helps academic institutions and university professors to integrate Alteryx into their accounting, finance, and business intelligence curriculums. The program even offers students free Alteryx licenses while they are in school, to assist them with their analytics studies.

"How can users embed more advanced analytics into their process flows, as needs arise?"

In addition to the code-free capabilities that Alteryx offers for data preparation and data blending, data transformation, and visualization, Alteryx incorporates advanced predictive and prescriptive analytics capabilities in the platform. Not only can Alteryx help users assemble diverse datasets into one place, employ descriptive analytics to understand past events and drivers, but it also provides advanced capabilities including machine learning algorithms that can be used to look ahead to future events, to make decisions, and take appropriate actions. We are excited about the future and putting immense augmented data analytics capabilities into the hands of users, for seamless integration to their business processes.

Dean Stoecker interview
www.alteryx.com

Conclusion

In this chapter, you have gained some familiarity with data preparation: the import and capture of source data, understanding what is represented in the array, and cleansing the data to ensure it is conformant and of high quality. We have demonstrated data manipulation techniques such as blending, joining, enriching, and sorting data to allow for enhanced analysis, to promote clear and accessible visualizations, and to enable further processing in subsequent steps. It is important that data analytics appears not merely as a theoretical topic often referred to throughout this book. Instead, we wanted to bring the topics and tools to life and to show the enhanced capabilities that self-service tooling can offer. The basic functionality illustrated in this chapter only scratches the surface of the rich suite of features offered by Alteryx. We did not set out to write a software manual; rather, we hoped to demonstrate a logical approach to applying formidable self-service analytics tooling to interrogate data when faced with real-world business questions.

While we have answered the questions posed about S&P 500 performance, identified industry trends, and uncovered single names that are outperforming the index in several dimensions from our limited-scope analysis, we want to emphasize that something larger was accomplished. We have structured the analysis steps in workflows that can easily be built upon – or tailored to answer new questions. With a larger set of data at hand, the workflows we have established could easily be expanded to analyze thousands of companies, spanning multiple markets and indices, with only minor changes to transformation steps and groupings. At period end, the analysis could readily be rolled or refreshed with several clicks of the mouse. While we have examined company and industry fundamentals only, the dataset could be enriched further with market data to provide color on stock performance, allowing us to track, compare, and examine other key ratios such as P/E (price earnings), P/B (price/book), and dividend yield ratios. This would enable more advanced analytic techniques to better understand correlations between accounting performance and stock performance – and in a perfect world, even to make predictions. *At least read through the conclusion before you call your broker!*

While the capabilities illustrated are powerful and can unlock actionable insights from data, managers in finance, accounting, and operations functions are motivated more than ever before by control and efficiency goals. While we began the chapter with five questions, and had a blank canvas to tangentially explore the data, managers often have less flexibility. They must capture and intake processing inputs, perform strictly regimented processing steps, and generate conforming outputs for distribution to internal and external consumers. Very often, the value proposition of self-service analytics tooling lies in the ability for end-users to structure the performance of processing steps in a tool to emulate system processing, in place of manual (and error-prone) spreadsheet work. Each time an operation in a dynamic workflow (such as blending, joining, enrichment, and transformation) can replace the manual construction of formulae, selections and copy/paste operations, comparisons and reconciliations, graphing or charting exercises, or any of the manual steps performed in spreadsheets, the likelihood of introducing processing errors has been considerably reduced. In place of the manual tail, we have lent structure to unstructured work steps, and we have forged a stable, well-defined, easily auditable workflow that can be invoked on demand – over and over again. Finally, each legacy manual processing step we have replaced with an automated workflow represents recurring time savings and an opportunity to recapture capacity for true functional ownership.

CHAPTER 7

Process Discovery: Identify Opportunities, Evaluate Feasibility, and Prioritize

In Chapter 6, we demonstrated Alteryx as a prominent vendor tool in the analytics suite. It was important to concretely show analytics in action and to reframe this book as a practical guide, rather than a work exploring only theories and hypotheticals. We tried to center our case studies on the most common use cases – ones that you are likely to encounter with only a superficial survey of your organization, rather than the more complex advanced analytics applications that are highly specialized, and may be more obscure and difficult to uncover. Now that you have seen at least one highly subscribed data analytics tool in action, you are likely excited to return focus to your own organizations and to begin deployment straight away. Well then, simply pull up your spreadsheet containing your groomed, ranked, scored, and prioritized backlog pipeline. You know the one – with valid opportunities neatly captured, with man-days of development effort estimated and resource costs assigned, showing which organizational, divisional, or department objectives are supported, and finally sorted descending by the dollar value of the benefits case.

We will wait right here to lift our glasses, in a toast to your success and upcoming promotion.

You may be thinking that we have missed a step somewhere. From where exactly does this rich backlog pipeline come? Where are all of these promising opportunities to be found? How did they get so neatly collated, groomed, and evaluated? Why shouldn't we be making more strategic systems implementations, rather than putting in place "rubber band and duct tape" solutions that serve to obscure system shortfalls? Let us provide an approach for you to begin to answer these questions.

In this chapter, we will logically build a business case for core systems first, but then point to residual activity in and around systems post-implementation – the manual tail. From there, we will introduce process discovery and discuss the role that various levels of the organization can play in driving process transparency and in surfacing process inefficiencies as opportunities to employ the data analytics tooling that was demonstrated in the previous chapter. We will take you through the production of process discovery artifacts based on hypothetical scenarios presented that will highlight process inefficiencies for redress. Finally, we will introduce automated process discovery tools, product bundles, and services that are available in the marketplace. This will lead neatly into Chapter 8, where we will pick up from where we leave off in this chapter. In Chapter 8, we will capture the problem statements and opportunities that were surfaced in our abbreviated process discovery examples and work through the extraction of key capabilities required of any viable solution to help you to solve for these opportunities. Importantly, you will be provided with a means to objectively evaluate them, both against organizational objectives and constraints – and against each other – to determine an order of priority.

Note that full texts can and have been written on the subject of the comprehensive performance of process discovery. We will attempt to familiarize you with the process, demonstrate its importance, and introduce you to important tools you may wish to adopt at your respective organizations, in only two chapters of this book – Chapters 7 and 8. The authors encourage you to explore the wealth of materials available, beyond the real estate we can dedicate to process discovery in this book.

Business Case for Systems versus Self-Service Data Analytics

Take for example a small organization with 100 employees generating $20 million in sales and grossing a pretax income of $6 million. Imagine for a moment you are the CFO surveying the organization for opportunities to scale, to cut costs, or to improve profitability. You remember that your payroll manager, Karishma, has come to you several times in the last two years complaining of manual work to perform the payroll cycle. Opportunistically, she has also pointed to the expense reimbursement process and highlighted that the function is so similar to her own, and maintains that she could combine the two and easily run both as a payroll and expense processing utility. Recently, she has made waves by threatening to quit, saying that she has studied hard to become a CPA and this low value-added work is hardly gratifying. That gets your attention.

You bring in a consultant, Joe Patrick from Consulting Solutions LLP, whose engagement team performs a study of the process. The procedures performed included the widespread distribution of a survey across the organization to gather the perceptions and inputs from participants who feel the pain. At the conclusion of this effort, you are surprised to see the staggering amount of time the payroll and expense function spends processing individual claims manually. Even more significant, you hear that the manual expense submission process and time sheet preparation takes each employee two hours per week – or roughly 5% of their workday, on average.

Joe Patrick, parroted by his full entourage in dark suits, makes you aware of a core technology system-based solution that should reduce the time and effort required to perform this work in the future. Several times, Joe referred to the need for a comprehensive top-to-bottom process discovery across the organization. In fact, at one point he broached the subject of whether you would consider hiring his firm for an automated process discovery engagement. You decline, on the basis that you were engaging the consulting firm for a specific purpose, are operating under compressed timelines, and would prefer that if and when the process discovery was performed, it was done in-house. However, one part of the pitch did get your attention. The consultant offers you a time and expense system at a cost of

EXHIBIT 7-1 Income Statement Impact of T&E Core System Implementation

Baseline

Sales			20,000,000

	# production employees	**60**	
	cost per employee	100,000	
Total Annual Production Employee Expense		**$6,000,000**	

Other Direct Costs		4,000,000	

Total Cost of Goods Sold			**$10,000,000**

Gross Profit			**$10,000,000**

Operating Expenses

	Selling Expenses			
	# sales people	10		
	cost per employee	150,000		
	Sales Force Salary Expenses		$1,500,000	
	Advertising		200,000	
	Commission Expense		500,000	$2,200,000
	Adminitrative Expenses			
	Office Equipment Expenses		$1,300,000	
	Office Supply Expenses		500,000	$1,800,000

Total Operating Expenses			$4,000,000

Net Income			**$6,000,000**

(continued)

EXHIBIT 7-1 Income Statement Impact of T&E Core System Implementation *(continued)*

After
  Investment

Sales			21,000,000
	# production employees	**57**	
	cost per employee	100,000	
Total Annual Production Employee Expenses			**$5,700,000**
Other Direct Costs			4,000,000
Total Cost of Goods Sold			**$9,700,000**
Gross Profit			**$11,300,000**

Operating Expenses
  Selling Expenses

	# sales people	10	
	cost per employee	150,000	
	Sales Force Salary Expenses	$1,500,000	
	Advertising	200,000	
	Commission Expenses	525,000	**$2,225,000**
Administrative Expenses			
	Office Equipment Expenses	$1,300,000	
	Office Supply Expenses	500,000	$1,800,000
Total Operating Expenses			**$4,025,000**
Software Amortization Expenses			$50,000
Net Income			**$7,225,000**

$50,000, that can be delivered within 120 days of contract signing. Is it worth the investment?

When it was only one individual making noise about work overload, you are sympathetic but not moved to immediate action. However, if you could eliminate this overhead task from the day of your 100 employees, it may be reasonable to assume that they may be 5% more productive. Perhaps your salesforce, representing 10 of the 100 employees, may generate $21 million in sales with their additional 5% productivity versus the $20 million baseline. On the cost side, perhaps you can meet that additional increased sales demand with three fewer production employees who currently number 60 of the 100 in your organization. Perhaps there is a bigger benefits case to be found, by digging a bit more into this payroll and expense opportunity.

Every organization of course has the opportunity to retrain and redeploy these individuals in line with their strategy, but to analyze the raw impact on efficiency and profitability, let's assume these individuals are no longer required at your organization. These three employees each earned $100,000 per year, and this amount now represents a savings on the cost basis which drops straight through to margins (refer to Porter's Value Chain in Exhibit 7-4). In this example, the investment in a $50,000 expense management system could potentially result in increased profitability of $1,225,000 in year 1, with an increase to $1,275,000 per year thereafter, in perpetuity. If you were the CFO, you would immediately approve an investment that provides a 20% increase in net income and cut that $50,000 check all day long! In the income statement shown in Exhibit 7-1, we have tried to make it clear where the tech spend and savings would cascade, resulting in a higher net income for year 1.

This is where automation can have a significant impact on profitability and efficiency. There are many reasons why systems implementations can yield significant benefits in quality of delivery, speed of execution, and overall process efficiency. If we accept the premise that *systems* can add significant value to both core and non-core work activities, why would we need data analytics, artificial intelligence (AI), and digital tooling such as robotic process automation (RPA), natural language processing (NLP), data enrichment and transformation tools, machine learning, and other tactical solutions in business and industry? Why are automation needs not met with systems alone?

Let's take a closer look at the payroll process and the expense reimbursement process, and let's assume the check was cut and the fit-for-purpose system was implemented 120 days thereafter, by Joe and his engagement team. After some normal teething issues, across all functions in the organization, individuals have more time to focus on their clear remit, undistracted by routine time and expense management tasks. You have just identified and addressed a prevalent use case in your organization, with the adoption of a system to improve process performance and efficiency. Job satisfaction is up, and you are counting your performance bonus already, and it is only September. You renew your subscription to the *Robb Report*; things are looking rosy, indeed.

When the dust settles several months later, on a whim, you call the consultants back in for a short meeting. You want to follow up on a point that had been made surrounding the need for an automation heatmap. When here previously, Joe Patrick had suggested that, even if we were not sold on the idea of a full automated process discovery engagement, at a minimum, we would need to perform a high-level process discovery to better understand the systems landscape and where employees were spending their time. Time and time again, he pointed to the need for a wide-scope process mapping exercise. He had mentioned that process mapping involves the creation of visual representations of process workflows, highlighting the discrete tasks performed daily across our functions, from start to finish. He said this was necessary to understand the current state of our processing environment and to uncover pain points that may represent opportunities to employ technology and process change to further streamline our organization. According to Joe, only then could we realize goals of improved control and efficiency.

As the engagement partner, Joe arrived at your office very prepared with very professional process maps that had been prepared for an anonymized competing organization, along with lengthy matrices detailing sample processes, time spent performing them, the probability of success in automating them with off-the-shelf tools, the proposed solution/tool, and the residual processing time anticipated post the automation release. On the sample materials, there were indicative daily rates for developers, along with build time estimates shown for each solution. You remain confident that the recent system implementation has significantly advanced the organization, but you walk out of the meeting more convinced than ever of the need for a detailed process discovery effort, as you believe that there still must be room to further streamline processing.

Walking back from the conference room, you see that someone is waiting outside your office. It is Karishma, whom you expect to be pleased with her new payroll system and resulting productivity and efficiency. By the look on her face, she may not be as pleased as you would have expected. Whatever her complaint, you reflect that she now has the time to loiter outside your office, which is progress in itself. You usher her in, motion for her to sit, and even before you can set down the stack of sample process flows and matrices that the consultants have left with you, she hits you with a list of further features and functionality that she says are absolutely indispensable must-haves that were neglected during system implementation.

She states that the payroll team must still work with the new system outputs to get them enriched with payroll rates from HR for journal entries, and tailored for reporting and other important uses. She very evenly explains that while the system provides great work-flow benefits in passing time sheets from the originator to the approvers and ultimately to the payroll team, additional functionality will be required to streamline outputs from the new system for further downstream processing. Also, there is a notable interoperability gap, in that your new system does not readily share or combine information contained in the HR system. It seems that altogether new use cases have been identified.

In one way, you are disappointed that your $50,000 expenditure was not the end of the story. That is what had been promised by the consultants, after all. However, at their final go-live presentation, they were able to demonstrate the utility of the application, and you had been convinced – and remain convinced – that the investment was money well spent. All too often, the original requirements documents that were fed to developers failed to anticipate all features and functionality required to seamlessly integrate the new system into the processing landscape.

You took notes throughout the session with Karishma and are able to summarize the functionality she requires succinctly at the conclusion of the meeting. You recommend that she logs these problem statements and features in the IT demand backlog so they can be addressed strategically in due time. However, she states that she has little hope that resources and funding can be secured during the next investment cycle. It is true that the core tech backlog has quite a few competing priorities with another processing system your organization has been planning to launch for the last two years. Although the time and expense system implementation was clearly a success, you wonder if there is something that can be done straight away to make life a bit easier for Karishma and the team. The function could operate more efficiently by automating some of the processing steps conducted with system outputs and other work around the edges of your new system. You need tactical tooling to bridge the gap while awaiting core technology to deliver the additional features and system interoperability enhancements.

Recently, you brought on board a new college graduate, Adam Goodman, who had mentioned that he is savvy with a few off-the-shelf self-service analytics tools like Xceptor and Alteryx. Adam is a promising young person, and you had been impressed that he is confident with data and automation. While Adam seemed overly informal at times and still shows signs of youth, you had been able to see beyond his three-day stubble and took the chance on him in hopes that he would turn out to be a great investment over the long-term. Currently, you have him providing some help with order management and answering vendor phone calls, which is fine for now. He is getting his feet wet and learning your business. Looking at the backlog list, you wonder if some of the demand items could be addressed with one of these tools, so you ask Adam to sit with Karishma to understand better what she does and to come back with a view on whether anything can be done with Alteryx. After all, we could quite easily purchase some licenses, if that would better structure the team's work, increase process quality and stability, and save her some time.

Adam marches into your office the following week, and you notice that he is freshly shaved this morning. Also, you see that he has put on his one 1960s thin *Mad Men* tie that you last saw that day back in May, when he arrived at your office for his interview. Maybe this is a good sign. You can't help but smile as you think of your own son and all of his antics as he finishes school. Clearly, Adam's project has gone well, and he has good results to report back. He must be bucking for a raise with that tie. *Good man, Goodman!*

You ask Adam where he got to with Karishma, what the real pain points were, and how he thought he could help. He informs you that, in two days sitting with the payroll team, he was able to shadow five timesheet review and approval processes and that there are, as he put it, "tons" of solid use cases for Alteryx. From the reformatting of data that is pulled from the new system, to the application of audit filters, to look-ups against employee HR records to pull pay rates and other static, to gathering input files for upload to the ledger – all of these were great use cases. In fact, Adam believes that with Alteryx, he can remove many of the independent processing steps performed by the team, and he can save them as much as two hours per day.

Adam is on his game today, and you are encouraged that he could be just the extra set of hands needed to help Karishma get some relief (*it must be the tie!*). If Adam can drive efficiency and put some structure around manual tasks, and perhaps rebuild a little capacity in Karishma's function, he will have more than paid for himself. Of course, we would also need to spend some money on Alteryx licenses or other tactical tooling, but you like that the solutions he raised do not require the over-subscribed technology team to build them, as would be required for a larger-scale application or system rollout. End-user tooling can be engaged by virtually everyone in an organization that is able to identify appropriate use cases and to navigate the increasingly user-friendly and accessible functionality that the tools offer. However, before you agree to let Adam relinquish his current tasks and go to work for Karishma and the payroll team for the next few months, you think that the process discovery exercise that the consulting partner had been so vocal in promoting may be in order.

As Joe Patrick made clear, this exercise should not only prove useful to helping you finally assemble much-needed documentation of how the organization fits together, but if it can help with the identification of a rich pipeline of opportunities, all the better. Now that you have Adam standing by and eager to help, you will want to keep him busy. Building the backlog can help him to reduce wait, build momentum, and increase transformation velocity overall across the organization. Additionally, the more processes that have been defined, documented, and evaluated for benefits will give color and context around headcount efficiency and footprint goals you have been discussing with the CEO. You promise Adam that once the detailed process discovery is completed, you will pull him into a meeting to discuss the outcome and whether it will make sense to redeploy him to address the opportunities identified. You tell him to sit tight for now. Crestfallen, he manages an "Ok dude, er. . .sir, no problem" before slinking away.

Process Discovery Phases and Methodology

Business process discovery, also called process discovery, is a collection of tools and techniques used to define, scope, map, describe, and analyze an organization's existing business processes. Along with business process modeling, process discovery is critical to making business process management (BPM) initiatives successful. Process discovery can be used to many ends, but we are introducing it as an approach to not only gather facts, allowing for deeper understanding and documentation of the organization and its business processes, but as a way to survey the processing landscape to identify pockets of manual processing that may represent opportunities to apply data analytics and automation tooling. As problem statements are encountered, it is important that enough detail is gathered to allow for assessing the size of the problems, the relative priority of addressing them when weighed up against the other opportunities surfaced, and which solutions may be appropriate to address them.

There are many ways to proceed with process discovery, but in its simplest form, it will include defining a target process and producing a set of project artifacts, and then analyzing them to determine where in the process there is considerable manual effort. These hotspots in the value chain can be evaluated further for a number of factors to determine whether they represent feasible opportunities to deploy data analytics or automation tools to increase control and efficiency. Typical evaluative factors include the type of manual effort, the level of complexity, the repetitive nature of the task, input stability, and the level of discernment and analysis involved in the process – and the variety of tooling you have at your disposal.

In the following sections, we will start with top-down process discovery steps and then proceed to the bottom-up steps, which are the most likely to be fruitful when it comes to identifying concrete opportunities to capture efficiency through the employ of data analytics tooling.

Top-Down: Organizational Context

To begin the process discovery, it is useful to look top-down from senior management's perspective. As a starting point, it is useful to describe in some detail the current business environment in which the company operates. Who are your customers? What industry do you operate in? Who are your competitors? Are there notable changes in your environment or marked trends in progress today? There are any number of templates readily available to assist with top-down process discovery, but we will remind you of three elegant universal tools that can help to prompt your thinking at the organizational-level – SWOT analysis, Porter's Five Forces, and Porter's Value Chain. High-level process discovery is unlikely to uncover clear opportunities to employ data analytics, but it will produce important context that points toward clear organizational objectives. Any change efforts that stem from lower-level or bottom-up process discovery must demonstrably support these objectives.

SWOT Analysis

Often it is useful to gather a group of senior executives to perform a strengths, weaknesses, opportunities, and threats (SWOT) analysis to give further context to the discovery. Looking at your core competencies and what your company does well can help to formulate or refine your identity and profile. Similarly, candidly calling out weaknesses and areas for improvement is the first step in mobilizing to redress them. However, your company does not operate in a vacuum. Over time, opportunities emerge that must be capitalized upon, and threats rear their heads for active (or even pro-active) management. Formulating actions and objectives which support the identified opportunities and which address the stated threats can follow from this exercise. SWOT analysis is an important exercise to formally recognize how your company operates and the environment it operates within. Stick to simple, and remember that a more complicated or "pretty" artifact does not make it intrinsically more valuable. It is the disciplined thought process that is most valuable here.

By way of example, we tried to highlight the considerations which would be brought to this exercise as we prepared Exhibit 7-2 as a sample artifact created for a fictional company. You can see that one company strength cited is that they have recently been able to scale their production to reduce the per-unit cost. This has resulted in an opportunity to penetrate a lower-income customer segment through altering the product mix. In this example, you can also see that one key focus area is opening up the Latin American markets. Currently listed as a weakness, it is also an opportunity – and a threat. In this example, you can see significant interplay of both internal and external factors that are neatly tied together in this format. The organization benefits from taking stock of their own performance and capabilities, as well as from recognizing environmental trends and developments. For better or for worse, this is a snapshot at a point in time; it is important to revisit and refresh this view with some frequency to ensure that it is kept current, both as the organization itself evolves and as external forces pulse and wane over time.

Porter's Five Forces

Many of these same environmental and external factors can be useful in assessing the competitive landscape in which the company operates. Porter's Five Forces (of Competitive Position Analysis)[1] is a tool to help executives to think through supplier power, buyer power, threat of new entrants, and substitutions, and how they interact to form the competitive landscape. While this tool is often used to help potential investors to evaluate whether or not to dive-in head first into a new industry, it can also be used to help executives to understand where they fit in and the forces they must continue to navigate in order to be successful. This additional high-level view can be an

EXHIBIT 7-2   Company SWOT Analysis

COMPANY SWOT ANALYSIS

	Strengths	Weaknesses
Internal	We have an extremely innovative and unique Product Offering stemming from significant investment in research and development.	Due to our R&D capabilities and strong reputation, the market expects innovative products from us quarterly. Meeting market expectations is not always possible.
	We have strong brand value which is valued at more than $500 million.	Our products are considered luxury items, due to our premium pricing. Our customer base is limited to high-income consumers.
	We have wide distribution network with 72 retail stores spread across 5 countries, and have strong online channels and trade partners.	We have not demonstrated our ability to penetrate important Latin American markets, due to lack of relationships and distribution channels.
	Due to scale, our incremental per-unit production costs have been reduced.	

	Opportunities	Threats
External	Due to reduced incremental per-unit production costs, we can now consider offering our cutting-edge technology in a no-frills format, to market to lower-income customers.	We face political obstructions in new markets, including recent opposition in Mexico.
	By varying our product mix, and developing lower cost products, we are better equipped to expand to emerging markets in developing countries.	Product substitutes have eroded the global market for our product by $10 billion.
	Our chief competitor has signaled they may be open to being acquired. We estimate that they currently enjoy an 8% global market share, and 40% market share within Latin America.	Due to the recent adverse court decision, we may not be able to legally protect our proprietary technology from competitors who have reverse-engineered our products.

important and beneficial step to framing organizational and industry context, and we have prepared a sample model and presented it in Exhibit 7-3. The idea is to ensure your organization recognizes these considerable forces at play that shape the environment in which you compete. For service organizations in particular, any notable or extreme developments across any of these dimensions point to the need for controlled, efficient, high-quality, and well-governed processing.

Again, simple is better. Preparing this view is about building consensus from thought-leaders and distilling their input to key messaging that can help to shape actionable objectives and strategy decisions. In the example shown here, we have imagined the industry forces at work for the same organization featured in the SWOT analysis in the previous section. You can see that the threat of substitutes features here, as does the price-sensitivity of customers, which was alluded to in the "weaknesses" quadrant of the SWOT frame.

Between the SWOT analysis and the Porter's Five Forces view of competition, when taken together, a picture begins to emerge of the featured organization. If the picture presented here gives the impression that the company may be in serious trouble, absent drastic countermeasures, the authors are good painters. The company does not enjoy broad-based market appeal, they are shut out of important geographic markets, and there are lower-cost substitutes popping up all around them. A strong leader will derive an approach to lead the organization to a better place when presented with these views. Considering and framing the backdrop properly can set the stage for a corrective course.

Porter's Value Chain

Having assessed your strengths, weakness, and who you are as a company, and having given thought to the prevailing industry forces at play, and the opportunities and threats presenting themselves, the next step is to take look more closely at the way your organization fits together. To assist with this introspection, we suggest leveraging a generic Porter Value Chain[2] template (Exhibit 7-4) and customizing it to reflect the nuances of your organization as you drop in your own primary and support activities and functions. Be careful to

EXHIBIT 7-3 Porter's Five Forces Model

PORTER'S FIVE FORCES MODEL

COMPETITIVE RIVALRY–MEDIUM

There is significant competition between brick and mortar retail stores versus online providers.

The industry has seen increase in advertising expenses.

With substitutes eroding the market for our product, it is less clear with whom we directly compete.

THREAT OF SUBSTITUTE PRODUCTS & SERVICES–HIGH

There are multiple product substitutes emerging. Product substitutes have eroded the global market for our product by $10 billion.

Our paper increase in market share is driven not by our sales growth but by diminishing demand in our segment.

THREAT OF NEW ENTRANTS–MEDIUM

High capital investment is a barrier to entry. Costly R&D activities drive product innovations and success in the premium market.

There has been interest from large players in introducing competing technologies in a less-expensive format.

BARGAINING POWER OF BUYERS–LOW

Buyers tend to be loyal to existing brands.

However, customers are increasingly price-sensitive, exhibiting high elasticity of demand during the recent business cycle downturn.

BARGAINING POWER OF SUPPLIERS–LOW

There are many suppliers who compete for scarce contracts in our industry. We routinely change suppliers when advantageous terms are offered.

THREAT OF NEW ENTRANTS

THREAT OF SUBSTITUTE PRODUCTS & SERVICES

BARGAINING POWER OF SUPPLIERS

BARGAINING POWER OF BUYERS

Competitive Rivalry

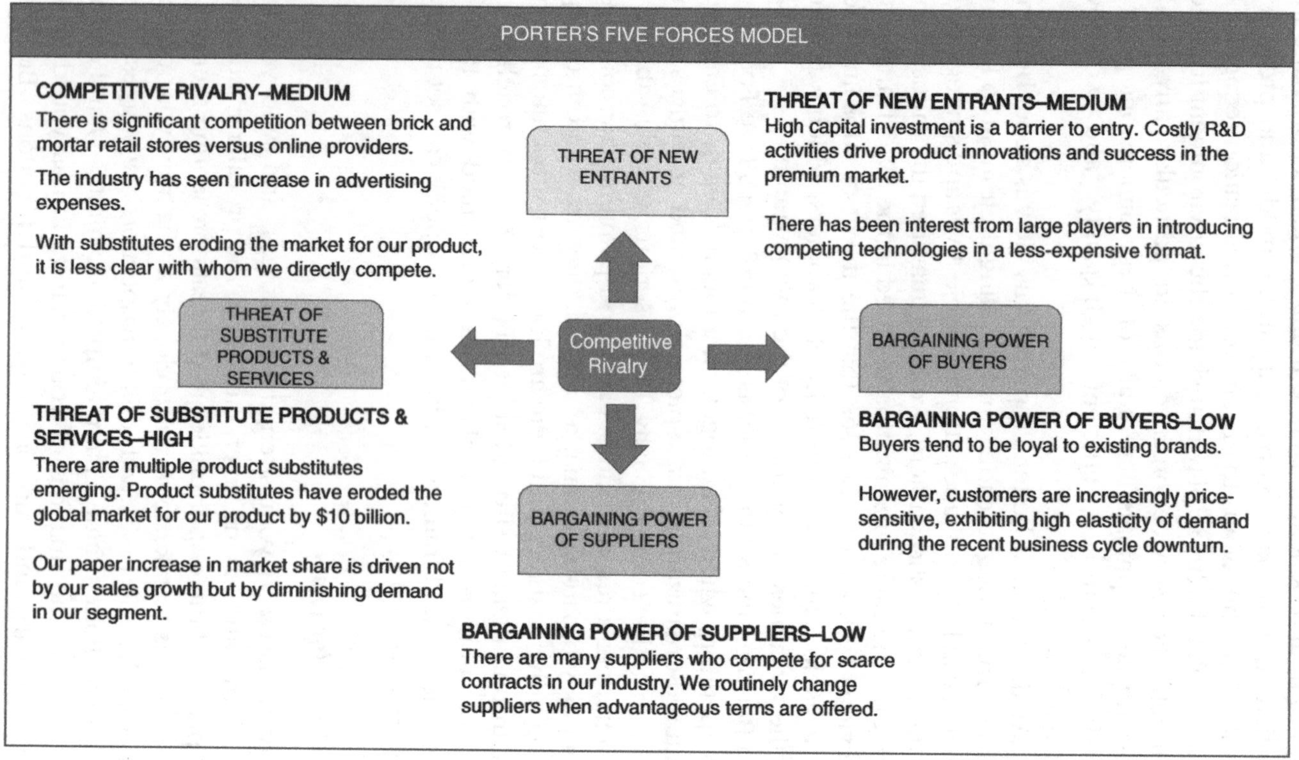

consider the firm infrastructure and technology landscape and how they influence the value creation you feature as primary activities.

One of the complaints with this frame is that some say it is especially appropriate for larger-scale organizations, whereas for niche firms it is less so. A software firm may not have inbound procurement or logistics concerns, at least to the same degree as would a manufacturer who transforms raw physical inputs. Might the technology development stripe, shown across the top as a support activity, more reasonably be considered a primary activity for a technology developer? Quite possibly – fair point. However, Porter would probably argue that there are categories of technology within the stack, a portion of which is still best classified as supportive, even while the technology products being developed in the core division of the technology developer may well fall into the operations category of primary activities, in Exhibit 7-4.

Keep in mind, this frame is not written in stone; the thinking still holds, even if the template is amended or customized to better suit, describe, inspire, or motivate your organization. Porter's talking point is that whether firms are manufacturers or service providers, whether they are in technology or logistics, identifying efficiencies in any of the firm's primary or support activities will ultimately increase margins. To bring it home, whether we ultimately capture opportunities

EXHIBIT 7-4 Porter's Value Chain

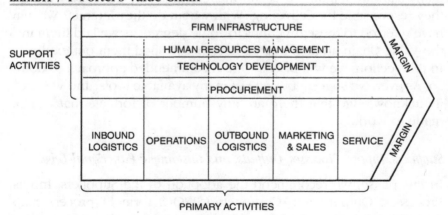

Source: Denis Fadeev, https://commons.wikimedia.org/wiki/
File:Michael_Porter's_Value_Chain.svg

to employ analytics within operations, marketing and sales, or service, the efficiency benefits realized can drive increased margins.

We argue that the exercise of thinking through this view is well worthwhile. Having performed the step, a clearer view emerges of where each activity falls in the schema, and how each activity relates to others in your organization. Further, a quick survey of each category of primary and support activities could point to areas rich in opportunities to boost efficiency. When this view is combined with the strengths and constraints observed from the SWOT analysis and with the competitive forces as surfaced from the Porter's Five Forces analysis, significant insight can be gained about the firm and the environment in which it operates. Perhaps most of all, it should again be obvious that controlled, efficient, and well-governed processing can drive a positive impact to margins. *Is anyone sensing a recurring theme?*

Top-Down: Functional View

Now that solid thinking has been put into understanding the environment in which the company is operating, you can move down to the next level to begin to describe the organizational functions. The next step is to prepare a view of your organization's functional hierarchy, to give color to the different parts of the organization. How many staff are aligned to each function? What do they do? What are they responsible for delivering? With whom do they interact? We may have referred to these functions to some degree, as we laid them into the Value Chain artifact, but we have not fleshed them out explicitly. In this section, we will discuss one recommended approach to doing so. As ever, we suggest but one of many available tools, and we readily acknowledge that there are any number of formats that can be made to work.

Suppliers, Inputs, Processes, Outputs, and Customers: Functional-Level

In this phase, we recommend the adoption of the Suppliers, Inputs, Processes, Outputs, and Customers (SIPOC) form of process map. A SIPOC is formatted into five columns, with one column for each of these dimensions. This view is more detailed than any that we prepared at the company level, as we are drilling into the summary view and breaking it out into multiple frames as we begin to explore the various departments and functions in the organization. *Peel the onion.*

At this stage, we recommend completing one SIPOC per department or function. Start by identifying and explicitly naming categories of internal and external "suppliers" to your departmental business processes in the first column, and then name the process "Inputs" that these suppliers provide, in the next column to the right. These are straightforward categories and tend to be relatively easy, but as you move to the middle column, Processes, it can be challenging to keep your 35,000-foot perspective, and you can easily get bogged down in the details. There is a time and a place for detail, but that comes at the next level of discovery. For now, try to group these into categories of processes that are roughly similar. If you are preparing a SIPOC for the HR function, you may wish to summarize the departmental processes in a few buckets like "Employee Onboarding," "Training and Development," "Performance Review and Feedback" or other appreciable broad categories of "like" activities, for which the function is responsible. It is easy to see that within training and development, there could be "external" training, "in-house specialty skills" training, or perhaps "compliance" training, but spelling them out at this stage is less useful, as it does not add appreciable color to the processes and responsibilities of the HR department, overall.

Here is where our use of the SIPOC to summarize the activities of the entire department takes things in a bit of a different direction, versus detailing the processing steps as we would do, were we preparing a SIPOC for a single process. Still, using the SIPOC in this way is quite useful, as it can help you to begin to think through the broad categories of functional processes, which you can then explore, explode, and define in greater detail when later we move to the Map and Measure phase (see the section Bottom-Up: Map and Measure). The idea is still to keep it relatively high level, and your completed SIPOC should still fit on a single page.

From "Processes" we can move to the penultimate column, "Outputs," where we can list the categories of deliverables that are produced in the prior column. Here again, you will need to keep a high-level perspective and group these into several categories of deliverables, rather than spelling out each of the hundreds or even thousands of deliverables that are produced, say, in the External Reporting function. Using this function as an example, you may wish to list several categories of deliverables. You may wish to have a single "Process" node for SEC reporting, and have outputs listed like "Annual Form 10-K," or "Quarterly Form 10-Q," or "Annual Report to Shareholders." To get at completeness, it is a good idea to use the "Suppliers," "Inputs," and "Processes" you have already captured to make sure there is a corresponding "Output" listed. By the time you move to the right side of the "Processes" column, the SIPOC nearly completes itself – it is all downhill from here. For each of the process "Outputs" or deliverables listed, they are each of course delivered to internal or external "Customers." The SIPOC can be completed by ensuring the customers (or categories of customers) to whom the "Outputs" are delivered are listed.

To illustrate the functional-level SIPOC, in Exhibit 7-5, we have drilled in to one department – the Time and Expense Processing Department, which is responsible for two main functions – expense reimbursement and completing the payroll disbursement cycle at our example firm. Note that there are only seven high-level processes in the middle column, as this is a high-level functional view. "Like" activities have been grouped into these very general process steps. Reading through these very quickly, we already get a reasonable sense of what the function is meant to do. At the bottom, Processing Goals have been clearly stated, along with Control/Governance goals and Quality Constraints. Note that the "Suppliers" column is important to show the functions that are involved. Also note the "Customers" column, which is useful to show whom the production steps impact. These two fields taken together can help us to perform our stakeholder mapping. At the top left, we see that there is a total of four dedicated employees involved, but that they may be working at capacity, given there is an indication that the department has an open headcount requisition.

There are any number of formats that can be used to diagram, describe, or illustrate a function, but the SIPOC is a great tool to convey in a single frame the tasks that a function performs, the size of the function, and any dependencies on other departments, functions, and stakeholders. Once completed for the first function, the same level of detail can be produced for as many departments or functions

EXHIBIT 7-5 Time and Expenses Department SIPOC

4 FTE, 1 Open Requisition

Time and Expense Processing Department SIPOC

Suppliers	Inputs/Systems	Process	Outputs	Customers
Employees seeking Reimbursement Employees on the payroll	Blank Expense Form Template	Employees Prepares/Submits Time and Expense Reports	Completed Expense Report Package Submission	Approving Managers or Payroll/Expense Team
Approving Managers	Blank Remittance Slip Template	Required Manager Approvals	Manager Approval	Payroll Team Expense Team
Expense Team	Required Expense Receipts	Expense Processing Procedures and Reviews	Packages Validated for Completeness	Expense Team
Payroll Team Human Resources Tax Department	Completed Expense Forms/Required Receipts HR Pay Rate Info Tax Withholding Data	Time Sheet Processing Procedures and Reviews	Rejected Reports	Payroll Team
Expense Team Payroll Team	Completed Time Sheets	Payment Remittance Slip Preparation and Payment Approvals	Approved Expense Reports and Approved Payroll slips	Cash Payments team
Cash Team	Completed and Approved Remittance Slips	Cash Disbursements Accounting Entries for Payroll Expenses and Expense Processing and Reimbursement	Completed Remittance Slips Payments and payment accounting entries	Employee Seeking Expense Reimbursement or Payroll Remuneration

Processing Goals: To promptly reimburse employees for qualifying expenses incurred for the benefit of the company and produce accurate accounting entries.

Control/Governance Goal: To ensure that company expense policies and procedures and payroll, holiday, and overtime procedures are followed.

Expenses Quality Constraints: SLA of 24 hours from Employee Submission to Expense Reimbursement Disbursement, Failure/Rework rate <5%.

Payroll Quality Constraints: Payment disbursements must be fair and accurate, timely based on published pay cycles, with Failure/Rework rate <.01%.

as are distinct within the organization. Try to keep consistent with respect to the level of detail shown. By starting with company-level frames, and then moving to these organization or functional-level views, you are achieving much in illustrating how your company fits together. Once they are created, you will be surprised at how many times you offer up and refer to these artifacts in meetings with others across your organization that can benefit from a single one-page frame to convey your high-level processes and functional deliverables.

The idea is to build the organizational documentation in a way that will allow you to peel the onion, layer after layer as you drill down to the process level. It is possible that even the functional SIPOCs may reveal some obvious areas of inefficient manual processing. However, depending on the scale and breadth of your organization, and the degree to which individual processes were summarized, we need to go one or even several steps deeper, to fully understand, document, and analyze functional processes. In the next section, we will begin to identify the areas within the organization that can most benefit from the employ of data analytics and automation tooling and to capture specific opportunities for our development backlog.

Middle Management: Define the Processes

The next step in our process discovery effort is quite similar to the last, but it involves delegation. While the first stages in the journey could be done by functional executives or department heads, to begin to put some flesh on the bones and to peel the onion a bit further, we now require the input of middle managers. It is from this level of the organization that strong process definitions can be extracted. More specifically, we can assign logical start and stop points for each of the processes we will uncover during the Map and Measure stage, to be covered in the following section.

Department heads and executives may know the types of processes that are performed across their domains and may even have some specific process knowledge surrounding services provided to flagship clients, but they may be less aware of process specifics, how processes that exist within departments and functions fit together, the order of operations required to generate outputs, and the handoffs between stakeholders that allow for the outputs from one process to feed into the next as inputs. If we go down below middle management and process owners directly to operators, the risk is that individual operators may not understand how the work they perform contributes to overall functional deliverables, or how their outputs are used by other teams and functions downstream. For these reasons, we recommend the intermediate managers as the starting point, when we are breaking out the high-level SIPOCs produced in the preceding process discovery steps to understand *individual* processes – where they start and stop, who consumes process outputs, and how the processes fit into the function, overall.

Suppliers, Inputs, Processes, Outputs, and Customers: Process-Level

Middle managers and process owners can now commence work to flesh out the processes that will ultimately be mapped and measured in the subsequent steps. They begin with the SIPOCs previously prepared at the functional level, and break out the general high-level process nodes (from the middle columns of the functional SIPOCs) to more detailed process listings. For each process on the detailed process list, middle managers should enlist their teams to define the starting points where processes begin and the stopping points where they end. For each process, it is also useful that the team produce a one-page process narrative. This is a quick summary document that highlights the goals of the process, the number of employees dedicated or involved in the process, the process inputs, the key processing steps, and key process outputs that are produced from the process, in narrative form. Careful attention must be paid to capturing the parties and functions that are involved, and whether they are suppliers to the individual processing steps or the next customers of the processing step outputs. *Does this ring a bell?*

You may be thinking that we are describing these lower-level processes in much the same way as we described the departments and functions in the Top-Down step above – and you would be right. In essence, we are saying that the next step is to iterate out all the stand-alone processes within the process categories and prepare individual SIPOCs for each of the individual processes performed within the departments or functions. By performing this next level of

SIPOCs, we are revealing the layer where the automation opportunities are most likely to exist – and where data analytics can play a key role in both structuring work and driving efficiency.

We will now drill a step further into the Time and Expense Processing Department. As we described earlier, they are responsible for two main functions – expense reimbursement and completing the payroll disbursement cycle. Now, with the help of middle managers and process owners to define the start and stop points, we can flesh out both processes more specifically. First, let's look at the written description of the expense submission and reimbursement process, which would have come from process owners and the operators performing the steps.

"The process begins when employees complete expense form templates (along with required receipts for any individual expenditures greater than $20) and either submit the package to managers for approval (if the report total is greater than $100) or submit the package directly to the Expense Team, if it is below the threshold. For the packages requiring approvals, managers review and either approve or reject, before the workflow moves to the Expense team. Upon receipt of packages by the Expense Team, they wait in a queue until they are pulled into WIP. At that time, the Expense team performs a completeness check to confirm that manager approval has been proffered where required, that all required fields have been duly captured, and that all required receipts have been submitted. They also apply audit filters which may or may not flag the entire expense report for a detailed review. If a detail review is performed as a result, and the report is deemed outside of policy, it would be rejected and sent back to the employee for amendment and resubmission. If the report is confirmed as accurate and within policy, the Expense team approves and completes a remittance slip, before forwarding both to the cash team. The Cash team makes the payments to finalize the process, and they record them with the appropriate accounting journal entries. On average, employees submit one expense report per month."

From this narrative, the middle managers and process owners have produced the expense reimbursement SIPOC shown in Exhibit 7-6. Since this is the first SIPOC representation of an individual process that you may have come across, spend a second to trace these process steps down the "Process" column. Look to the left to see what inputs are required and whom the providers of those inputs are. Look to the right in the "Outputs" column to see what each processing step is meant to produce. As ever, look at the stakeholders in the "Suppliers" and "Customers" columns to see the interactions and dependencies with other functions. Hopefully, the readers are convinced that the process SIPOC has satisfactorily translated the written process description into a visual representation neatly summarizing the process.

There are some other gems that have been captured as well. At the top left in the header, we can see that there are two employees dedicated to this process, and we can see that of the two teams, this is the team that has the open headcount requisition, indicating that they are operating at or above capacity. Across the bottom of the diagram, we see that the processing goals have been explicitly stated, along with control/governance goals and quality constraints. Note that if any additional descriptions would be useful in your organization, they can be quite readily added to your own artifact template and made standard going forward. The idea is to convey the process clearly in a single-page frame.

We have successfully exploded the functional-level SIPOC to pull out the first process, but there is still another process for which the function is responsible. Let us turn our attention to the time sheet submission and payroll process to more fully flesh it out, as part of our detailed process discovery. We will start again with the process narrative, or the verbal description that would have been provided by process owners and the operators performing the steps, as necessary.

"The process begins when employees complete Weekly Time Sheet Reports, leveraging blank templates. Each employee must submit their time every week in order to get paid. If employees worked overtime, they submit their Time Sheets

EXHIBIT 7-6 Expenses Submission Review/Approval/Reimbursement SIPOC

2 FTE, 1 **Open Requisition** → Expense submission review/approval & reimbursement

Suppliers	Inputs/Systems	Process	Outputs	Customers
Employee Seeking Reimbursement	Blank Expense Form Template	Employee prepares/submits Expense Report (along with receipts for any purchases > $20).	Completed Expense Report Package Submission	Approving Managers or Expense Team
Approving Managers	Completed Expense Form and required receipts	If Expense Report total AMT > $100, Manager Approval Required	Manager Approval	Expense Team
Expense Team	Forms Flagged for Audit Review	Expense team ensures required receipts included and performs completeness check. Audit Flag Filters Applied.	Completeness Validated Packages	Expense Team
Expense Team	Blank Remittance Slip Template	Reports flagged for Audit are detail reviewed and returned to employees if rejected or require correction.	Rejected Reports	Employee Seeking Reimbursement
Expense Team	Approved Reports	Expense team prepares remittance slip and approves payment.	Approved Expense Reports	Cash Payments team
Cash Team	Completed Remittance Slips	Cash team receives approved expense reports, makes reimbursement payments & journal entries.	Completed Remittance Slips	Employee Seeking Reimbursement
		Employees receive payments and remittance slips, any process failures escalated for remediation.	Completed Payments and Accounting Journal Entries	Employee Seeking Reimbursement

Processing Goals: To promptly reimburse employees for qualifying expenses incurred for the benefit of the company and produce accounting entries.

Control/Governance Goal: To ensure that company expense policies and procedures are followed.

Quality Constraints: SLA of 24 hours from Employee Submission to Payment Disbursement, Failure/Rework rate <5%.

to managers for approval. For those Time Sheets requiring approvals, managers review and either approve or reject, before the workflow moves to the Payroll Team. Upon receipt of Time Sheets by the Payroll Team, they wait in a queue until they are pulled into WIP. At that time, the Payroll Team begins by performing a completeness check to confirm that required manager approval has been proffered when overtime is reported, that all required fields have been duly captured, and that any holidays claimed are on the approved holiday calendar. At that point, any incomplete Time Sheets are returned to the submitters for amendment and resubmission. The Payroll team goes on to apply audit filters, which may or may not flag the Time Sheet submission for a full detailed review. If a detail review is performed as a result, and the Time Sheet is deemed inaccurate or outside of overtime policy, it would be rejected and sent back to the employee for amendment and resubmission. Next, a check is performed to ensure that the employee is in fact eligible and entitled to any claims for paid time off. If the Time Sheet is accurate and within policy, the Payroll team calculates the payroll based on the hours or calendar days worked, the employee's pay rate as sourced from HR, and the tax withholding information as provided by the tax department. Finally, the team approves the payroll disbursement and prepares a remittance slip, before making a journal entry to record the payroll expense (dr. Payroll Expense) and to set up the payable liability (cr. Wages Payable). At this point, they forward the remittance slip to the Cash team. The payroll item then sits in a "wait" queue until it is pulled into WIP by the Cash Team. Once taken up, the Cash Team makes the payroll disbursements to add the approved payroll item to the payroll calendar batch. To finalize the process, the Cash Team makes the appropriate accounting journal entries to reflect the cash movement (cr. Cash) and to offset the payable liability (dr. Wages Payable)."

The middle managers and process owners have translated this verbal narrative to produce the following Time Sheet and Payroll Cycle SIPOC (Exhibit 7-7). Again, take a moment to trace these process steps

EXHIBIT 7-7 Time Sheet Submission Review/Approval & Payroll Cycle SIPOC

2 FTE

Time Sheet submission review/approval & Payroll Cycle

Suppliers	Inputs/Systems	Process	Outputs	Customers
Employee	Weekly Time Card Blank Time Sheet Report Template	Employee prepares/submits Weekly Time Sheet Report	Completed Expense Report Package Submission	Approving Managers Payroll Team
Approving Managers	Completed and Approved Report	If Time Sheet Contains Overtime Weekly Total Hours > 40, Manager Approval Required	Manager Approval	Approving Managers
Payroll Team	Reports Flagged for Audit Review	Payroll team confirms holidays listed are on approved list, ensures vacation day eligibility. Audit Flag Filters Applied.	Validated Reports (with audit flag or without)	Payroll Team
Payroll Team	Audited Time Sheet Reports	Time Sheets flagged for Audit are detail reviewed and returned to employees if correction required.	Rejected Time Sheet Reports or Validated Reports	Employee Seeking Reimbursement
Human Resources Tax Department	Corrected/Validated Reports, HR Pay Rate Data/Tax Withholding Data	Payroll team prepares remittances, approves payroll disbursement, makes Journal Entries (dr. payroll exp, cr. Payable).	Approved Time Sheets/Remittance Slips and Accounting Journals	Cash Payments Team
Payroll Team	Completed Payroll/ Remittance Slips	Cash team receives approved payroll slips. Makes payroll disbursements/journal entries (dr. payable, cr. Cash).	Completed Payroll Disbursements and Accounting Journals	Employees are fully paid.
Cash Team		Employees receive Friday payroll disbursements, following holiday calendar. Any failures escalated for remediation.		

Processing Goals: To perform timely payroll cycle in accordance with applicable labor laws and to generate proper accounting journal entries.

Control/Governance Goal: To ensure that company payroll, holiday, and overtime policies and procedures are followed.

Quality Constraints: Payroll disbursements must be fair and accurate, Failure/Rework rate <.01%.

down the Process column. Look to the left to see what inputs are required and whom the providers of those inputs are. Look to the right in the Outputs column to see what each processing step is meant to accomplish. As ever, look at the stakeholders in the Suppliers and Customers columns to see the interactions and dependencies with other functions.

Following the artifact minimum standard, some additional annotations have been made. At the top left, we can see that there are two employees dedicated to this process. The processing goals have been explicitly stated, along with control/governance goals and quality constraints. Note that again, they have managed quite neatly to convey the process in a single-page frame that would allow someone to understand the process – and the need for the process – all at a single glance (or certainly after a five-minute study).

Bottom-Up: Map and Measure

Next comes the detailed portion of our process discovery. The Map and Measure phase is about gaining a better understanding of processes under review and gathering as much data as is useful to inform the analysis to follow. The data that must be collected is driven by the questions you are asking. If the goal is to investigate, measure, and improve the rate of failure for a broken process, you may start by assembling failure metrics showing the rate and impact of failures, both to confirm there is in fact a problem and to establish a baseline upon which to improve. From there, you would likely break down the process into finer detail to begin to understand where in the process flow the process breaks down. This would provide the data that is required to move to the analysis phase, where you would then ask the "Five Whys" to begin to uncover root causes, or perhaps you would use intensive data analytics to correlate variable observations to failures and to predict failures based on these observations. Simply put, the Map and Measure phase of process discovery is where key information is gathered to allow for data-driven analysis.

For our purposes, we are performing process discovery to visually spell out target processes in enough detail to make them readily understood. We are interested in understanding the degree to which individual processing steps are manual-intensive or error-prone *and* the time required to perform them in the current state. Therefore, the baseline data we will collect during this phase needs to be enough to allow us to better understand key processes and their manual-intensive pain points, and to diagnose where pockets of opportunity exist that can benefit from deployment of self-service data analytics tools. The control and efficiency opportunities must be evaluated to distill the problem statements to the use cases they represent. Use cases must then be matched with appropriate tools that offer the potential solution for them. Finally, the opportunities can be compared to arrive at a logical and informed order of priority. Just as importantly, project, investment, and risk governance procedures must be followed to protect the value of the growing data analytics portfolio.

Process Map (Swim Lanes)

Starting with the process-level SIPOCs that were created in the last step by middle managers, process owners and the day-to-day operators must be enlisted to perform Map and Measure for each of the in-scope processes. This step is closely related to business process mapping. We will visually illustrate the process, detail how inputs and outputs are consumed at which steps, and track the movement of work products through the workflow to generate final deliverables. The first artifact required is a process flow diagram. More specifically, the format we recommend is the swim lanes process flow diagram, as it can most easily show not only the steps involved but also the handoffs and interactions between stakeholders and functions during the production process.

    Let's demonstrate the use of swim lanes by revisiting the expense submission and reimbursement stream for which a process-level SIPOC was produced. Given that the original process narrative has already been digested to produce the SIPOC, we have a great head start. We need only to translate the SIPOC format to the more visual swim lanes format in several steps. First, ensure all of the suppliers and customers each have their own lane, in the order in which they feature in the SIPOC, moving down the page. In our example, we will label the top lane as Employee (who submits the expense report), followed by Approval Manager in the second lane, the Expense Team in the third lane, and finally the Cash Team in the bottom lane. We have now established lanes for all of the teams and individuals involved in the process. Only those steps performed by those teams or individuals will be added to their respective lanes. Next, pull the Process steps as summarized in the middle column of the SIPOC, and drop them into the flow diagram, moving from left to right across the page in the order they are performed. Remember to add them to the correct lanes, depending on who performs the step. Arrows can be used to indicate the next logical steps in the progression or any feedback loops at decision points such as reviews and approvals.

At this stage, we now have produced the backbone of the swim lanes diagram, but we need to add a bit more color. First, we will clearly highlight the process start and conclusion steps, as they were defined by middle managers and process owners. This formally demarcates the in-scope process from the overall value chain. But given the purpose of our analysis, we want a bit more information to jump off the page. Remember why this exercise is being performed. We are interested in identifying manual work steps that may represent an opportunity to deploy analytics tooling for automation. From our process narrative, there were three steps which seemed to be performed manually: Completeness Checks, Detailed Review Procedures, and Remittance Preparation. It would make our diagram more meaningful if we take the step of highlighting these process steps as focal points for later analysis. We will use "Manual!" boxes to draw attention to process steps where significant manual effort is required. Review the process flow swim lanes diagram presented in Exhibit 7-8 and compare it to the original process-level SIPOC prepared earlier (Exhibit 7-6), to see that this format better conveys details of the process such as which teams and individuals perform which steps, the handoffs between individuals and teams, and even communicates a further dimension of interest – the highly manual processing steps that we may wish to analyze further.

Now we will perform the exercise once more, this time for the time sheet and payroll cycle. Again, we have at hand the neatly organized SIPOC, which was derived from the written process narrative. Again, we list out the suppliers, producers, and customers in their own individual lanes, in the order in which they feature in the SIPOC. As before, we will drop in the Process steps as summarized

EXHIBIT 7-8 Expenses Submission/Reimbursement Swim Lanes Process Map

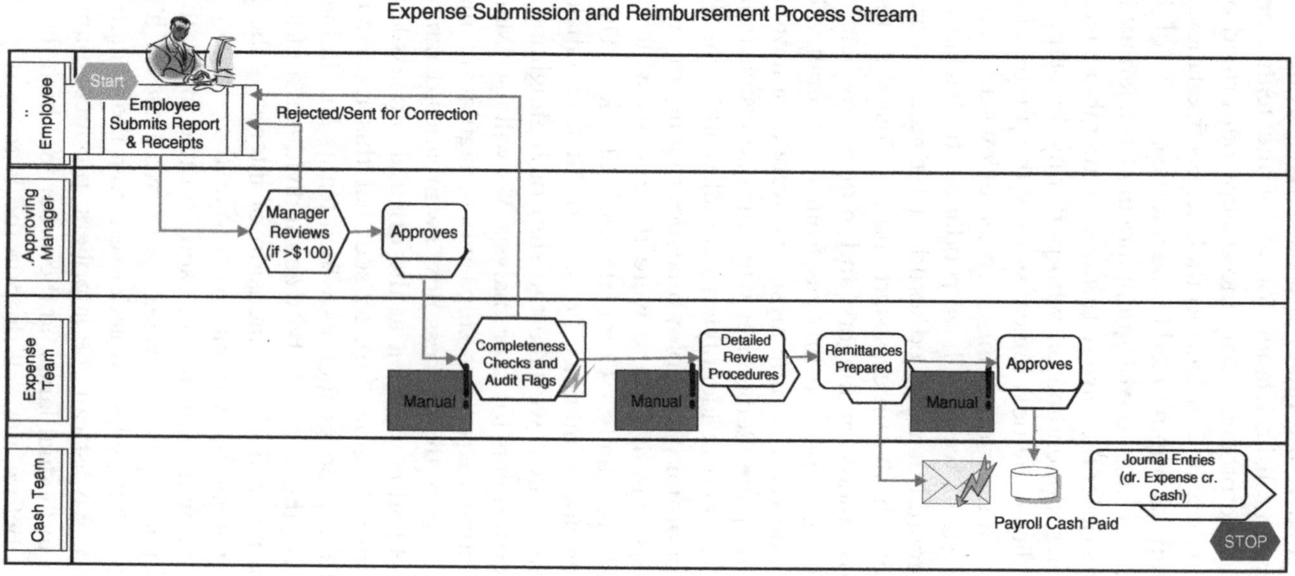

Expense Submission and Reimbursement Process Stream

in the middle column of the SIPOC, moving from left to right across the page. We will clearly highlight the starting point and the conclusion steps in the workflow, and we will use the manual boxes to clearly highlight where significant manual effort is required (and ultimately where in the process flow opportunities to employ self-service data analytics tools are likely to be identified). Again, review the process flow swim lanes diagram in Exhibit 7-9 and compare it to the process-level SIPOC shown in Exhibit 7-7. It should be obvious that we have put some flesh on the bone. Our new frame conveys more detail around the process steps, including who performs them, and which warrant further attention. Hopefully, taking you through the SIPOC and swim lanes process mapping exercises has been useful, and you are beginning to get excited about leveraging both formats, as you turn back to your own organization.

One additional goal we have in performing the comparisons of "like" processes is to ensure they are performed consistently to the extent possible. Enforcing a consistent process model across functions, while ensuring that bespoke variances are minimized, is key to building scale. Where workflow differences are identified, the disparities should be fully reviewed and either normalized and brought into line or the divergence should be well-considered and fully justified. As you review and compare the two functional swim-lane process maps we presented in Exhibits 7-8 and 7-9, do you notice anything inconsistent about the two processes? *Hint: Look at the accounting journal entries performed by the cash teams in the two examples. Now look at the accounting journal entries performed by the expense team and the payroll team.*

By reviewing the process flow in these simple diagrams, one process disparity is easily discernable. You can see that in the expense process, the expense team does not make accounting entries to set up the payable, whereas in the payroll process, the payroll team does in fact make the expense entry. There may be a great reason for this processing deviation, but then again, it may be a historic oversight. The point is, that by visually depicting the "like" processes, it draws the eye very naturally to bespoke divergences that warrant consideration by process owners and middle management alike. In Exhibit 7-10, we will make this process divergence extremely obvious by highlighting the journal entries process steps with a callout box in both diagrams.

EXHIBIT 7-9 Time Sheet Submission/Payroll Swim Lanes Process Map

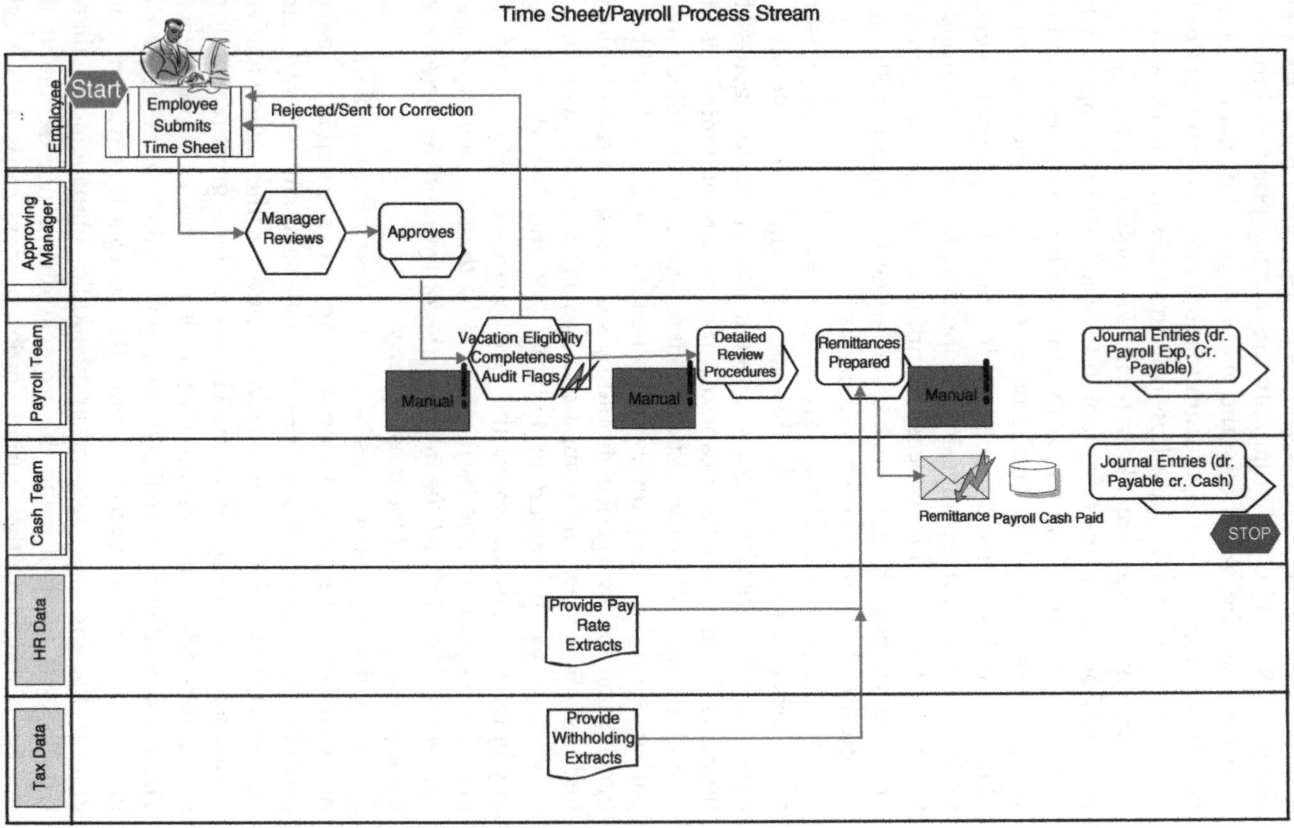

Time Sheet/Payroll Process Stream

EXHIBIT 7-10 Annotated Process Maps – Divergence of "Like" Processes

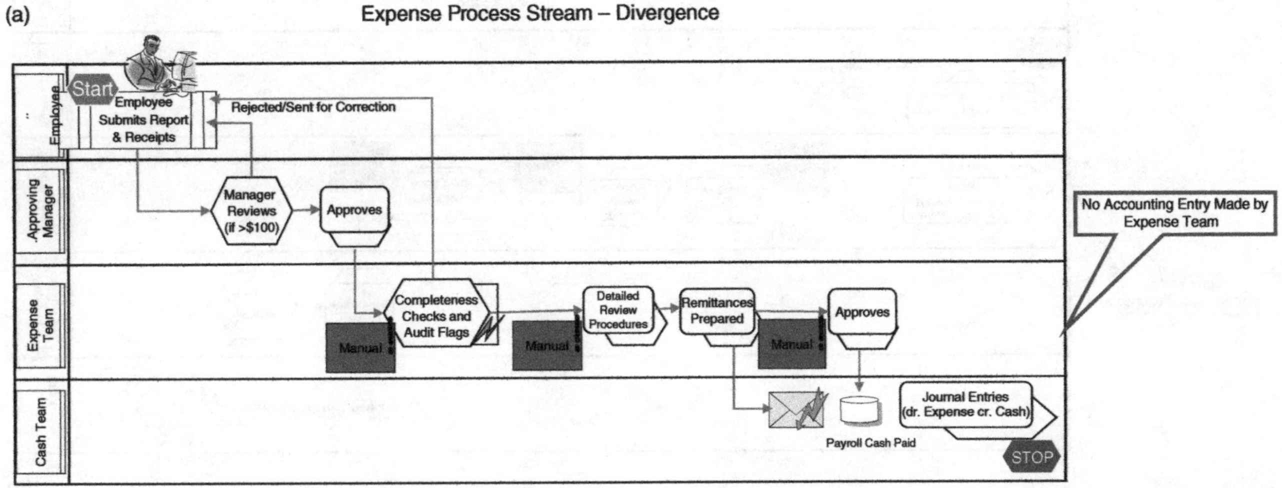

(a)

Expense Process Stream – Divergence

No Accounting Entry Made by Expense Team

(continued)

EXHIBIT 7-10 Annotated Process Maps – Divergence of "Like" Processes *(continued)*

Time Sheet/Payroll Process Stream – Divergence

(b)

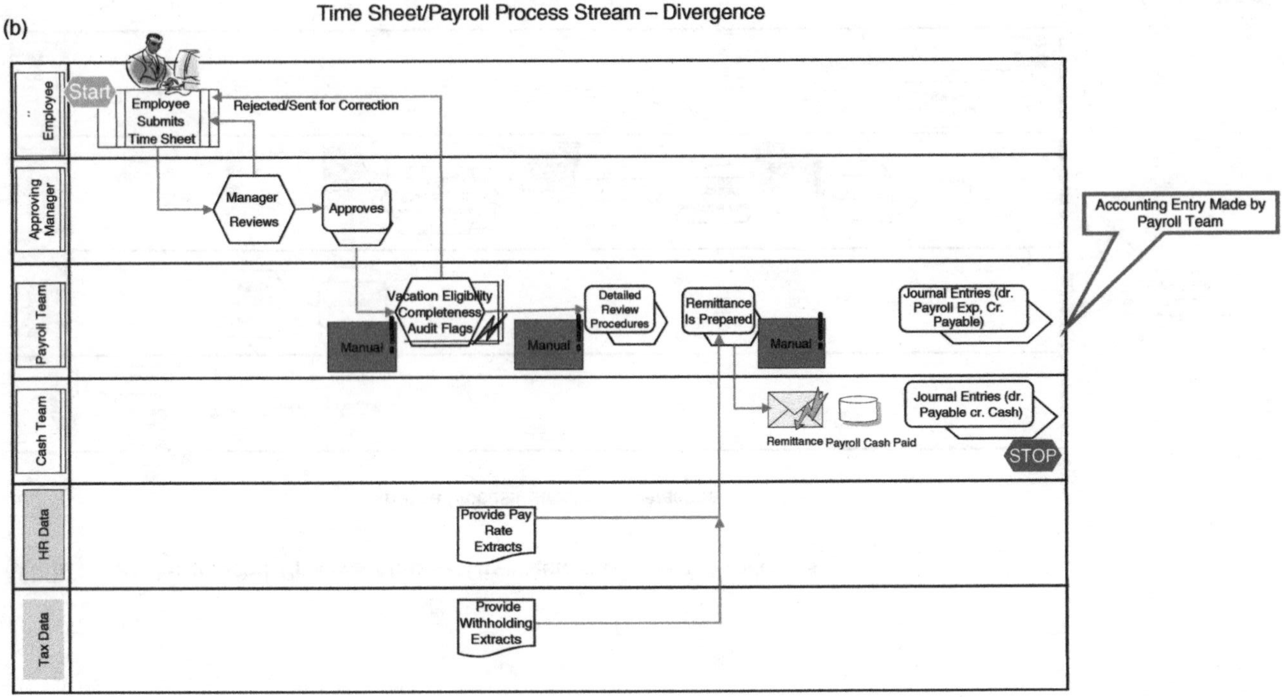

Measure (Elapsed Time)

Now that we have performed the "mapping" portion of our Map and Measure, we can add another layer by overlaying an elapsed timeline onto our SIPOCs. Where we have identified processing steps that are ripe for automation, we need to collect some baseline process time metrics that will allow us to compare opportunities for prioritization, and as well as allow us to retrospectively gauge how we moved the needle post go-live. To this end, we should go back to process owners to gather some baseline process times across the process steps. In the next section, Automated Process Discovery, we will discuss some automated process discovery tools which can capture and log the elapsed time spent in applications, but for purposes of our example, we will capture this by interviewing operators to determine the time spent performing processing steps. In some cases, a more accurate estimate of the time required to complete processing can be gleaned by directly observing operators as they perform processing steps. This is a more objective approach that is less subject to biased perceptions or exaggeration.

The information gathered from the interviews gives us the sense that it takes employees on average 30 minutes to prepare and submit their expense reports. Managers typically spend 15 minutes or less reviewing the reports before the expense team receives the packages. So far, all appears reasonable. The expense team performs their completeness check which takes 10 minutes – *fine, not bad*. However, when the expense team proceeds to manually apply audit filters to flag reports for a detailed review, we see that on average this step takes a full 20 minutes for each expense report!

We drilled in with the process owners to better understand this manual step. We learned that this step involves looking at the historical rejection rate of reports submitted by the employee, to determine if there is any pattern of abuse that would make this submission high risk. All expense reports submitted by employees with a rejection rate of greater than 20% are flagged for a detailed review. Additionally, the company expense policy is relatively strict when it comes to ensuring that the per person expenses are within specified limits. This means that the full list of attendees must be tallied from the report, and meals may not exceed the allotted limits for breakfast

($20/person), lunch ($35/person), or dinner ($75/person). Further, there is a policy rule stipulating that when multiple attendees are at company events, the highest-ranking individual must pick up the tab. This is a control that was implemented to ensure that manager approval is meaningful, objective, and legitimately performed by someone not in attendance at the event. Finally, the reports are reviewed for compliance with a gift limit of $40. This control was put in place to prevent the appearance of bribery. If any of these audit criteria are met, the report is flagged to the high-risk queue for a detail review. We believe this process step represents an opportunity to employ tooling, and therefore we are flagging this step as an opportunity.

Next, we learn that the detailed review process takes 25 minutes on average, if it is performed. However, in speaking with the process owners, we find that only 1% of all expense reports are flagged for the detailed review, and we further learned that the detailed review results in a rejection 95% of the time. This tells us that the process appears effective, and further that discernment and brain power are being used to manage these exceptions. Therefore, given the relatively small number of detailed reviews that are performed, we do not believe there is the same large opportunity to build efficiency with this control step as there is with the audit flag step outlined above.

To finish the process, the expense team prepares a remittance slip, and they approve the reimbursement payment, usually in about 10 minutes, before handing off to the cash team for the final payment and the required accounting journal entries. The timelines in these final steps appear reasonable. We already noted that we will log the process disparity, noted around the fact that the expense team does not make any accounting entries for a later review and normalization.

A simple way to display the timeline is by adding an elapsed timeline column onto our SIPOC adjacent to the processes, as we have done in Exhibit 7-11. Note that we have color coded the measurements to highlight the time-intensive processing steps with orange (to denote some inefficiency) and red (to denote that the processing step should be looked at closely for automation). For the red Audit flag step, we have called out that this step requires 20 minutes of manual effort to draw attention to this opportunity.

EXHIBIT 7-11 Expense Process SIPOC with Elapsed Time and Opportunities

			Expense submission review/approval & reimbursement			
2 FTE, 1 Open Requisition						
Suppliers	**Inputs/Systems**	**Elapsed Time**	**Process**		**Outputs**	**Customers**
Employee Seeking Reimbursement	Blank Expense Form Template	30 Mins	Employee prepares/submits Expense Report (along with receipts for any purchases > $20).		Completed Expense Report Package Submission	Approving Managers or Expense Team
Approving Managers	Completed Expense Form and Required Receipts	45 Mins	If Expense Report total AMT > $100, Manager Approval Required		Manager Approval	Expense Team
Expense Team			Expense team ensures required receipts included and perform completeness check. Audit Flag Filters Applied.		Audit Flag Filters Applied Manually – (~20 Mins)	Expense Team
					Completeness-Validated Packages	
Expense Team	Forms Flagged for Audit Review	75 Mins	Reports flagged for Audit are detail reviewed and returned to employees if rejected or require correction.		Rejected Reports	Employee Seeking Reimbursement
Expense Team	Blank Remittance Slip Template	100 Mins	Expense team prepares remittance slip and approves payment.		Approved Expense Reports	Cash Payments Team
Expense Team	Approved Reports	115 Mins	Cash team receives approved expense reports, makes reimbursement payments & journal entries.		Completed Remittance Slips	Employee Seeking Reimbursement
Cash Team	Completed Remittance Slips	125 Mins	Employees receive payments and remittance slips, any process failures escalated for remediation.		Payments and Payment Accounting Entries	

Processing Goals: To promptly reimburse employees for qualifying expenses incurred for the benefit of the company and produce accounting entries.

Control/Governance Goal: To ensure that company expense policies and procedures are followed.

Quality Constraints: SLA of 24 hours from Employee Submission to Payment Disbursement, Failure/Rework rate <5%.

Now we will perform the same analysis on the time sheet and payroll process to see if we can detect opportunities to streamline processing. We will again gather baseline process time metrics that will allow us to compare opportunities for prioritization. To this end, we turn back to our process owners to gather current state process times across these steps.

The information gathered from the interviews tells us that it takes employees on average 30 minutes to prepare and submit weekly time sheets. Managers spend 15 minutes or less reviewing the reports when overtime is submitted. The payroll team spends 5 minutes determining whether holiday hours submitted are for recognized holidays. If not, they must investigate whether the employee was eligible for leave, based on their remaining leave balance. So far, all appears reasonable. However, we learned that the payroll team manually applies audit filters to highlight time sheets that require a detailed review. We see that this takes a full 10 minutes on average for each time sheet.

We drilled in with the process owners to better understand this manual step and how the filters are applied. We learned that this step involves looking at the historical rejection rates for employees to understand if there is any pattern of abuse that would make this submission high risk. All time sheets submitted by employees with a rejection rate of greater than 20% are flagged for a detailed review. Additionally, for certain departments, policies are in place to specifically prohibit overtime. Therefore, when overtime is submitted, a check is performed to refer to the employee record in an HR system extract to confirm that overtime is allowed in their department. If it is not allowed, there are some circumstances where exceptions may be appropriate, but further documentation is required in such cases. Further, at certain company real estate locations, employees are not allowed on site when the lobby is not staffed with security. Therefore, any hours submitted outside of normal business hours are run against facilities lists to flag those with business hours guidelines. These are scrutinized very closely, and therefore all such cases are flagged for a detailed review. We believe this step represents an opportunity to employ tooling to run these validations more efficiently, and therefore are flagging this as an opportunity.

Next, we learn that the detailed review process takes 15 minutes on average, if it is performed. Just as in the expense reimbursement process, the process owners confirm that only 1% of all time sheet submissions are flagged for the detailed review. When the detail review is performed, it is not done needlessly, as they result in a 92% rejection rate. This review process control appears to operate effectively, and the step warrants discernment and brain power. Therefore, given the relatively small number of detailed reviews that are performed, we do not believe this step represents a significant opportunity to build efficiency.

However, for approved time sheets that can move on to be fully processed for the payroll, a significant manual process exists which takes a staggering 30 minutes per employee. The payroll team must manually look up pay rates that have been transmitted from the HR system. They must likewise look up the tax withholding amounts, which are transmitted from the tax department. Both of these inputs are required in order to allow for the system to calculate the amounts due to the employee for the current pay cycle. We believe that this step is laden with opportunity to build efficiency with data analytics tooling. Accordingly, we call this out on the SIPOC. Once the payable amounts are calculated, the payroll team prepares remittance slips, then posts the accounting journal entries to debit payroll expense and to credit the payable liability before sending the remittance slips and approvals to the cash team for payment.

The cash team receives the approvals and remittance slips and funds the payroll by moving cash to satisfy the amounts owed to employees. Once complete, they likewise post an accounting entry to reduce the payable liability with a debit versus a credit to cash. This completes the payroll cycle. Refer to Exhibit 7-12 to see the added elapsed time column, as well as the callouts of the manual pain points embedded in the process.

We have now completed our somewhat limited process discovery exercises, leaning heavily on process narratives, swim lanes diagrams to visually depict and compare "like" processes, and on the SIPOC as a tool to summarize inputs, process steps, and outputs, along with key stakeholders. We emphasize again the vast number of tools that can be used to frame functions and processes. There are just as many tools, tricks, and best practices for measurement and analysis, but it was important to demonstrate a clear, quick and dirty way to surface opportunities. While in our example, we examined a

EXHIBIT 7-12 Time Sheet/Payroll SIPOC with Elapsed Time and Opportunities

2 FTE

Time Sheet submission review/approval & Payroll Cycle

Suppliers	Inputs/Systems	Elapsed Time	Process	Outputs	Customers
Employee	Weekly Time Card Blank Time Sheet Report Template		Employee prepares/submits Weekly Time Sheet Report	Completed Expense Report Package Submission	Approving Managers Payroll Team
		30 Mins			
Approving Managers	Completed and Approved Report		If Time Sheet Contains Overtime Weekly Total Hours > 40, Manager Approval Required	Manager Approval — Audit Flag Filters Applied Manually — (~10 Mins)	Approving Managers
		45 Mins			
Payroll Team	Reports Flagged for Audit Review		Payroll team confirms holidays listed are on approved list, ensures vacation day eligibility. Audit Flag Filters Applied.	Validated Reports (with audit flag or without)	Payroll Team
		60 Mins			
Payroll Team	Audited Time Sheet Reports		Time Sheets flagged for Audit are detail reviewed and returned to employees if correction required.	Rejected Time Sheet Reports or Validated Reports	Employee Seeking Reimbursement
		75 Mins		Approved Time — Pay Rates/Withholding Applied Manually — (~20 Mins)	
Human Resources Tax Department	Corrected/Validated Reports, HR Pay Rate Data/Tax Withholding Data		Payroll team prepares remittances, approves payroll disbursement, makes Journal Entries (dr. payroll exp. cr. Payable).	Approved Time Sheets/Remittance Slips and Accounting Journals	Cash Payments Team
		105 Mins			
Payroll Team	Completed Payroll/ Remittance Slips		Cash team receives approved payroll slips. Makes payroll disbursements/journal entries (dr: payable, cr. Cash).	Completed Payroll Disbursements and Accounting Journals	Employees are fully paid.
		115 Mins			
Cash Team			Employees receive Friday payroll disbursements, following holiday calendar. Any failures escalated for remediation.		

Processing Goals: To perform timely payroll cycle in accordance with applicable labor laws and to generate proper accounting journal entries.

Control/Governance Goal: To ensure that company payroll, holiday, and overtime policies and procedures are followed.

Quality Constraints: Payroll disbursements must be fair and accurate, Failure/Rework rate <.01%.

single function and mapped only two discrete processes, imagine that the scope of discovery was widened to survey *all* processes across *all* functions and departments in the company. Chances are high that there would be the makings for a rich and promising backlog that could keep Adam Goodman wearing his thin tie for months. Being mindful that any process efficiency realized across functions can lead to increased margins, we can see that an ambitious effort to uplift, structure, and automate manual-intensive processes could have a highly material impact on the expense base in medium- to large-scale organizations.

Automated Process Discovery

The process discovery exercise demonstrated in this chapter was effective for our stated goal, which was to uncover pockets of high-touch processing activities that represent manual pain points, where we believe we can employ data analytics tooling to capture efficiency and to increase control. However, our information was largely gathered through interviews with those who own or perform the processes. This can be effective, for sure, but there are also limitations to this approach.

A first limitation is that you are relying largely on anecdotal evidence to uncover manual processing steps. What some individuals or even departments consider to be extremely painful may be taken as a matter of course by others or in other areas. Some operators may set a high bar on their expectations of system functionality, whereas others may have operated in a largely manual environment for most or all of their careers. Due to the amount of influence some process owners enjoy, they may be more successful in attracting focus and resources on their individual pain. We have all encountered these personalities (*reader in the blue shirt, we are looking at you. . .*). When surveying a large organization for pockets of opportunity, it can sometimes be the loudest voice that propels it to the top of the priority list, not necessarily the most inefficient process that offers the best control or efficiency gains to the organization. Instead, we propose that the best use of available resources "gets the oil," rather than the "squeakiest wheel."

A second limitation is that you are relying on individuals to volunteer pain points, when there are sometimes motivations to keep these under the radar. For instance, from our expense and payroll discovery exercise, let's imagine that the four individuals are over-stretched with the current manual processes. To get the job done, they have themselves been claiming significant overtime pay. Might they be at least slightly reticent to streamline the manual process, if it results in cutting their time-and-a-half pay above 40 hours? As another example, in today's cost-conscious environment where head-count costs are under continued scrutiny, imagine that in some dark corridor in the processing plant, there is a mid-chain function which performs *only* the manual portion of a value chain, before handing over to another function who turn their unpolished inputs into a more shiny and valued output. The tendency may be to deem the entire mid-stream function to be low value-added and ripe for auto-mation and ultimate elimination. In such cases, it is no surprise that the entire department is not forming a stampede line to get some long-needed attention on their low-efficiency processing steps. You get the point.

In certain environments, a more data-driven approach would certainly be more objective and fruitful than relying on vocal and proactive stakeholders to step forward with great ideas. What if we could use software that could track time in applications, and capture mouse clicks and system actions in event logs? Process mining software can perform many of the steps we performed together in the preceding sections, when it comes to the bottom-up Map and Measure portion of process discovery.

Process mining software captures actions and events which occur over a discovery period at the system level or the cross-enterprise technology stack level and analyzes this data with algorithms that can detect slow, high-touch, or manual-intensive work steps. In some cases, automated process discovery tools even allow the tracing of user-level actions, following their processing steps over time. When this analysis is combined with process narratives from process own-ers and operators, it can be used to generate detailed process maps, and even heatmaps to highlight operations that may be a good fit for automation with data analytics tooling like RPA. These flagged hot-spots of manual activity can be a great place to focus a more detailed process discovery where further information is required. Opportunities can then be captured, compared, and evaluated on a number of dimensions to establish a logical order or priority of attack based on control metrics, efficiency metrics, or investment metrics like ROI. Currently, a number of tools are available to track key strokes across applications in the performance of processes, to capture transaction metrics, and even importantly to categorize such processes by complexity, to highlight those that may offer solid use cases for automation. Today, consulting firms have combined their suit of automated process mining software with their significant engagement management expertise into a bundled process discovery product offering and are actively marketing to medium- to large-scale organizations. Additional services and outputs on offer include Visio and BPMN process map preparation, the generation of SOPs, and the performance of time and motion studies. Common process discovery and process mapping tools in use today include Signavio, iGrafx, K2, Promapp, and Kissflow.

There are great benefits to the automated process discovery approach as well as limitations that must be managed. Starting with the benefits, these tools and service bundles can greatly accelerate the timeline by which you can survey the organization for processing inefficiencies. The approach can also be cost effective when the production slowdown caused by the manual discovery steps is avoided. Further, by analyzing large amounts of observational data embedded in system event records, the software can sometimes glean insights that business analysts alone may miss.

However, there are clear limitations as well. The first is that no matter how sophisticated the software, it is meaningless without the spine of SME knowledge putting the analysis results into perspective. You are still reliant on process owners and operators to fill in the knowledge gaps, but to a lesser extent than if they are the source of all details regarding process steps, time estimates, and pain points. Further, one dimension that automated process discovery software does not consider is the required level of personal interactions, the level of customer service being performed, or the exact circumstances surrounding the discovery observation that may impact the measures being captured. The software will not know that the process was slowed to ensure white-glove service for a flagship client, as the observations are captured. Nor will it know that the process observation occurred on a day where volumes were down and performance substandard, due to the fact that the observation occurred the Monday after Super Bowl night, and the process was exceedingly. . . sloooow.

Irrespective, this tooling can be extremely useful to building a rapid understanding of how users interact with systems across the enterprise in the performance of their roles. For organizations that do not have a strong understanding of where to start, it can help with objective transparency by eliminating the hidden human biases and motivations that we considered at the top of this section. Importantly, it can help organizations create an achievable automation plan.

Conclusion

We have covered a lot of ground in this chapter. We began by taking stock of the organization's strengths and weaknesses internally, as well as the opportunities and threats that are emerging at this point in time externally. We also analyzed the elements that Porter believes best describe the competitive landscape. Finally, we introduced Porter's Value chain as an artifact that can prompt executives to articulate key (primary) functions and the supporting functions which contribute to making them successful, and which reminds us that *any* process improvements can lead to increased margins. These artifacts, taken together, can spark thinking by proactive executives and help them to forge a strategy to move the organization forward by setting clear and actionable objectives.

We next fleshed out the Time and Expense function, leaning heavily on the SIPOC as a visual tool to summarize inputs, process steps and outputs, and key stakeholders. Drilling down a level, we used the same tool to spell out two target processes, at least in enough detail to allow for the identification of manual processing steps that are likely to represent opportunities to employ tactical data analytics tooling. The result of our efforts was that we did in fact uncover several manual-intensive processing steps that could benefit from Alteryx or other self-service tooling. Finally, we introduced automated process discovery as a product bundle that can help organizations jump-start their automation journey.

We emphasized throughout that we were choosing to highlight only a small selection of the vast number of tools and formats that can be used to frame functions and processes. We can attest to there being just as many tricks and best practices for measurement and analysis, depending on the questions posed. However, we felt it was important to demonstrate a clear, quick-and-dirty means to surface opportunities. While this may have provided some useful discovery steps to take back to your respective organizations, we are not quite done. So far, we have only uncovered some problematic manual steps that we believe could *perhaps* benefit from data analytics tooling. We have more work to do to capture the opportunities in an opportunity matrix and lay the groundwork for the heatmap that can effectively highlight where inefficiencies live. We will also need to match use cases to tooling, before sizing up the build effort and benefits to arrive at a logical priority sequence. In Chapter 8, we will pick up where this process discovery leaves off, to illustrate the steps involved in grooming discovered opportunities into a tidy backlog, and to bubble up the best opportunities to the top of the list, in priority order.

Notes

1. Michael E. Porter, 1979. "How Competitive Forces Shape Strategy," Harvard Business Review (Vol. 57, No. 2), pp. 137–145.
2. Michael E. Porter, 1985. "Competitive Advantage: Creating and Sustaining Superior Performance," New York: Free Press, p. 37. Unchanged. Link to License: https://creativecommons.org/licenses/by-sa/3.0/deed.en.

CHAPTER 8

Opportunity Capture and Heatmaps

As alluded to in the previous chapter, simply being aware of some number of inefficient processes and several problem statements across the organization is not what we consider to be a well-groomed, investment-controlled, prioritized, and actionable backlog. However, the work we performed together in Chapter 7 has uncovered some diamonds in the rough. Given we have captured some baseline process time data, if we estimate the residual tail post-implementation, we have the data points we need to articulate a benefits case for each opportunity highlighted during process discovery.

In this chapter, we will capture the problem statements and opportunities that were surfaced during discovery and logically build data-driven business cases for them. Next, we will demonstrate how to extract the key capabilities required of viable solutions (use cases) before matching solutions to these opportunities. Once the opportunities have been sized for the expected effort required to solution them, and with benefits cases fully developed, we can objectively evaluate the items in the listing against project acceptance criteria, organizational objectives and constraints, and against each other – to determine an order of priority. The final prioritized backlog can be shown in an automation heatmap format to visually communicate the viable opportunities and the various dimensions considered for project selection through the judicious use of red, amber, or green (RAG) ratings. *Ceteris Paribus*, we would give primacy to solutions that redress a high degree of manual pain, that represent minimum complexity such that we have a high confidence of success, and that require only minimal time and effort to deliver. *Start with the golden unicorns.*

To conclude the chapter, we will introduce two concepts that will be useful to industrializing self-service data analytics as a growth area in your organization. The adoption of workflow tooling for the self-service portfolio can hasten the organization-wide process discovery effort, by empowering process owners across the landscape to identify and self-report opportunities. By structuring the change management workflows in a tool, we can be assured that control and governance objectives are met (as highlighted in Chapters 4 and 5). Finally, we will introduce the use case library as a tool to log and broadly communicate key details of the innovations made across the organization. As success grows, it can be referred to by process owners across the landscape to spark their thinking, such that replication opportunities are swiftly identified and innovations can be built upon and additively enhanced.

Opportunity Inventory Matrix

We used the detailed process discovery steps in Chapter 7 much as a geologist might use ground-penetrating radar to survey a vast tract of land for irregularities, to hone in on underground features for further study. EUREKA! The needle is going crazy. We have found some features of interest. However, until they are down on paper (is that still a thing?), you cannot commence the further study. As opportunities are identified, we will first capture them in an Opportunity Inventory Matrix, so that we can gather the detail required to understand the use cases and how to solve for them, the relative sizing and benefits of any remediation work, and the logical order of attack for the issues raised. In the following sections, we will distill the opportunities identified in the process discovery exercise from Chapter 7 to build a concrete Opportunity Inventory, which may yield the first trickle of viable opportunities for our groomed backlog. The goal is to build a pipeline of valid and feasible opportunities to pull from as our self-service capabilities grow and mature.

Capturing Problem Statements

Let's begin by capturing the problem statements we uncovered in our elapsed time-annotated SIPOCs above (see Exhibits 7-11 and 7-12), in a simple Opportunity Inventory. This involves five steps. The first is assigning a process identifier (Process ID). Best practice is to use a two-part code consisting of a readily identifiable department or function code, with an added unique integer, as many opportunities can exist with the same function (you will thank us later for reminding you to do this, when the list grows from a few items to a few thousand). Next, assign the opportunity a short name in five words or less (Process Name). Then, looking at the callouts in the exhibits, summarize the problem statement in a single sentence (Problem Statement). Next, iterate the process steps that are performed manually, being careful to spell out each step specifically (Process Steps), rather than lumping them together. This will be important information as we move to the fifth step, which is to submit a technology request to your core tech teams for the required enhancements and functionality. Always remember that any tactical data analytics builds should be considered a stopgap measure with a limited shelf life, until the strategic solution can be delivered behind it.

Review Exhibit 8-1 to see the beginnings of an Opportunity Inventory taking shape. We have a 3×4 matrix that allows us to easily capture and refer to opportunities. The Process Steps column has allowed us to flesh out some requirements that we used to log three separate core technology enhancement requests. *Do we have a tactical tool that can help with these?*

Uncovering Use Cases

We have neatly begun with an Opportunity Inventory Matrix, which is the first step in capturing our backlog. However, in reading the process steps, we need to distill these a bit further to understand the use cases, so that we know which tool to pull out from our time-worn medical bag of data analytics technologies (old-school, we know). In reviewing the first Time Sheet process, we see that we need to enrich a record with a historic Time Sheet rejection rate from

EXHIBIT 8-1 Opportunity Inventory Matrix

Process ID	Process Name	Problem Statement	Process Steps
TE0001	Payroll Process Audit Flags	Audit flag filters are performed manually, adding 10 minutes per employee to cycle time	Review submitter for historical Time Sheet rejection rates. If >20% then High Risk – flag for review. If overtime is claimed, check HR system extract to confirm employee's department allows overtime (or for exception approval). Check real estate site for hours restrictions policies. Determine if hours claimed are outside of policy.
TE0002	Payroll Process Payroll Calculation	Lookups for Pay Rates and withholding rates performed manually, adding 15 minutes per employee to cycle time	Enrich Remittance Slip by lookup of pay rates HR system and tax withholding from Tax department to calculate pay.
TE0003	Expense Process Audit Flags	Audit flag filters are performed manually, adding 20 minutes per employee to cycle time	Review submitter for historical Expense Report rejection rates. If >20% then High Risk – flag for review. Check that meal expenses are within limits: breakfast ($20/person), lunch ($35/person), dinner ($75/person). Where submissions refer to multiple attendees, identify highest-ranking individual in HR system to ensure it is the submitter. If gift code selected, claim code may not exceed $40.

the HR file, based on an employee name or identifier. We then need to compare the historic rejection rate to value ranges to understand the risk profile assigned to this particular Time Sheet. This is a join and enrichment activity. Fine, but what other processing steps are contained in this demand item? If overtime is claimed, we need to perform an additional check against the HR file that allows us to determine if the employee's department-specific policies allow for overtime. If yes, great, but if not, we will need to look for an exception approval or flag this Time Sheet for a detailed review. This is also a join and enrichment activity. Finally, we need to perform a third join against the HR file to obtain the employees' real estate locations to understand if the hours are restricted in their locales. If so, we need to compare the claimed hours versus the policy hours to understand if there is an outer join or exception. The use case here can also be classified as a join and enrich. Finally, if any of these factors result in a violation, the individual Time Sheet must be flagged for a thorough and detailed review. We have now extracted the use cases - the simple capabilities required for the needed solution.

In reviewing the second Time Sheet process opportunity (TE0002), we see that to prepare the remittance slip, we need to enrich the record with pay rates from HR file, based on an employee name or identifier. We then need to perform another join and enrichment to pull the withholding rates from the tax department data file. This is a very similar functionality to what was required for the first solution (TE0001), except that we have a final step which is some multiplication to derive the pay amount, based on the rates that have been captured. Therefore, we need the capability to do some simple math. Let's perform a similar exercise for the final opportunity to see if there is any additional functionality required.

In reviewing the third Expense Reimbursement process opportunity (TE0003), we see that to prepare the remittance slip, we need to enrich the record with a historic Expense Report rejection rate from the HR file, based on an employee name or identifier. We then need to compare the historic rejection rate to value ranges to understand the risk profile that is assigned to this particular Expense Report. This is a join and enrichment activity. The next step is to compare individual meal claims versus the policy limits. This is a join, enrich, compare, and flag use case. We then need to perform another join and enrichment from the HR file to understand who of the attendees at the corporate event is the highest ranking by corporate title. That highest-ranking individual and the individual claiming the expense must be one and the same. This is a join and enrichment activity as well. Finally, any claims coded as gifts must be compared against the gift policy limit of $40. This is also a join and enrichment activity. Taken in total, we now understand the functionality required to solution the use case.

Review Exhibit 8-2 to see what has been added to our Opportunity Inventory. We have hidden several columns to fit the exhibit neatly on the page. But you can see that we have added the Strategic Core Tech Request column to capture the references that correspond to the strategic enhancement request we have raised for the additional functionality. Again, this is an important control point to ensure that tactical solutions have a limited shelf life and are in place only until the strategic systems fill the gap in our wake. From the Process Steps column, you will see that we have added the Use Case Functionality, where we have noted the distilled functionality, as captured above.

Solutioning

Before we dig into solutioning, remember that the work at your company is performed by employees with varying degrees of technical, subject matter, and even spreadsheet proficiency. Of course, we need to be careful to consider how to best employ them to their fullest potential, but just because they deem a process to be painful, and claim that it warrants automation, does not make it so – but it could mean that. Perhaps there is a training gap. Maybe there is a skills gap. Perhaps we do not have the right employee in the seat. There are many ways to move the needle on key performance indicators (KPIs) like processing time, process quality, process fails, and the amount of rework. We must be careful not to become fixated on our automation tools, and we must be open to considering any number of ways to attack a problem, as we endeavor to match solutions to problem statements.

That brings us to the Tactical Tooling column, where we have identified that Alteryx could perform each of the required steps. We say again that there are a large number of off-the-shelf vendor

EXHIBIT 8-2 Matching Tools to Use Cases

Process ID	Process Steps	Strategic Core Tech Request Reference	Use Case Funtionality	Tactical Tooling
TE0001	Review submitter for historical Time Sheet rejection rates. If >20% then High Risk – flag for review. If overtime is claimed, check HR system extract to confirm employee's department allows overtime (or for exception approval). Check real estate site for hours restrictions policies. Determine if hours claimed are outside of policy.	JIRA TE-76492	Join & Enrich, Flag	Alteryx
TE0002	Enrich Remittance Slip by lookup of pay rates HR system and tax withholding from Tax department to calculate pay.	JIRA PR-76496	Join & Enrich, Simple Math, Flag	Alteryx
TE0003	Review submitter for historical Expense Report rejection rates. If >20% then High Risk – flag for review. Check that meal expenses are within limits: breakfast ($20/person), lunch ($35/person), dinner ($75/person). Where submissions refer to multiple attendees, identify highest-ranking individual in HR system to ensure it is the submitter. If gift code selected, claim code may not exceed $40.	JIRA EP-77109	Join & Enrich, Simple Math, Flag	Alteryx

applications from which to choose. The solution you elect will be partially dependent on the vendor management decisions your company has made and the ongoing relationships that may have been built. However, we have gone through the steps systematically to understand the required functionality and feel confident that we have selected the appropriate tool for what amounts to only an abbreviated list of needs. If we imagine the lengthy list of opportunities that we would be faced with, had the bottom-up process discovery exercise been carried out more broadly across the organization, we might see use cases where repetitive data entry is required, which may make the use case a better match for Robotic Process Automation (RPA). We might see the need to analyze enormous datasets, to classify data points, and propose an action, as would be appropriate for machine learning (ML), or we may encounter a need to glean meaning from vernacular in order to further perform operations or process steps, which may be best addressed through natural language processing (NLP). If the problem statement or use case relates to flexible visualization or reporting, we would have unzipped the dashboarding section of our medical trunk to pull out Tableau or QlikView, for example. However, as you saw in Chapter 6, Alteryx is quite well suited for the use cases we have uncovered, in consideration of the process complexity, the repetitive nature of the actions, the specific analysis steps required, and the ultimate actions being performed.

Given our small sample, we are lucky indeed that a single tool can help us to drive operational efficiency and increase control. Let's say it is determined that for all three of these opportunities, an Alteryx build is deemed to be in line with the functional or departmental objectives, and we have the relationship and licenses in place to employ this tool to meet these demands. We are ready to roll up our sleeves to get down to business. But wait! Which opportunity do we tackle first? Are they all a "go"? We do not know which of the projects meet our project acceptance criteria, based on the benefits they offer. To answer these questions logically, we need to capture a bit more information to inform the decision. Let's return to our opportunity matrix and add some of the limited quantitative details we captured during discovery.

Benefits Cases

The primary currency of processing functions today is time savings and increased process stability. Opportunities to build efficiency and to reduce the manual tail performed outside of systems are those that will rise to the top of the prioritization queue. For each of the three opportunities captured from Chapter 7, we have some basic information that will allow us to build a benefits case. Let's take a closer look at each in turn to see what we can glean as potential benefits.

For TE0001, we said that manually applying the payroll audit flag filters is a manual process which takes 10 minutes to complete. The first step is to convert this value to the common denominator we will use universally to measure time savings. In our case, we will use hours. Therefore, the baseline process time is .17 hours (10 minutes). We will also assume that post-implementation, we will still have a small residual tail. Usually, this is the time it will take to initialize the workflow. Let's assume that the operator will spend one minute (or 0.02 hours) running the Alteryx workflow, if it is ultimately prioritized and built. Let's capture this residual manual tail in our opportunity matrix to detail out the benefits. When we subtract the residual processing time from the baseline processing time, we can derive the direct benefits case for our build. In this case, it is calculated as follows: .17 hours less .02 hours = 0.15 hours. Building this Alteryx workflow has the potential to build .15 hours of efficiency in the day for each Time Sheet that is processed. In terms of pain assessment, going back to our narratives, we believe that this task overall can be deemed to represent a "medium" level of pain.

For TE0002, we said that performing the payroll manual calculation from HR pay rates and Tax Withholding rates is a manual process which takes 15 minutes to complete. Here, the baseline process time is .25 hours (15 minutes). Again, we will assume that post-implementation, we will still have a small residual tail. Let's assume that the operator will spend 90 seconds (or 0.03 hours) running the Alteryx workflow, if it is ultimately prioritized and built. Let's capture both the baseline process time as well as the residual manual tail in our opportunity matrix. When we subtract the residual processing time from the baseline processing time, we can derive the direct benefits case for our build. In this case, it is calculated as follows: .25 hours less .03 hours = 0.22 hours. Building this Alteryx workflow has the potential to build 0.22 hours of efficiency in the day for each Time Sheet that is processed. In terms of pain assessment, again going back to our narratives, we believe that similar to TE0001, this task can be deemed to represent a "medium" level of pain.

Next, we will analyze the third opportunity. For TE0003, we said that to manually apply the Expense Report audit flag filters is a manual process which takes 20 minutes to complete. Here, the baseline process time is .33 hours (20 minutes). Again, we will assume that post-implementation, we will still have a small residual tail. Let's assume that the operator will spend 1 minute (or .02 hours) running the Alteryx workflow, if it is ultimately prioritized and built. Let's capture both the baseline process time as well as the residual manual tail in our Opportunity Matrix. When we subtract the residual processing time from the baseline processing time, we can derive the direct benefits case for our build. In this case, it is calculated as follows: .33 hours less .02 hours = .31 hours. Building this Alteryx workflow has the potential to build .31 hours of efficiency in the day for each Time Sheet that is processed. In terms of pain assessment, we believe that this task represents a more significant level of pain to the Payroll Team and therefore can be deemed to represent a "high" level of pain.

Taken together, we now have a view of the relative benefits of each opportunity, respectively. Review Exhibit 8-3 to see the benefits that have been added to each line in our Opportunity Inventory. If we were to get started today on a single one of the opportunities, our eye might scan the page and fall upon TE0003, which appears to offer the greatest benefit.

However, we still may not have the full picture. The reason is that we have not yet considered the number of times per month that each process is performed, here and elsewhere. By adding cycle metrics, we derive the full efficiency that can be gained by taking them forward.

For TE0001, we know that the Time Sheet submission and approval process is completed each week in our example enterprise. We also know that there are 100 employees. Therefore, if we assume that each employee must submit their Time Sheet, and that there are four weeks during the month, we can use a multiplier of 400 (4 × 100). This

EXHIBIT 8-3 Building Benefits Cases

Process ID	Process Name	Problem Statement	Use Cases Funtionality	Tactical Tooling	Baseline Process Time	Residual Process Time (Post-Implementation)	Hours Saved per Month
TE0001	Payroll Process Audit Flags	Audit flag filters are performed manually, adding 10 minutes per employee to cycle time	Join & Enrich, Flag	Alteryx	.17 hours	.02 hours	.15 hours
TE0002	Payroll Process Payroll Calculation	Lookups for pay rates and withholding rates performed manually, adding 15 minutes per employee to cycle time	Join & Enrich, Simple Math, Flag	Alteryx	0.25 hours	.03 hours	.22 hours
TE0003	Expense Process Audit Flags	Audit flag filters are performed manually, adding 20 minutes per employee to cycle time	Join & Enrich, Simple Math, Flag	Alteryx	.33 hours	.02 hours	.31 hours

means that the monthly savings is not .15 hours, but a full 60 hours of efficiency that can be gained through automating this process.

TE0002 was also an opportunity that was identified for the payroll and Time Sheet submission and approval process. Like TE0001, it is completed each week for the 100 employees. Therefore, we can again use the multiplier of 400 (4 × 100). This means that the monthly savings is not .22 hours, but a full 88 hours of efficiency that can be gained through automating this process.

TE0003 was an opportunity identified from the Expense process, rather than Time Sheet submission and approval process. We said that on average, each employee submits one Expense Report per month. Therefore, if there are 100 employees at the company, we can use a multiplier of 100. This means that the monthly savings is not .31 hours, but a full 31 hours of efficiency that can be gained through automating this process.

Notice that before the cycle metrics were considered, we were intent to begin work on TE0003, which offered a greater benefit at .31 hours than did TE0002, which offered a slightly smaller benefit of .22 hours. However, when we consider the number of times the process is performed each month, TE0002 offers a far more significant efficiency benefit. Further, notice that once the cycle metrics are taken into consideration, these three opportunities total 179 hours of benefit. That equates to roughly one FTE (full-time employee) worth of effort, if we consider the 45-hour work week as normal, and we assume that on average there are four weeks in a month.

Remember that the function was stretched and had recently requested a requisition to add an employee to the function (refer to the top-left corner of Exhibit 7-6). Through the identification of three use cases to employ self-service data analytics capabilities, we may build enough efficiency to forego the hiring of an additional resource for the team. Therefore, the savings of these three builds can be directly quantified by the total cost to the organization of hiring, compensating, providing real estate and workspace, and providing benefits to an additional employee. This efficiency metric is referred to as "headcount avoidance" and can readily be expressed in dollars. Later in the chapter, in the section Multiplier Effect of Replication Opportunities on Project Benefits Case, we will discuss an additional benefits multiplier that can be considered for projects that have widespread replication opportunities across the organization. For now, we have been able lay out the benefits cases for each of our three opportunities and to express them in a common term for ready comparison – hours saved per month. Attaching a dollar value to a project can be persuasive to stakeholders and sponsors, so it may be worth translating hours saved into fractions of the average employee dollar cost, depending on organizational culture and quasi-normative preferences. See Exhibit 8-4 for the additional benefits case information we have captured in this exercise.

Sizing Build Efforts

We have derived one side of the equation, the benefits cases for each of the opportunities. However, as we know, automation builds are not free; rather, they represent an investment in time and money, and they often represent an opportunity cost. Subject matter experts (SMEs) are diverted from their core functions, and once project development resources are deployed, they have reduced ability to take up the next project in the queue. Accordingly, we need to consider these costs which can offset the benefits cases we derived in the previous section.

Different solutions have different types of costs associated with them. In Chapter 7, our CFO elected to purchase a core technology system-based solution from Consulting Solutions LLP at a cost of $50,000. In Chapter 2, we discussed that cloud-based artificial intelligence solutions can come with a monthly subscription fee, with add-ons based on the modules and functionality elected by the consumers. Here, we are considering the deployment of Alteryx to solution our opportunities. Alteryx, like many off-the-shelf data analytics tools, requires an investment in the cost of acquiring software licenses, whether individual or enterprise-wide. However, for our purposes, we will assume that our company has already purchased the licenses, and there are no incremental software costs attributable to each build. Taking licensing out of the equation, the obvious costs that are of interest to us are the required investments in time and resources for the development of each solution.

We are considering Alteryx as a self-service tool, meaning that process owners themselves, rather than dedicated technology teams, are equipped with data analytics tools and can avail themselves of

EXHIBIT 8-4 Benefits Cases with Cycle Metrics Multiplier

Process ID	Process Name	Problem Statement	Tactical Tooling	Baseline Process Time	Residual Process Time (Post-Implementation)	Hours Saved per Month	Cycle Metrics/ Replication Opportunities?	Total Opportunity (Hours Saved per Month)
TE0001	Payroll Process Audit Flags	Audit flag filters are performed manually, adding 10 minutes per employee to cycle time	Alteryx	.17 hours	.02 hours	.15 hours	400 = 100 employees × 4 weekly Time Sheet cycles per month	60 hours
TE0002	Payroll Process Payroll Calculation	Lookups for pay rates and withholding rates performed manually, adding 15 minutes per employee to cycle time	Alteryx	.25 hours	.03 hours	.22 hours	400 = 100 employees × 4 weekly Time Sheet cycles per month	88 hours
TE0003	Expense Process Audit Flags	Audit flag filters are performed manually, adding 20 minutes per employee to cycle time	Alteryx	.33 hours	.02 hours	.31 hours	100 = 100 employees on average submit 1 expense report per month	31 hours
								179 hours

the functionality on offer to make their processes more robust, efficient, and scalable. This eliminates the need to perform a detailed costing of each of these builds, as there is no explicit cost associated with process owners and operators taking the initiative, other than the opportunity costs named above. However, as a matter of completeness and to illustrate the sizing process, we will progress with a high-level sizing estimate.

To simplify the illustration, we will make certain assumptions that will allow us to complete the sizing with ease. First, we will assume that all individuals developing the workflow earn an average hourly rate of $51. Next, we will assume that a single process owner or operator can develop, test, and implement the solution without the input of any other team member. Further, we will assume that all of the project governance steps, as introduced in Chapter 4, can be performed by the same resource. Therefore, we will round up to assign development days in full day increments to cover some of the overhead associated with sound governance.

Now that we have detailed our sizing assumptions, let's review the process steps for each build in turn to give us a sense of the development effort required. We realize that, absent workflow development experience with Alteryx, this will be difficult to do. However, by reviewing the number of process steps and their complexity, we should be able to identify builds which will require more work than others. In contrast to large-scale systems development efforts, where a lot hinges on delivering on time and within the allotted budget, for "small" automation projects it is common to accept indicative sizing estimates often expressed in hours or days.

Looking first at TE0001, we see that there are essentially three audit flag tests which are performed. The first is to look up the employee's Time Sheet rejection rate and to assign a high-risk flag. The second step is to confirm that an employee is overtime-eligible based on her department. The third is to ensure that the hours claimed are consistent with policy in the employee's real estate location. We will estimate that these three process steps can be automated in a single day of development. You will have to take your authors at their words for now that this is reasonable, until such time as you get a feel for the tooling and capabilities – and it is. If we extend our hourly development cost to an 8-hour day, we have a one-time development cost estimate of $408 for TE0001. When we weigh this up against the 60 hours of productivity it offers each month in perpetuity, this is a slam dunk.

Looking next at TE0002, we see that there are essentially two enrichment steps to pull back employee pay rates from the HR system and the Tax Withholding rates from the Tax system. We said that some simple math is required as well, to extend the hours claimed to derive gross pay and withholding amounts. Because of the additional multiplication extension operation, we will rate this use case as higher in complexity than TE0001. Particularly given the level of scrutiny to which the output can be subjected, given the importance of accuracy to our personnel and as the payroll cycle is subject to regulation, this build may also warrant a higher risk rating, as was covered in Chapter 5. However, though slightly more complex, we represent that these three process steps can also be performed in a single day of development. Once more, if we extend our hourly development cost to an 8-hour day, we have a one-time development cost estimate of $408 for TE0002.

Finally, we will consider TE0003. We can see already that there appear to be more enrichment steps needed here than were required for either of TE0001 or TE0002, above. We have a similar enrichment to pull the rejection rate based on an employee identifier to understand if the Expense submission is high risk. This is much like the step performed in the Time Sheet process TE0001 above, but there are additional steps that must be performed for each of the itemized expenses contained in the Report. There is a test to ensure all meals are within the policy limits, and checks to ensure that the submitter is the most senior employee at the company event, and finally there is a test performed on expense line items that are coded as gifts to ensure they are within the gift policy limits. Due to the sheer number of enrichments and tests that are required to solution this opportunity, we believe it has higher complexity and will take longer to develop, *Ceteris Paribus*. Accordingly, we will incrementally increase our estimate by one day and assign the build a development time of two days. As for costing, if we extend our hourly development cost to an 8-hour day and multiply times two days, we have a one-time development cost estimate of $816 for TE0003.

See Exhibit 8-5 for the build sizing information we have captured in this exercise.

EXHIBIT 8-5 Sizing Build Efforts

Process ID	Process Steps	Baseline Process Time	Residual Process Time (Post-Implementation)	Hours Saved per Month	Replication Opportunities?	Total Opportunity (Hours Saved per Month)	Hourly Dev Cost	Dev Days	Cost Estimate (8 hr Dev Day)
TE0001	Review submitter for historical Time Sheet rejection rates. If >20% then High Risk – flag for review. If overtime is claimed, check HR system extract to confirm employee's department allows overtime (or for exception approval).	.17 hours	.02 hours	.15 hours	400 = 100 employees × 4 weekly Time Sheet cycles per month	60 hours	$51.00	1	$408.00

(continued)

EXHIBIT 8-5 Sizing Build Efforts *(continued)*

Process ID	Process Steps	Baseline Process Time	Residual Process Time (Post-Implementation)	Hours Saved per Month	Replication Opportunities?	Total Opportunity (Hours Saved per Month)	Hourly Dev Cost	Dev Days	Cost Estimate (8 hr Dev Day)
	Check real estate site for hours restrictions policies. Determine if hours claimed are outside of policy.								
TE0002	Enrich Remittance Slip by lookup of pay rates HR system and tax withholding from Tax department to calculate pay.	0.25 hours	.03 hours	.22 hours	400 = 100 employees x 4 weekly Time Sheet cycles per month	88 hours	$51.00	1	$ 408.00

| TE0003 | Review submitter for historical Expense Report rejection rates. If >20% then High Risk – flag for review. Check that meal expenses are within limits: breakfast ($20/person), lunch ($35/ person), dinner ($75/person). | .33 hours | .02 hours | .31 hours | 100 = 100 employees on average submit 1 expense report per month | 31 hours | $51.00 | 2 | $816.00 |

(continued)

EXHIBIT 8-5 Sizing Build Efforts *(continued)*

Process ID	Process Steps	Baseline Process Time	Residual Process Time (Post-Implementation)	Hours Saved per Month	Replication Opportunities?	Total Opportunity (Hours Saved per Month)	Hourly Dev Cost	Dev Days	Cost Estimate (8 hr Dev Day)
	Where submissions refer to multiple attendees, identify highest-ranking individual in HR system to ensure it is the submitter. If gift code selected, claim code may not exceed $40.					179 hours	$51.00	4	$1,632.00

Admittedly, this is the "finger in the air" type of sizing, but it was at least helpful to identify that the third opportunity appears to be more complex and has a greater number of discrete processing steps contained within it. We have now begun to develop a significantly rich Opportunity Matrix that is painting a fairly detailed picture of what is entailed in each opportunity. However, we want to take this even further.

Project Acceptance Criteria and Organizational Constraints

Now that we have a view of the use cases, the benefits cases, and the relative sizing of our opportunities, we are getting close to having our groomed backlog, but we still have to overlay our project acceptance criteria. These are affirmative statements of standards that if met, will allow us to proceed with a project. These could be based on project costs ("We will accept projects with a cost of less than $2000."), the benefits case ("We will accept projects that are projected to save at least 25 hours per month."), the amount of pain ("We will focus our efforts on improving the lives of operators. Therefore, we will accept projects with a pain assessment of 'medium' and 'high.'"), or the stated focal areas for automation or process streamlining ("Our automation effort is focused on improving control in our Regulatory Filing process, given the sanctions we received during the last reporting cycle. Therefore, we will only accept projects coded as 'Regulatory' with a project code beginning in 'RR.'"). A further acceptance criterion may be based on the use case presented ("We will accept projects that can be solutioned with self-service data analytics tools, but given the over-subscribed Robotic Process Automation backlog, we will pass on projects which require RPA resources."). These become important in the final identification of projects to take forward.

We must also overlay any organizational or departmental constraints. In contrast to project acceptance criteria, we are using organizational constraints to mean the limits and boundaries imposed on all projects by the organizational or functional strategy. Refer to Exhibit 5-3 to review an example of the evaluation of the alignment of digital transformation tooling with stated functional goals. We want to ensure that any projects taken up do not operate counter to organizational strategy – the goals and objectives established and handed down by senior executives. An example of an organizational constraint could be "Our strategy is to reduce dependence on external vendors. Therefore, we will reject any projects which build further dependence on our vendor relationships."

For our purposes, there are a few acceptance criteria that we will stand up to help us evaluate the opportunities. Given this is the first batch of Alteryx builds, we will begin with a statement surrounding complexity or probability of success. Therefore, our first acceptance criterion will be as follows: "Given we are in early stages of our digital journey, we will accept projects with low complexity and a high probability of success, and we will cautiously evaluate opportunities with medium or high complexity and medium probability of success. This may sound obvious, but it is important that we set the stage for all participants clearly and uniformly. It is important not to "bite off more than we can chew," and an early failure at this point in the journey could lead to negative press, setting the program back severely. In early stages, sponsors must take care to protect perceptions of the analytics program until the results can speak for themselves.

A second criterion we will put in place weighs project costs and benefits. As a general rule, an organization would accept any project where the internal rate of return (IRR) is greater than their cost of capital, so long as the return is as good as or better than alternatives. However, we will set a somewhat arbitrary benchmark and establish our second acceptance criterion as follows: "Given current costs of labor and available investment budget, we will accept projects offering time savings at a cost of $1,000/monthly hour saved. We will decline projects where time savings are more expensive." In point of fact, all three of the identified opportunities come at a price well below this acceptance threshold, based on the project costs and benefits cases we have established previously.

It may be that a third criterion is warranted, to carve out where we live in the self-service data analytics space. Remember from Chapter 7 that the loudest voice or the "squeakiest wheel" is not always the best use of project resources (only sometimes). Let's add some objectivity to the project selection process with the statement that "We will evaluate and accept automation opportunities in descending order of control or efficiency benefits, not only high touch and painful processes (in the opinion of the operator)." This puts subscribers on notice that there is an objective standard adhered to during the project selection process. In the next section, we will put all of the pieces together, including project costs and benefits, project acceptance criteria, and organizational constraints, to arrive at a "go/no go" decision and order of priority.

Automation Heatmap and Prioritization

One way to visually communicate the opportunities backlog is by color-coding the various dimensions considered for project selection in red, amber, or green (RAG). As a rule of thumb, red is bad, amber is of concern, and green is good. In general, the sparing use of red is recommended during updates with senior executives. Your authors can attest to the chilling effect that a column of red status assessments can have during a project call. The one time, however, that red can work to your advantage is in describing a baseline against which you have moved the needle to the green. By tactfully representing the opportunity landscape with colors, we can readily convey the thought-process behind project selection and resource deployment decision-making.

Let's color-code our own opportunity short list now. To begin, we add several fields to our Opportunity Inventory Matrix. First, we will capture the Pain Assessment. TE0001 we will rate as "Medium" or moderate, based on our process narrative. We will color-code this cell with an amber or orange color. TE0002 and TE0003, respectively, we will show as "High," based on the characterizations from process owners and operators, and we will color-code the pain assessment cells as red to indicate that they are very painful processing steps. Next, we will capture Build Complexity. We said that TE0001 would be the easiest based on the processing steps and use case functionality that was noted, and we will accordingly rate it with a build complexity of "Low" and color-code the cell as green. The TE0002 use case featured the same join and enrich requirement, but required the additional simple math functionality to derive gross and net pay, so we will assess the complexity as "Medium" or moderate. You guessed it, we will fill the cell with amber or orange. For TE0003, given the number of tests required to ensure the expense reports were within policy, we will assess the complexity as "High" and set it off from the rest with the oft-dreaded red.

Next, we will add a column to capture our assessment of the likelihood of success in consideration of the tooling we have matched to the opportunity. For TE0001, we are highly confident that we can automate the Payroll Process Audit Flag process through the use of Alteryx. Accordingly, we will assign the level of confidence as "High" in the Likelihood of Success column. The same goes for TE0002, even though it introduces the new requirement of simple math, as we have said. However, for TE0003, we will conservatively set the opportunity apart from the others, given the increased build complexity. We will assess the likelihood of success at "Medium."

Given the effort represented by these opportunities, and in consideration of pain assessments, projected benefits, build complexity rankings, and the likelihood of success, we come to a final column which is a "go/no go" column we will name "Recommended?" For the first opportunity – with a moderate amount of reported pain, a low build complexity, and a high likelihood of success – we will happily recommend this project. Of course, we will do a last-minute check to ensure it is in line with our Project Acceptance Criteria and any Organizational Constraints. We are in luck – we can proceed. For our second opportunity, TE0002, the pain was assessed as "High," but the build complexity was moderate. We believed that there is a high likelihood of success. Accordingly, we can also recommend this project, after a review of our Project Acceptance Criteria. However, for the third opportunity, TE0003, we rated it with a "High" build complexity and only a moderate likelihood of success, which is hardly ideal as a first venture into self-service data analytics. As we mentioned, we need to protect the "baby." That said, strictly speaking it is still allowed, based on our Project Acceptance Criteria, which stipulates that we would carefully consider these more complex projects. For now, we will indicate a "Maybe" as our final recommendation to ensure it is considered more fully – perhaps after TE0001 and TE0002 are bedded down successfully.

Remember that we began with an Opportunities Matrix, which contained good detail surrounding the opportunities, use case functionality, and proposed solutions. It also contained much of the cost and benefit analysis we ultimately relied upon to select our opportunities. However, by adding color to the equation, we can readily convey our logic at a glance and paint a picture for our stakeholders as to where we should be spending our time and why. See Exhibit 8-6 for the visually explicit Automation Heatmap we have produced in this exercise.

EXHIBIT 8-6 The Automation Heatmap

Opportunity Inventory-Process Heatmap
Time and Expense Cycles

Process ID	Process Name	Use Cases Funtionality	Tactical Tooling	Total Opportunity (Hours Saved per Month)	Dev Days	Cost Estimate	Pain Assessment	Build Complexity	Likelihood of Success	Recommended?	Priority
TE0001	Payroll Process Audit Flags	Join & Enrich, Flag	Alteryx	60 hours	1	$408.00	Medium	Low	High	Yes	2
TE0002	Payroll Process Payroll Calculation	Join & Enrich, Simple Math, Flag	Alteryx	88 hours	1	$408.00	High	Medium	High	Yes	1
TE0003	Expense Process Audit Flags	Join & Enrich, Simple Math, Flag	Alteryx	31 hours	2	$816.00	High	High	Medium	Maybe	3
					4	$1,632.00					

Project Acceptance Criteria

Given the early stage of our Digital Journey, we will accept projects with low complexity & high probability of success. Will cautiously evaluate opportunities with medium complexity & probability of success.

Given current costs of labor and available investment budget, we will accept projects offering time savings at a cost of $1000/monthly hour saved. We will decline where time savings are more expensive.

We will evaluate and accept automation opportunities in the descending order of control or efficiency benefits, not only high touch and painful processes (in the opinion of the operator).

Note that the first color-coded column speaks to internal clients' perceptions of pain, whereas the next two columns, Build Complexity and Likelihood of Success, speak to the difficulty of successfully implementing the automation. Note that at the end of the day, the bottom-line column is the "Recommended?" column, due to the fact that it is informed by all other columns and whether, in consideration of them, the project is a "go" (or a "no-go"). The ideal opportunity would have a red pain assessment but would be green across the board from there. This would indicate that there would be a large benefit to taking up the project, but the project itself is quite manageable.

This brings us to our last step which is to arrive at a logical order of priority for the opportunities we have captured. TE0003 we will give the lowest priority, given the inherent complexities for the build, and in light of our limited experience with the tooling. Putting them in ascending order, we will give this a priority of "3" (last place). In consideration of the "High" pain assessment for TE0002, as well as the fact that it promises the most significant benefit at 88 hours saved per month (roughly .5 FTE), we will give preference to this build, *Ceteris Paribus*, and give this first priority ("1"), leaving TE0001 in second place with a "2." A perfectly legitimate alternative course would be to take up TE0001 first, given it features the lowest build complexity rating, to build confidence, before following it up with TE0002.

The order matters; you will find that there are any number of organizational, perceptional, or personality nuances that inform your approach to prioritization, as you build experience in this regard. For our purposes, determining the priority sequence was a simple exercise, in light of the very few opportunities under consideration and the little information we provided regarding the personalities involved. When your organization matures along the digital spectrum, you will find that the Opportunity Inventory Matrix grows more substantial and considerable each day. Remember, you are looking for "bang for the buck" and to make the most impact with a limited resource pool.

Going back a step, often managers have an idea of where opportunities for automation lie – at least anecdotally. However, just because process owners have highlighted their process as highly manual and very painful does not necessarily mean that we should prioritize the area and deploy every data analytics tool at our disposal to make it more efficient when there are other opportunities that promise even higher benefits. When we embark on an automation strategy, we must optimize resource deployment based on data-driven decision-making, rather than on impressions, characterizations, and speculation. It is important to validate that you are attacking the right processes. The order of attack and prioritization needs to make sense. Capturing a rich Opportunity Inventory Matrix allows us to organize and evaluate opportunities in a more pragmatic, objective, and thoughtful way.

In our example, we scanned the organization for pockets of opportunity across several processes, and that is a model which is often used when a specialized automation function has been carved-out. However, keep in mind that a more organic pattern of growth will emerge, when the door is opened to self-service data analytics tooling at your organization. Advanced capabilities will be in the hands of the process owners to deploy at will. Give a kid a bat, and she will definitely take a swing. Give Alteryx to process owners, and . . . You get the point. Rather than objectively and discerningly weighing up projects to ensure they are consistent with functional and organizational objectives, process owners may quickly see the flexibility the tool offers to perform many of the tasks that today are performed in spreadsheets. While this is a natural evolution, it is important that the right tools are brought thoughtfully to bear on the right problems and that automation efforts support management goals. Here again, your authors must stress the importance of building strong investment governance around analytics programs in *advance* of adoption at scale to force due consideration of these principles. Once the cat is out of the bag, it becomes unnecessarily challenging to retrofit governance over a broad user-base that has developed bad habits.

Workflow Tooling

Now that you have worked through the exercise to capture problem statements and opportunities in an Opportunity Inventory Matrix, you can see that to quantify a benefits case and to size a build effort, we need a good amount of standardized information. Once we have it, there is a reasonably consistent and repeatable runbook that can be used by a program manager to flesh out opportunities for ready comparison. Perhaps you can also imagine the amount of back and forth effort it may take to pry this information out of busy and sometimes uncooperative process owners and operators. Now, imagine that your data analytics capabilities have been well-publicized and have achieved great renown across your organization, and you have a steadily growing demand pool. You may be in need of some help.

For all of the reasons above, one solution that makes a lot of sense in an environment of abundant demand is to adopt a self-service *workflow* tool. A workflow broadly refers to a sequence of activities that must occur in order to transform inputs to outputs. In our case, we demonstrated the need to capture basic qualitative and quantitative inputs that were evaluated to arrive at a viable solution, a go/no-go decision, and an order of relative priority. We laid out a logical sequence of steps to assemble this information in the previous sections of this chapter. What if requests could be logged by process owners directly in a workflow tool, for your consideration and prioritization as a self-service data analytics program manager, when operators are motivated to do so by process pain?

Once process owners begin the self-service capture and supply of opportunities directly in the workflow tool, they will serve you up an Opportunity Inventory Matrix quite directly, without "sniffing out" opportunities from process narratives and SIPOCs. As requests come to the front door, they can be rejected outright if they are not feasible use cases for tooling you have on offer. If, however, the opportunities under consideration are viable, the benefits are appreciable, and the opportunities meet project acceptance criteria and are within organizational constraints, they can be moved to your backlog for prioritization. If ultimately prioritized and taken up, the projects would be advanced through a customizable workflow that may include such project stages as Detailed Requirements Gathering, More Information Needed, Backlog, Work in Progress, In UAT, Pending Release, and Delivered. Your organization may have its own nomenclature in use to describe the various stages of project delivery, which you would be free to adopt and specify during the initial configuration of the workflow tool.

A number of providers such as Atlassian (JIRA and Trello), Kanban Tool, Kanbanize, Pipefy, Asana, Axosoft, Wrike, and others have developed workflow tooling that can help to structure requests by ensuring minimum information requirements are met (e.g., benefits cases, use cases, project requirements, process description and pain points), by specifying a clear path for work activities, and by forcing conformity with governance precepts (e.g., a reference to a core technology request must be captured in order for a user to submit a tactical solution request, or evidence of signoff and the employee ID of the signatory must be captured to promote a build to production). Further, the visual work board features (such as Kanban Boards) can give transparency to the number of demand items, the number of projects currently in progress, and the number of successful deliveries achieved during the period – all in real time or low-latency near real time. JIRA, in particular, has made its way to service desks and technology departments within large organizations as a tool of choice. It is a considerable graduation, indeed, when the function matures and industrializes to the point that you can turn on the spigot and have a ready-made backlog of opportunities delivered to your front door by process owners and operators to solution, prioritize, progress, and control.

As your data analytics journey unfolds, you will begin to consider such factors as time-in-wait and project velocity, development resource bottlenecks, and project artifact retention (for control-minded stakeholders). Of course, it will be critical to demonstrate program benefits, along the way, through detailed reporting on benefits delivered. Structuring inbound requests in a logical way, while ensuring that enough input is captured from process owners at early stages, can save much of the back-and-forth that inevitably results in project delays. Centralizing all analytics efforts in a single platform allows for a clear picture of what is in flight, what is next, how the program is performing, what is being delivered and to whom, and the cumulative benefits realized. Remember the adage introduced in Chapter 2: "You can't manage it if you can't measure it." Workflow tooling can help meet many of the project governance objectives laid out in Chapter 4, and the risk governance objectives covered in Chapter 5. Perhaps most importantly, it can help to hasten the pace of change within your organization.

The idea is to gather a rich pipeline of opportunities to rationalize, validate, and drop into the backlog to draw from, as project resources are available. Shifting the opportunity-sourcing responsibilities directly to process owners is one way to get buy-in through cultivation of a shared sense of responsibility for digital advancement. It is also an effective way to develop specialization and preserve focus, as those with data analytics build expertise do not have to get up from the table to survey the organization for the next opportunity; instead, they can keep their heads down and nose to the wheel. The result is increased transformation velocity across the organization, as "wait" queues within project stages are reduced, and throughput is ultimately increased.

Additionally, the more processes that have been defined, documented, and evaluated for benefits will give color and context around headcount efficiency and footprint goals. If we think that across a department, at least 20% of the tasks can be automated, then an 8% annual headcount efficiency target in year one is not unreasonable at its face, assuming project and technology resources can be allocated to the goal. The use of a workflow tool to centralize opportunities, to redraw roles and responsibilities, and to archive project artifacts for robust project governance and investment governance will be a game-changer, as the data analytics program advances along the digital maturity spectrum toward industrialization.

Use Case Library

As we described in the preceding section, workflow tooling can advance the organization as the self-service data analytics program is industrialized at scale. Another way to lay the groundwork for scale is to create a Use Case Library, where an entry is made for each data analytics build, to log its inputs, outputs, and transformation steps, along with the analytics solution used, a copy of the final configuration, and the project team and specialists who built it. The idea is to build awareness around success stories, to incrementally syndicate and build upon the knowledge gained elsewhere in the organization, and ultimately to repurpose, customize, and plug-and-play previously developed functionality more broadly.

Note: The fields referenced above for the Use Case Library overlap significantly with those required for *risk* governance as covered in Chapter 5, but also for *project* governance and *investment* governance as discussed in Chapter 4 and in the "Opportunity Inventory Matrix" section presented in this chapter. It is easy to see that the use of a workflow tool to assemble and centralize all project details can be useful in enabling a variety of cuts to satisfy governance procedures and program reporting.

Some organizations feature success stories in data analytics newsletters or in executive town halls to recognize successful analytics deployments and to formally praise innovators embracing digital tooling to great effect. Managers and process owners, for their part, may pay close attention to innovations emerging elsewhere in the organization, to see how they might leverage the work done for replication in their own areas. Use Case Libraries can be important tools that are often referred to, as digitalization becomes part of the organizational DNA. If it can advance the organization and speed the adoption of digital tooling, it is worth its SharePoint space many times over. We should be careful not to forget that just as the rest of the organization can benefit from process efficiency measures, so too can the change organization, itself. Repurposing project data points already captured in the creation of a Use Case Library view can serve to promote widespread adoption and turbocharge the organization in its digital journey.

If we refer back to Exhibit 8-5, we see that at least the first processing step is in common between TE0001 and TE0003. In both cases, the first step is to "Review submitter for historical rejection rates." Although the data source differs between these two demand items, it is quite likely that there would be common steps contained in the Alteryx workflow logic for each, respectively. Therefore, once

TE0001 is soundly addressed with an Alteryx solution (it is first in our priority order), when TE0003 is ultimately picked up, it may well be worth the time to refer back to the completed build workflow for TE0001, to review the logic used to accomplish this step. Further, it might be useful to consult the project team who were involved in implementing the solution for TE0001. This illustrates the benefits of the Use Case Library. If use case functionality is well described and captured uniformly across the data analytics landscape, similar efforts can be made simpler by learning from and incrementally building upon prior successes. *Why reinvent the wheel?*

Multiplier Effect of Replication Opportunities on Project Benefits Case

Let us introduce the multiplier effect for projects that have widespread replication opportunities across the organization. We imagine for a moment that you are presented with a major advanced analytics machine learning project with complex algorithms under consideration – one that is highly technical and costly to build at $1 million. You believe that if it is successful, it could yield an efficiency benefit of 13 FTE (who individually cost $100,000 per year to employ). If successful, these individuals could be redeployed elsewhere in the organization. After consulting your HP-12c (Hewlett Packard financial calculator), you determine that this opportunity represents a benefits case of $1.3 million. However, given the complexity, you are only 80% confident that it can be built effectively, and you are quite aware that it may take a significant amount of time to work out the teething issues, even if the build is technically successful. Therefore, the expected benefit of the build is tempered to $1.04 million. Last, your organization has an investment constraint that requires a one-year breakeven. We see that this project is viable and makes it in above the line, but only just. The year one net benefit is a moderate $40,000.

The $1 million up-front investment will raise eyebrows for sure and will be difficult to attract from sponsors and investment gatekeepers. Further, you are aware that a machine learning build requires significant partnership and involvement from IT, who in your experience have been just as quick to own successes as they are to deflect failures at your expense. (We are presenting a hypothetical interpersonal dynamic that can influence decisions and actions. We are in no way painting our fine technologists in IT with a demonic brush.) It is true that the benefits case, when viewed in perpetuity, is staggering, but you are also aware that your organization rarely looks beyond the one-year horizon. After all, your bonus is only paid based on what you did this year, irrespective of the cumulative aggregate efficiency savings contributed in your decade with the firm. *What have you done for me lately?*

Nicole Mayor, a process owner from Operations, approaches you with a differently structured idea. She has identified an opportunity to save every employee in her area 15 minutes per day. You are thinking to yourself that you don't even get out of bed unless an opportunity saves 50 hours per month, but you hear her out – you are a professional, after all. The pain point she relates is that each employee must gather the inputs to their daily processes from a number of sources, including opening emails and downloading detachments, downloading system reports, and capturing published market data from web-based applications. Even though an honest quantification comes in at 15 minutes, she is aware that performing this task can very often take much longer. The process itself can distract operators from other priorities, and of course the task is low value-added and banal. To address it, she proposes rerouting the input file emails to shared mailboxes, and pointing Alteryx to them to "listen" for input arrivals and to capture them when received. To automate the extraction of system reports, she proposes deploying modular, limited-scope Bots to launch the systems, navigate the report menus, and finally to download extracts for further local processing.

Given that Nicole has a total of 10 employees in her area including herself, the benefits case for this opportunity totals 150 minutes per day or 2.5 hours (15 minutes per employ saved). For simplicity, let's generously call this one third of an FTE. We can readily arrive at a benefits dollar value by multiplying by the $100,000 average employee cost, to arrive at an annualized benefit of $33,000 in perpetuity. Not bad at all, given that the total sizing for the robotics build comes in at five days, and the Alteryx build comes in at three days to source the data for the team in total. But what makes this a home run is that this problem statement and use case persists across the entire organization.

Across the company, nearly everyone is reliant on processing inputs sourced from systems and emails. Very quickly, you realize that this is a problem with a far greater benefits case than the 15 minutes per day across the team of 10. Taking the widespread replication opportunities into consideration, there is a far greater multiplier to consider. You amend your benefits case formula as follows: 100 employees × 15 Minutes saved per day = 1,500 minutes saved per day. This equates to roughly three FTE. The dollar value of the benefits case can be determined again by multiplying the three FTE times the average employee cost of $100,000. Nicole has brought a seemingly small opportunity that, when replicated broadly, can yield $300,000 in benefit – in perpetuity. The work can be started immediately without vying for the $1 million investment. These simpler analytics builds can be delivered with a high probability of success, with very little up-front costs, with the year one benefit of 7× over the investment-intensive machine learning opportunity under consideration. Particularly because you are interested in the one-year time horizon, it is clear which opportunity bubbles to the top of the priority list, given the circumstances we have imagined for this example.

This is the multiplier effect that replication opportunities can have on project benefits cases. We have crafted this example to make the numbers work, and it is well noted that machine learning opportunities often come with far more moderate price tags, but we wanted to illustrate a point. It is important to take an organizational view and to look beyond your area when you consider innovation. Ideas that have broad appeal with significant replication opportunities should be considered for the full measure of benefit they can ultimately register.

Conclusion

In this chapter, we began by capturing the problem statements we uncovered through the process discovery exercises illustrated in Chapter 7. From there, we worked to build out a rich Opportunity Inventory Matrix by distilling the use cases from problem statements, matching tools to use cases, building out benefits cases for each opportunity, and sizing the build efforts once solutions have been identified. These are the foundational steps in creating a backlog of automation opportunities.

Once the opportunity detail was properly captured, project acceptance criteria and organizational constraints were overlaid to ensure the right opportunities were considered and that projects selected for advancement were in line with functional strategy. We stressed the importance of the upfront establishment of data analytics program governance, which is particularly important with self-service tooling, due to the hyper-organic growth pattern it can follow. Once process owners and operators become aware of the control and efficiency benefits of structuring their manual processes, the floodgates will be opened, and the tidal wave must be kept in check.

Once we had rationalized the opportunities identified, we finally arrived at the makings of an opportunity backlog. Building a solid pipeline of viable and conforming opportunities sheds light on the scale of opportunities to be found across the organization. Redrawing project team roles and responsibilities to land responsibility for opportunity identification with process owners can provide lift to the analytics program by allowing those with analytics development skills to keep laser focus on reducing time-to-market and increasing throughput. As work in process items roll off the line to completion, such specialists can simply pull in the next work item from the neatly groomed backlog, rather than taking hands off keys to engage in the next process discovery effort. We further demonstrated the color coding of the opportunity backlog to create the Automation Heatmap. This artifact is useful in justifying and visually communicating the priority assessment for senior stakeholders.

We then turned to two topics related to industrializing data analytics at scale. We first introduced workflow tooling functionality and common off-the-shelf tools like Atlassian JIRA that allows us to ensure that minimum information standards are met, as opportunities come in through the front door. The information assembled must be enough to evaluate project benefits and costs, arrive at a solution, and to prioritize demand items for acceptance into the backlog. Once taken up, the workflow tool serves to structure work steps and project phases in a standard and transparent way, to ensure consistent compliance with project governance procedures that can be directly embedded in the workflow, and to keep a near real-time record of demand items, throughout the build life cycle to ultimate delivery.

We then introduced the Use Case Library as a tool to capture and communicate the innovations delivered broadly across the organization. Key project details are captured such as problem statements and use cases, solutions implemented to address them, and the benefits realized from the efforts. Process owners can refer to the Use Case Library to keep abreast of innovations emerging elsewhere in the organization. Where similar problem statements exist in their own areas, they have a leg up in understanding what can be done to solution for them and to whom to go for advice. For this purpose, project subject matter experts (SMEs) are often recorded, not only to give them firm-wide recognition for their accomplishments but also to encourage the growth of informal personal networks and the formation of an analytics community. Organizations should encourage SMEs to lend a hand when other managers wish to leverage the work previously accomplished – and to build on it additively. The Use Case Library is particularly important when there are widespread replication opportunities for delivered innovations. Remember the multiplier effect that replication opportunities can have on benefits cases. Modular solutions with a narrow scope that can be broadly deployed across the organization should be selected over one-time bespoke solutions, *Ceteris Paribus*.

In Chapter 7, we demonstrated means of surveying the organization to document how functions fit together, to understand the processes within them, and to uncover manual and time-consuming process steps that represent opportunities to deploy data analytics to increase control and capture efficiency. In Chapter 8, we have demonstrated a process for the capture, evaluation, solutioning, and prioritization of the opportunities discovered. Taken together, the topics presented should be enough to allow readers to turn their eyes toward their own organizations. We hope you feel well equipped to steer your organization through an informed process discovery and to oversee the assembly of an opportunity backlog from the pain points encountered. Armed with a better understanding of emerging data analytics capabilities, you may feel less intimidated by acronyms like RPA, NLP, OCR, AI, IoT, and the others we have presented. Having seen Alteryx in action in Chapter 6, you may be eager to take the first steps forward, or you may already be diving in headfirst. Irrespective of the level of digital maturity at your own organizations, it is important to continually demonstrate the benefits realized from the program and to avoid falling victim to a lack of governance discipline that can erode the value of the analytics program at one fell swoop.

Glossary

A

Analytics Process Automation (APA) Delivers end-to-end automation of analytics, machine learning, and data science processes; enabling the agility needed to accelerate digital transformation. With the Alteryx APA Platform you can automate processes, embed intelligent decisioning, and achieve better business outcomes (Alteryx).

Application Programming Interface (API) The standards instructions and rules that allow computer programs to interact. Frequently refers to allowing one system to source data or services from another.

Artificial Intelligence (AI) The theory and science of development of computer systems and processes that can consider facts and variables to perform processes that typically require human intelligence – optical character recognition, speech recognition, observing variables for compound decision-making, language translation, and more.

B

Backlog, or Project Backlog This is the queue where the prioritized list of features, functionality, and other build requests have been staged (by product managers) as they await being pulled into a sprint or pegged to a release, as technology development bandwidth becomes available. This term is often used in Agile, and it is one of the "wait" queues.

Benefits Case Expected benefit for delivering a project. The benefits case is often used to justify the deployment of dollars, development resources, and focus versus other competing alternatives.

"Black Box" Processing and Testing Processing structured in a tool which is typified by a lack of adequate process documentation or change management artifacts. When discreet processing steps and workflows have not been memorialized effectively as a data analytics build is developed, the result is a "hidden" process, whose effectiveness can only be assessed from the outside, by feeding raw data inputs through the engine and reviewing the output, in order to determine what transformation has occurred.

Business Intelligence The strategies and technologies used by business enterprises to analyze historical data and business information along with current observations of performance, to predict future operational performance.

Business Process Management (BPM) Is a discipline aimed at optimizing business activities and processing workflows. It can involve process mapping and measurement, process change analysis, and implementation steps including modeling, execution, control, and automation. BPM is conducted to ensure systems, processes, and stakeholder interactions support enterprise goals.

C

Classification The process of specifying (or finding a function to assign) classifications to an observation in a dataset, based on training parameters. In Machine Learning (ML) Classification, a computer model or program is trained based on sample training data to separate observed values into discrete categories.

Center of Excellence (CoE) Automation and related governance efforts may be centralized in an Automation Center of Excellence (CoE) function that supports firm-wide analytics and automation efforts. Depending on the model in place, the level of staffing, and the maturity of the function, the leadership, technologists, and specialists in this function may be charged with the development of analytics best practices that are syndicated across the organization, or they may be charged with all analytics development and delivery, itself.

Comprehensive Capital Analysis and Review (CCAR) The Federal Reserve Bank's annual review process aimed at assessing whether banks have adequate capital to withstand increased economic stress. We have introduced CCAR as a driver of increased regulatory focus on data governance and specifically on data lineage. Though this example is relevant to banks and holding companies, it is useful to infer sound data governance practices from regulatory guidance in play.

D

Dashboards A collection of metrics and visualizations of critical key performance indicators necessary to manage a process, business, department, or enterprise – often in a single view. Increasingly dynamic and interactive, they can offer context in a visually rich frame that the communication of a single fact or value can fail to do.

Data Analytics The science and art of processing increasingly large datasets to understand relationships and patterns in the data. Increasingly, this term is used to refer to the disciplines and technologies surrounding data interrogation and evaluation to allow for data-driven answers to business questions.

Data Blending Data blending refers to the process of joining two different tables of data using a unique identifier. Data blending allows for data from different sources to be brought together and unified to create adequately rich records in support of further analysis.

Data Cleansing Data cleansing refers to the process of ensuring data is clear of formatting issues and cleared of null values or erroneous entries. Data that has gone through data cleansing is ready for data enrichment, further analysis, and visualization.

Data Democratization Making digital information readily available to consumers broadly across organizations. Tooling advancements such as dashboards and APIs are removing data barriers, such that IT alone are no longer required as brokers of data to non-technical users.

Data Governance Aimed at ensuring that high-quality data is the starting point for all data processing in enterprise systems and for offline processing, this is the set of internal overarching policies and procedures for managing the availability, integrity, usage, and security of data across an organization.

Data Enrichment Enrichment refers to the process whereby an original data array is added to by merging data from another source, to produce an adequately rich dataset for the next set of processing steps.

Data Loading In extract, transform, and load (ETL), loading refers to the process whereby adequately rich and transformed datasets are loaded to platforms or systems for the next set of processing steps.

Data Mining The process of analyzing a large dataset to discover patterns, uncover relationships, or generate new information.

Data Normalization   In the case of a single attribute, normalization is the process of consolidating like values into a single conforming uniform value. In the case of loading or mastering data into a single array, it implies standardizing the values to the master format, and mapping the attributes from a source file to the correct fields in the master array.

Data Science   Broad field incorporating preparation and use of data systems, through statistics, mathematics, and algorithms, and processes, aimed at the extraction of information insights, or knowledge generation.

Data Scrubbing   Procedures whereby data errors, including missing or incomplete data, incorrect data, and data redundancies, are corrected to ensure a high-quality dataset.

Data Transformation   In ETL, transformation is the process of converting data from one structure or format to another for further processing.

Data Visualization   Visually representing information and key performance indicators (KPIs) with the use of charts, graphs, images or pictures, and diagrams to communicate clearly and efficiently.

Descriptive Analytics   An area of statistics and advanced analytics that uses statistical methods to parse, search, and summarize historical data to understand patterns, business trends, or changes.

Diagnostic Analytics   An area of statistics and advanced analytics that seeks to understand why events occurred. This root cause analysis is aimed at uncovering causation and correlations. Along the maturity continuum, diagnostic analytics follows descriptive analytics but is less mature than predictive analytics or prescriptive analytics.

Document Management Software (DMS)   The use of a computer system and software to store, manage, and track electronic documents and electronic images that have been captured with a document scanner in place of paper-based documents and information. Most associated with the concept of a "paperless office."

E

End-User Computing tools (EUCs)   For purposes of this book, we are defining these as the (over–relied upon) suite of tactical tools like Excel and Access where outside-of-systems processing is being carried out. One key premise of this book is that strategically, processing should be performed in systems, but the manual tail can be structured and reduced by supplementing or supplanting EUCs and spreadsheet processes with data analytics tooling.

Extract, Transform, and Load (ETL) ETL is an acronym for extract, transform, and load, which are key steps in data mastering.

F

Full-Time Employee (FTE) FTE is an acronym used to generically refer to a full-time employee, usually in relation to either the cost of salary and benefits for a single headcount or in relation to the average workload contribution made by one team member. "For this fiscal year, we must reduce our salary expense by $2 million, which equates to 10 FTE in your department." "The benefits case for this Robotics build equates to an efficiency gain of 3 FTE."

G

Garbage In, Garbage Out (GIGO) This acronym is an idiom or aphorism used to convey the idea that processing outputs are only as good as the data they rely upon at the outset. An incredibly precise process that is based on faulty inputs will result in faulty outputs.

I

Intelligent Character Recognition (ICR) Computer-based interpretation of handwritten, printed, or manually entered characters for capture, recognition, and retention, for later reference or for further processing.

Interoperability We are using this term to refer to the ability of one system to invoke or utilize the features, functionality, or *data* contained in another system. It is observed that many of the accommodation work steps performed in spreadsheets could be avoided if upstream systems were fully interoperable.

K

Key Performance Indicators (KPIs) Those metrics process owners and management use to measure health and performance of their business, or a process within it.

M

Machine Learning (ML) The field of study encompassing computer algorithms that can automatically improve through continued observation and increased experience based on mathematical models and sample data.

Material Non-Public Information (MNPI) This is the name given to text, data, and transactional detail, which has the potential to move the market for a given security or derivative. This information must be carefully safeguarded from disclosure to external parties, and even within the organization, access entitlements should be controlled and limited. Trading based on this information before it is public can give rise to charges of insider trading.

Markets in Financial Instruments Directive (MiFID) II European Union financial regulations aimed at promoting fairness and transparency in financial markets, and at protecting the marketplace in the event of a market crisis. We have introduced MiFID II as a driver of increased regulatory focus on data governance and specifically on data lineage, as trade data must be captured over time in order to allow for post-mortem retrospection by regulators, in the event of an adverse event.

Metadata Data about data. This data is used to provide information about other data, attributes, values, records, or arrays. There are many types of metadata, including statistical, structural, and administrative, among others.

Model Risk Governance This is the set of overarching policies and procedures for managing the development, testing, risk assessment, and validation of models where estimates, probabilities, and calculations are used. Model risk governance is increasingly regulated in the financial services setting.

N

Natural Language Processing (NLP) One of the longest-standing dimensions of artificial intelligence using linguistics and computer science to improve how computers capture, analyze, and process large volumes of human language data. Enlists a number of technologies, including speech recognition, language translation, natural language understanding, and natural language generation.

O

Optical Character Recognition (OCR) Computer-based or electronic conversion of images to machine-encoded text, often from scanned documents. OCR is best used to capture, recognize, and interpret standard text characters and can be used to process and retain vast numbers of large documents, for later reference or for further processing.

P

Personally Identifiable Information (PII) A classification of sensitive data that is known to allow for the association of an attribute value to an individual. Examples are Social Security numbers, taxpayer IDs, credit card numbers, phone numbers, and arguably many other data points. This information is high risk, given it can be maliciously used for violation of privacy, identity theft, or even fraud.

Predictive Analytics An area of statistics that deals with extracting information from data in order to predict outcomes, behaviors, and trends. In machine learning (ML), predictive analytics evolves beyond descriptive analytics and diagnostic analytics, as training data and algorithms are used to calculate statistical probabilities of future events and to predict future outcomes.

Prescriptive Analytics An area of statistics and advanced analytics that is aimed at determining the best available course of action, based on assigned parameters and on predicted outcomes. In machine learning (ML), prescriptive analytics is the most evolved in the analytics continuum, as it leverages descriptive analytics, diagnostic analytics, and predictive analytics, to assign or designate a course of action to predicted future events and outcomes.

Process Discovery The process by which existing business processes are scoped, defined, mapped, described, and analyzed in a target organization. We are introducing it as the means by which opportunities to employ data analytics tooling can be uncovered in your organization.

Process Memorialization Memorialization refers to the documentation of processing steps that convert data inputs to data outputs in the finance, accounting, or operations settings.

R

Return on Investment (ROI) Return on investment is a financial performance measure that considers expected or realized costs and benefits. It is the benchmark frequently used to evaluate and compare alternative investment opportunities to determine whether they will provide sufficient cash flows to warrant investment.

Reference Data The standardized set of data attributes and values that describes transactions. The values of reference data are typically stable and slow to change. One example would be a reference data field that captures the state where a transaction was processed. The values to select from would be a (relatively) stable list of the 50 US states.

Robotic Process Automation (RPA)   Refers to software that can be programmed to replicate basic, high-volume, and repetitive data input (and other) processing steps across multiple applications to replicate or emulate human performance.

S

"Small" Automation   Refers to the rapid introduction of flexible process-level automation, often to supplement core system function-ality - interoperability, transformation, or reporting features not yet in place. The self-service data analytics tooling referred to throughout the book fits within this definition, in contrast to larger-scale invest-ment in strategic system implementations, which are slow-to-market and tied to investment cycles.

Standard Operating Procedures (SOPs)   This portion of process documentation is detailed step-by-step instructions describing how to undertake a task. It is recommended that they are written and illustrated at the level that an untrained operator could perform the process in the event of staff turnover.

Static Data   Data that consists of set values that are not likely to be updated once captured. This term is used in contrast to dynamic data or formulaic data that is based on changing variables. In spread-sheets, static data is the portion of a data array that is not based on formulas, as opposed to the cells or fields that are formula-driven or references to other variable cells.

Straight Through Processing (STP)   The ability to decrease both cycle time and the costs of transaction processing through the employ of systems to eliminate manual intervention process steps in a workflow.

Systems Development Life Cycle (SDLC)   Refers to the tradi-tional stages of hardware and software development projects that start with feasibility, includes requirements gathering, prioritization, coding, user-acceptance testing, and continues through system deliv-ery and beyond. The life cycle typically involves a large number of sponsors and stakeholders – from end-users and business analysts, to product managers and technologists. In contrast to "small" automa-tion, the process typically extends across several investment cycles over a number of years.

T

Training Data Observations which are run through machine learning algorithms to "teach" models to make predictions. This initial set of observations serves as an initial load to allow for initialization. As the universe of observations is widened, the algorithms can be fine-tuned – hence the name "machine learning."

Turing Test Alan Turing, 1950 – This test is widely used to assess whether computer software that is meant to emulate a human interaction is successful, meaning that the humans cannot readily discern that they are interacting with a machine.

U

Use Cases Situations in the current state processing environment, in which it is appropriate to employ a product, service, or technology. In the data analytics environment, these are short descriptions (often no more than one sentence) of functionality that can easily prompt recognition and a binary "needed" or "not needed" in the mind of analysts. Use cases are captured to allow for analysts to understand where tooling can be deployed and to allow for widespread replication of previously developed solutions.

User Acceptance Testing (UAT) The testing and validation steps performed by end-users to confirm that one or many code change(s) is/are operating effectively, based on specified requirements.

Index

A

Accounting profession
   data analytics technologies
     usage, 170–171
   digital transformation
     usage, 171
Accounting work,
     automation, 132
Accuracy (data
     governance goal), 62
Algorithms, usage, 37
Alignment matrix, creation, 67
Alpha characters, numeric
     characters (contrast), 102
Alteryx, 24, 54, 179, 229
   business transformation
     capability, 216
   capabilities, user adoption/
     deployment, 216
   chart (creation/viewing),
     browse tool (usage), 195e
   control/efficiency,
     increase, 215–216
   data, link, 185
   dataset selection,
     enhancement, 193e, 194e
   ETL build deployment, 66–67
   feedback, 216

filter tool (data transformation
     tool), usage, 193e,
     208e, 212e
functionality, 182–196
functions, flexibility, 60
industries, 201–206, 205e–206e
IT trend analysis, 206–210
manual processing,
     reduction, 215–216
market trend analysis (group
     data), summarize tool
     (usage), 197e
non-IT industry data
     (removal), filter tool
     (usage), 212e
sample tool (data
     transformation tool),
     usage, 194e
self-service capabilities, 196
sort descending, usage, 204e
sort tool (data transformation
     tool), usage, 193e
training, availability, 217
transformed dataset
     (examination), browsing
     (usage), 208e
trend analysis (data
     transformation), summa-
     rize tool (usage), 207e